Boulevard of Broken Dreams

ALSO BY PAUL ALEXANDER

Ariel Ascending: Writings About Sylvia Plath (Editor)

Rough Magic

Death and Disaster

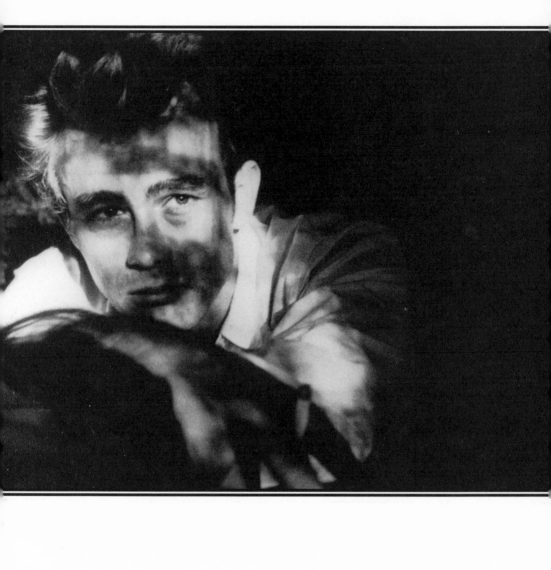

Boulevard of Broken Dreams

THE LIFE, TIMES, AND LEGEND OF JAMES DEAN

Paul Alexander

VIKING

VIKING
Published by the Penguin Group
Penguin Books USA Inc., 375 Hudson Street,
New York, New York 10014, U.S.A.
Penguin Books Ltd, 27 Wrights Lane, London W8 5TZ, England
Penguin Books Australia Ltd, Ringwood, Victoria, Australia
Penguin Books Canada Ltd, 10 Alcorn Avenue, Toronto, Ontario, Canada M4V 3B2
Penguin Books (N.Z.) Ltd, 182–190 Wairau Road, Auckland 10, New Zealand

Penguin Books Ltd, Registered Offices: Harmondsworth, Middlesex, England

First published in 1994 by Viking Penguin, a division of Penguin Books USA Inc.

1 2 3 4 5 6 7 8 9 10

Copyright © Paul Alexander, 1994
All rights reserved

Photograph credits appear on page 313.

LIBRARY OF CONGRESS CATALOGING IN PUBLICATION DATA
Alexander, Paul, 1955–
Boulevard of broken dreams : the life, times, and legend of James
Dean / by Paul Alexander.
p. cm.
ISBN 0-670-84951-0
1. Dean, James, 1931–1955.   2. Motion picture actors and
actresses—United States—Biography.   I. Title.
PN2287.D33A84   1994
791.43′028′092—dc20
[B]   93-42180

Printed in the United States of America
Set in Bodoni Book

For Chris
For James Stein
And in memory of Don Elgin

It ended—with his body changed to light,
a star that burns forever in the sky.

—"The Flight of Quetzalcoatl,"
an Aztec poem

Author's Note

All of the dialogue included in this book is reproduced from primary and secondary sources such as books, magazine articles, journals, and taped interviews with individuals who knew James Dean. None of the dialogue is imagined; it is as close to what was said as I can get.

—P. A.

Contents

Boulevard of Broken Dreams

A
Lost
Boy

1. So we think of James Dean who was the quintessential rebel—rebel against the establishment, against society's traditions and mores, against conformity of any kind. Think of him now and we see what has become a cliché. Dressed in a pair of blue jeans, a white T-shirt, and a red nylon zip-up jacket, he stands hunched over slightly with his head cocked to one side, his eyes squinted just so, his hands stuffed in his front pockets. A Chesterfield dangles from his lips. When Jim Stark struck this pose in *Rebel Without a Cause*, Dean's most famous picture, the look was not a cliché at all. It was new, startling, dangerous. Before Dean came along, boys didn't dress this way, and they sure didn't casually stare at someone with such resentment, such contempt. Although most of Hollywood didn't expect him to, Dean connected with an audience eager to hear what he had to say. He entered into the public's consciousness on a national level in the middle of the fifties, a decade defined by social conservatism and political repression. Like a stern but dispassionate father, Dwight Eisenhower, the former general, executed his job as president with no greater agenda than to maintain the status quo. At the same time, Joseph McCarthy, helped by Roy Cohn and a young Robert Kennedy, did his part to uphold what he considered to be the American way of life by cashing in on the Red Scare and carrying out a government-endorsed witch-hunt against Communists that terrorized the whole of the creative community. As the federal government embraced oppression, the rights of the individual were thought to be less important than protecting society's standards. There was, of course, a backlash, especially among the younger generation entering adulthood in the fifties. In various segments of the country, young people openly rebelled against their parents, their schools, society in general. In this climate of discontent James Dean appeared. Symbolizing the very ideas of individual rights and rebellion, he appealed to an entire generation of young people who adopted him as their hero. Girls idolized him. Boys dressed like him, spoke like him, stood like him. They wanted to *be* him. "Just think of all the James Deans," Andy Warhol would one day say, "and what it means." So we do. We think of all the James Deans and what it means and when we do we think of him.

Supple lips accented the cheekbones of his delicate, angular face while almond-brown hair highlighted the light blue of his round "bedroom" eyes. That was the face; on-screen it was luminous, unforgettable. Then there was the body. Well-built if not muscular, he carried himself like a wrestler although, when he wanted to, he could move with the subtle grace of a ballet dancer. And that walk. Preening, proud, he strutted through a room, or, just the opposite, slouched like a precocious child. Either way, he got a person's attention. Only his speech was more remarkable. "Slurred uncommunicative speech," one magazine called it at the time his pictures were released.

But besides his good looks, there's another reason we remember him. He did what few actors had done before, or have since. He brought something new to sex—an ambiguity, an openness, an androgyny that had not been there with other Hollywood stars. If the girls fell in love with him—and they did—in their own way boys fell in love with him too. During adolescence, almost every teenage boy feels sexually drawn to another boy at some time. Dean played on this attraction. By doing so, he embraced the uncertain nature of sexuality, which can be profoundly threatening to many people. He also actively cultivated contradictions. He was masculine—there was no doubt about it—yet he was also soft, vulnerable, *feminine.* The complexity in his sexuality came through in his movie roles. In *East of Eden* he plays the wounded, vengeful brother who longs to be loved by his father, his brother's girlfriend, *and* his brother. In *Giant,* especially in the early scenes, his character is defined by his uncertainty and indecision. In *Rebel Without a Cause,* Judy falls in love with Dean's character, but Plato does too, and Dean responds the same to both. In the picture Plato says he wants Jim Stark to be his father; the adoring stares he gives him, though, are certainly not those of a son. James Dean may have been the first American teenager, as he was called after his death, but he was also the first male star to fashion an androgynous image. In the fifties Dean became the counterpoint to figures like Gary Cooper, Clark Gable, and John Wayne—or Dwight Eisenhower, for that matter. The older generation represented oppression and repression, Dean freedom and progression.

During his brief career, he made only three pictures yet his contribution to modern acting is so significant it seems he made many more. He was just twenty-four when he died yet he accomplished more—in terms of quality if not quantity—than almost all of his contemporaries who have lived to be much older. He's been dead for nearly forty years yet the legend that emerged after he died is as vital today as it ever was.

In fact, when we think of him now, we think of that legend. Which makes sense. The legend has lasted longer than he lived. It started on a cool autumn afternoon on the last day of September in 1955 on a stretch of highway north of Los Angeles, near Cholame. Accompanied by his mechanic, Rolf Weutherich, Dean was speeding up the road in his Porsche Spyder 550 while the setting sun caused the sky to fade into a shade of gray almost exactly the same as the Porsche's. Then suddenly, seemingly out of nowhere, a Ford sedan coming at him in the other lane made a left turn across his lane. Unable to brake or to swerve quickly enough, Dean smashed into the side of the Ford. His neck snapped on impact. He was dead by the time an ambulance got him to a local hospital. Over the coming weeks and months, spurred on by the posthumous release of *Rebel* and *Giant,* a myth formed around Dean. As time passed, it grew, until eventually, like other artists who died before they should have—Diane Arbus, Robert Mapplethorpe, Sylvia Plath—he would become more famous in death than he had been during his lifetime. Ironically, one reason for that fame was the tragic circumstances of the death itself.

He was a beautiful gifted genius who died young. That was the legend. He was a deeply troubled young man who both amused and bewildered his family and friends with his demanding personality and obsession with acting. That was the person. What was there about the person that allowed the legend to be born?

One cold February night in 1957 in Kyoto, Japan, not quite a year and a half after James Dean died, Truman Capote was interviewing Marlon Brando in his suite in the Miyoko hotel. Brando was in Japan to shoot Joshua Logan's adaptation of James Michener's novel *Sayonara,* and Capote had come there to talk to Brando for a profile of him he was writing for *The New Yorker.* In their interview Capote asked Brando about Dean. It was, Capote noted, "a question that [Brando] seemed surprised to have been asked." Brando answered nervously. "No, Dean was never a friend of mine. I hardly knew him. But he had an *idée fixe* about me. He used to call up. I'd listen to him talking to the answering service, asking for me, leaving messages. But I never spoke to him. I never called him back." Brando was interrupted. When he returned to Capote, he continued. "Dean listened to me. He knew he was sick. I gave him the name of an analyst, and he went. And at least his *work* improved. Toward the end, I think he was beginning to find his own way as an actor. But this glorifying of Dean is all wrong. That's why I believe the documentary"—Robert Altman was preparing to make one on Dean and wanted Brando to narrate it—"could be important. To show he wasn't a hero; show what he really was—a lost boy trying to find himself."

Though Brando's assessment may be true, over the years Dean has become much more than that to, as of today, three different generations of admirers. He's assumed a place in our collective consciousness we've reserved for a mere handful of people. Maybe only Marilyn Monroe and Elvis Presley are more famous around the world than he is. And yet what was there about Dean that made him so special? What contributed to his becoming "a lost boy trying to find himself"? What exactly did Brando mean when he called Dean "sick"?

Dean was born in 1931 in Marion, Indiana, but not too long after he turned six his family moved to Los Angeles because Dean's father, Winton, got a better job there. Over the next three years, Dean grew unusually close to his mother. Then suddenly she died of cancer and Winton, unable to care for his son, sent him back to Indiana to be raised by Winton's sister. In the Dean mythology his status of de facto orphan is a key element; it seems to explain his deep-rooted insecurities and neurotic behavior. Whatever the reason, while growing up, he learned to channel his insecurity by throwing himself into his art. As a mature actor, he was willing to go too far, to flirt with the edge, to do what most actors never dream of doing. He dared to strive to be "real" on film, to show how an actual person would really respond in the world the film is capturing. Rejecting the polished style of the classically trained actor, he was rough, emotional (if it was called for), even occasionally out of control and inarticulate, but always honest, always *in the moment.*

In the end he may not have gone as far as he would have liked in his personal life. Evidence suggests that the image his studio projected to the public had nothing to do with the private life he actually lived. Warner Bros. painted him as a young, virile Casanova who dated one Hollywood starlet after another; in fact he was not like that at all. "Basically," one producer would put it, "he lived his life as a homosexual." If that is so, if he did have to compromise so vital an area of his personal life as his sexuality, that too was a tragedy, and perhaps a much more poignant one than the tragedy that unfolded on the early evening of September 30, 1955, when a driver who says he didn't see Dean coming pulled out in front of Dean's beautiful sleek Porsche.

2. In *Marilyn*, his 1974 biography, Norman Mailer addresses a central problem he had in writing about Monroe—her tendency to embellish events in her life or simply to make them up. "Some of them [episodes thought to be true]," Mailer contended, "were written by Marilyn, which is to say, by Marilyn as told to Ben Hecht, a prodigiously factoidal enterprise printed as Sunday supplement pieces in 1954. Hecht was never a writer to tell the truth when a concoction could put life in his prose, and Marilyn had been polishing her fables for years. No team of authors contributes more to the literary smog that hangs over legend than Marilyn ben Hecht." Mailer coined a phrase for these half-invented episodes based loosely on fact but still essentially works of fiction—*factoids*—and documented a string of them in Monroe's biography.

In the case of James Dean, the same sort of factoid pops up with more or less the same frequency. In the Dean legend he's said to have written about his mother, while trying to break into show business as a young man living in New York City, "My mother died on me when I was nine years old. What does she expect me to do? Do it all alone?" Yet a similar quote is attributed to him at another point in his life when, as a high-school student, he got into a fight, ended up being expelled, and that night sought refuge at his mother's grave. "What do you expect me to do?" he's supposed to have said while standing at the grave. "Do it all alone?" Which of these versions is true? Are they both true? Or are they both factoids? There's written evidence of the first, scrawled in Dean's almost illegible handwriting in the flyleaf of a book, so we can assume that it is at least partially true. But did he only echo in writing a comment he'd made to his mother's grave years before? With Dean, it's hard to tell since, as with most creative artists, he would gladly invent the details of his life if it made for a better story. After all, in an actor's life, the line between fact and fiction must be thin, simply because the actor does what he does.

Yet there are other reasons why Dean's biography has become full of factoids. First, at the end of his life and following his death, the Warner Bros. publicity department released biographical information about him to establish Dean as a salable commodity, not to tell the truth about his life. If facts had to be changed, they were changed. The primary concern was marketing Dean properly so that the corporation could earn money. Second, after his death, as the Dean legend endured, friends and family who survived him—and there were many since he died so young—invented and reinvented Dean's life story by telling it over and over to a never-ending stream of fans. Finally there's the problem of acquaintances who, barely knowing Dean, embellished the scant details of their friendship with him. Take Shelley Winters. She may have seen Dean occasionally at Hollywood parties in 1954 and 1955, but they were certainly not friends. "Jimmy was currently having a mad affair with Vampira—they probably made love in her coffin, from which she introduced the TV broadcast of old horror movies," Winters wrote in *Shelley II: The Middle of My Century.* She then went on to describe an occasion on which, Winters says, Dean lost a bet to her and, as a result, had to go to her therapist for a single visit at her expense. Since it is highly unlikely that Dean either had an affair with Vampira or made love to her in her coffin—he didn't even particularly like her, as he revealed to Hedda Hopper once when he dismissed Vampira as being "inane" and "infantile"—the accuracy of the story about the lost bet and the visit to the therapist is open to question.

Another person who has exaggerated his acquaintanceship with Dean is Dennis Hopper. Through the years, on television talk shows and in print, Hopper has offered an array of stories about Dean. According to Hopper, Dean was supposed to have gone into a monastery for the last three days of his life, a story that defies all existing evidence concerning the way Dean spent his final days. According to Hopper, Dean talked to him about his mother, a subject he almost never discussed with anyone, not even his lovers. According to Hopper, Dean revealed to him his secret of acting one day after Hopper grabbed him, threw him onto the hood of a car, and demanded to know how he did what he did, a story the very premise of which is dubious since Dean never would have allowed anyone to treat him in such a hostile manner. In actuality, though, Hopper had a small part in *Giant,* an even smaller one in *Rebel Without a Cause.* Dean probably knew him about as well as he did any other extra or bit player.

When writing a life, a journalist must sort out as best he can what information he believes is real and what he believes is invented. After that, he shapes his facts into a narrative. This is not an easy job, particularly if he keeps running across factoids, told on television or published in books and magazines, that are presented as if they are true but aren't. Then again, even Dean's hometown of Fairmount, Indiana, seems to be a product of the imagination. So do its inhabitants. Go there; look around. It's as if one has stepped into a Norman Rockwell painting—quaint stores, pretty neat houses, and quiet streets with names like Main and Elm and Sycamore. Talk to the people and they'll tell a folklore of the town that easily could have been imagined if it's not. For a lost boy trying to find some pattern of logic to his life, Fairmount must have been an extremely puzzling place.

Jimmy
Dean

1.   In the town's folklore it's said that Fairmount, Indiana, because it was the home of Bishop Milton Wright, the father of Wilbur and Orville, was indirectly responsible for the invention of the airplane. It's also said that Fairmount was indirectly responsible for the invention of the car. That's because local townspeople believe the town was the site of the creation of the first motor-run vehicle since in 1888 Orlie Scott and his two assistants, Charles T. Payne and Nathan Alpheus Armfield, built in a garage on East Washington Street a carriage that would be powered not by a horse but by a motor. When the contraption crashed just north of town, not far from Park Cemetery, the wreck was sold to Elwood Haynes of Kokomo, whom history credited with the invention. It's said that in 1903 Cyrus Pemberton sold the world's first ice cream cone and that somewhere between 1885 and 1907, the years he ran his lunch wagon, William "Bill" Dolman made and sold the world's first hamburger. Where did these historic events occur? Fairmount, or so it's said. The airplane, the automobile, the ice cream cone, the hamburger—all, then, are in debt to Fairmount for their creation. That's not bad for a tiny town, fifty miles north of Indianapolis, whose population throughout most of the twentieth century has hovered somewhere between two and three thousand. Maybe that's why in the 1980s the directors of the local museum adopted as a motto for the community "Fairmount—Home of Distinguished People." It was either that or the unofficial motto the town had used for years, "Fairmount—Indiana's Center of Culture." The town was called this, according to a published local history, because Fairmount had been home to so many "college presidents, writers, lawyers, scientists, doctors, actors, farmers, artists and teachers of national and even international fame."

These are the *myths* that enrich Fairmount's history, but some *facts* about the town are just as compelling. Founded in the early nineteenth century by Joseph Winslow, one of James Dean's distant relatives, who had come from the East through the Cumberland Gap to Indiana in search of a better life for himself and his family, Fairmount would remain essentially a farming community. For miles on end around the town lay rich flat fields on which farmers grew crops, mostly corn and beans, and raised animals, mostly pigs and cattle. Just before 1900 a group of businessmen set up the Fairmount Mining Company with the purpose of producing natural gas, which was indigenous to the area, but unlike Jonesboro and Gas City, two communities near Fairmount, the natural gas business never dominated the town's economy the way farming did. Just as agriculture defined Fairmount's financial life, religion dictated its social milieu. Through the town's history many residents have been members of the Society of Friends, commonly known as Quakers, a conservative Christian sect that believes in nonviolence, strict adherence to the truth, and the importance of the congregation over a minister in their religious services. At a Friends' meeting, which takes place in a meeting hall, not a church in the traditional sense of the word (although meeting halls are referred to as churches), no preacher presides. Instead, anyone moved by the Spirit can speak.

In Fairmount, in the decade before World War II, the Quaker community was large enough to support two Friends' meetinghouses. First Friends Church was located in Fairmount itself. The other had been established near Back Creek, a small, slow-moving stream that ran to the north of town, and was named, as a result, Back Creek Friends Church. Still, there was more to Fairmount than Friends churches— and the Baptist church, the Christian church, the Church of God, the United Methodist church, and the Wesleyan church, all of which were also located in the town. Besides Xen Edwards's drugstore, Citizen's Bank, the Palace Theatre, and Little's Koffee Kup, Fairmount had a post office, a tavern, a hardware store, a library, a high school, a supermarket, a cluster of small stores lining Main Street, and an office that belonged to Old Doc Holliday, the general practitioner who had delivered the majority of the young people in Fairmount. The houses, mostly two-story wood-frame structures, were built around the business district. That, though, was about it. If a person needed a hotel, a hospital, a restaurant, or even a wider variety of stores, he had to go to Marion, a small city about ten miles up the road with a population of somewhat less than fifty thousand.

It was from Marion that in late 1931 a young couple, married for more than a year and the parents of a new baby boy, moved back to Fairmount. Actually, the young man, Winton Dean, was from Fairmount originally, whereas his wife, Mildred Marie Wilson, came from Jonesboro. Her father, John Wilson, a former barber in Marion, now ran a farm, which he rented on shares, between Gas City and Upland. Her mother, Minnie Mae, kept herself busy raising her five children (Mildred, who was nicknamed Millie, was the next to oldest) until she died of cancer when her youngest child, Ruth, was six. Millie had gone to high school in Jonesboro where, among other activities, she had starred on the women's basketball team, the Jonesboro Crickets. Tall, stout, handsome, Winton was a pleasant, hard-working

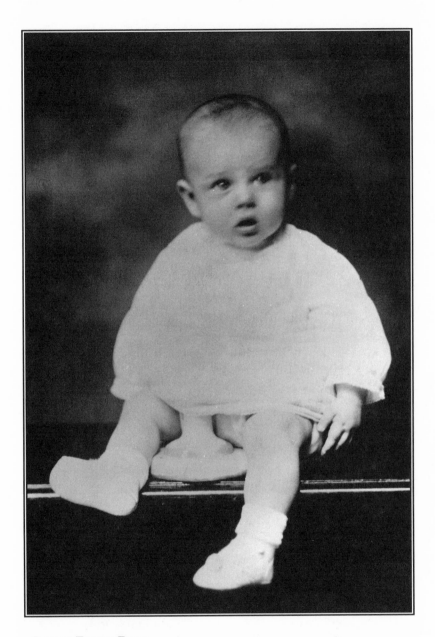

James Byron Dean

Mildred Wilson Dean, Winton Dean,
and five-month-old Jimmy

young man who, like most of the Deans, had a keen if subdued sense of humor. Slender and beautiful, Millie loved the arts, especially poetry, which she sometimes recited in church. Winton and Mildred met while Mildred was sharing an apartment with two other young women in Marion, had a passionate romance, and, on July 26, 1930, took out a marriage license at the Grant County courthouse in Marion. Later that same day, a local clergyman, Zeno Doan, married them. Winton was twenty-two, Mildred twenty. After the ceremony, they stopped in Fairmount at the home of some friends, David and Hazel Payne, to tell them that they had just gotten married but had no place to go on their honeymoon. The Paynes insisted that they stay with them. So they did, for the next two weeks. It was after those two weeks that the Deans set up housekeeping not in Fairmount or Jonesboro or Gas City, which would have been most logical, but in Marion in a cramped apartment in a building called the Seven Gables, located on the southwest corner of East Fourth and McClure streets in the central part of the city. Why Winton and Mildred Dean chose to move there instead of Fairmount, where they could have been closer to family and friends, became obvious soon enough, at least to those who really knew the couple. Mildred was pregnant, it turned out—and she had been for several weeks by the time she and Winton had gotten married.

In those first months of marriage, Winton went about his job in Marion at the Veterans Administration Hospital, where he had finished his training to become a dental technician. Because the country was in the middle of the Great Depression, Winton considered himself lucky to have a decent job, although the Deans, like most newlyweds, were extremely pressed for money. While her husband worked, Mildred spent her days fixing up their apartment and getting ready for the birth of their baby. Then, on the evening of February 7, 1931, only six months and twelve days after she and Winton were married, Mildred felt her water break and she went into labor.

Winton called the family physician, Victor Cameron, who came right over. A few hours later, at two o'clock in the morning on February 8, there in the Deans' apartment in the Seven Gables, Mildred gave birth to a son. Weighing eight pounds and ten ounces, he was a healthy, alert baby. After some thought, Winton and Mildred decided to name him James Byron. It seems probable that the Deans named their son for James Amick, a dentist with whom Winton worked, and Byron Vice, one of Winton's friends. Yet it's also possible that Mildred named him James simply because she liked the name (she didn't *have* to have a reason) and Byron because her favorite poet was the English Romantic George Gordon, Lord Byron. Whatever the reason, James Byron is the name the Deans chose, and during his life it would be the sort of name that would be altered or molded into several different forms. Jim, Jimmie, Jimmy, Deanie, Deaner, Jimmy Byron, James Byron—these were just a few variations friends and family would use throughout the years.

In the strictest sense of the word, Jimmy—and that's what most people would call him most of the time—was an unwanted child. He was not merely unplanned. His mother had gotten pregnant at a time when couples did not generally conceive children out of wedlock since doing so resulted in social disgrace. From all indications, though, once her pregnancy had become a reality to her, Mildred had ended up wanting Jimmy. After he was born, she held him, cuddled him. She doted on his every move, as any devoted mother would. In her own mind, Jimmy had become the child she always wanted, whether he was or not. "Millie was a very loving and giving person," says Ruth Wilson Stegmoller, Mildred's youngest sister. "She adored Jimmy. She adored her son."

But Winton was different. For him, in the summer of 1930, each passing day brought a new and heightened sense of anxiety. As week after week went by and Mildred had still not started her period, Winton became more worried. May turned into June. Soon it was July. Before long, Mildred had missed not one period but two, so they couldn't deny what was happening any longer. Finally Winton and Mildred got married. Then six months and twelve days later, there he was— Jimmy, the physical evidence of Winton and Mildred's night of plea- sure. Whenever Winton, a man considered by his friends to be distant and remote, picked up his son, Jimmy must have felt subconsciously, even from the first days of his life, that his father was what he was— cold and unloving.

Winton and Mildred waited for enough time to pass to blur the dates of their marriage and of Jimmy's birth. Then they moved to Fairmount and settled in a clapboard house on the corner of Washington and Vine streets. They lived there for several months—the newspaper boy would notice Jimmy, a curious, rambunctious infant, crawling around on the living room floor—before they moved two more times. First they stayed briefly with Winton's parents in Fairmount; next they moved into a tiny house near Back Creek Friends Church on a farm owned by Winton's brother-in-law, Marcus Winslow. The farm, one hundred and eighty acres just off Sand Pike Road, was originally owned by James Winslow, the Fairmount founder who had come west a century ago. Marcus had lived on the farm since he and Ortense, Winton's sister, had gotten married. Along with Charles Nolan, Win- ton and Ortense were the children of Charles and Emma Woolen Dean. In Grant County, Indiana, the Deans went back as far as Jim- my's great-great-grandfather Cal, who was buried in Park Cemetery. For three generations, the Deans had chosen farming and auction- eering as ways to make a living. From the time Jimmy was big enough to sit on his lap, Grandfather Dean would sell him off in a mock auc- tion, usually to Jimmy's grandmother. Just big enough to respond to what was happening, Jimmy seemed fascinated by his grandfather's fast talking. Auctioneering, the Deans pointed out with pride, is really a form of performing.

From all accounts, Jimmy was a happy baby. At two he spoke in

complete sentences. At three he started drawing pictures with crayons. Once he had begun coloring, Mildred could hardly get him to
stop. At this time Jimmy had lots of nosebleeds and he fainted
occasionally—the only two traits that made him different from other
preschool children—but the doctor said he'd outgrow these problems.
And he did. In time it became obvious that Jimmy was going to be
both curious and stubborn, traditional Dean personality characteris-
tics. For years, Hazel Payne would tell the story about the afternoon
Winton and Mildred brought Jimmy out to the house on Beaver Dam
Lake into which the Paynes had moved after they left Fairmount. On
the day of the Deans' visit, Hazel had given up looking for her favorite
belt, which she had lost. Within minutes of walking through the front
door, Jimmy, not much bigger than a toddler, came wandering into the
living room from another part of the house, belt in hand. To punctuate
her story, Hazel swore she had never seen a child as inquisitive as
Jimmy. As for his tendency to be stubborn, Winton would one day say
this: "You'd try to order him to do or not do something and he'd just
sit there with his little face all screwed up and closed. It didn't take
you very long to realize that you weren't going to get anywhere with
him. Spanking didn't help. Scolding didn't. And you couldn't bribe
him. But you could always reason with him, or appeal to his better in-
stincts." Interestingly, the comment says as much about Winton as it
does about Jimmy. It seems appropriate that Winton would notice his
inability to control Jimmy, since it had been the very fact of Jimmy's
existence over which Winton had had no control, or at least not
enough to do anything about it.

Eventually the Deans got tired of living on the farm and moved
back to Marion, although their life in Marion didn't differ much from
their life in the country. Winton worked; Mildred kept house and
mothered Jimmy. By reading books and reciting poetry to him,
Mildred did all she could to interest Jimmy in the arts. As he grew
older, Jimmy came to enjoy drawing with his crayons so much that

Mildred had trouble getting him to stop and do other things, like play and eat. In 1936, not long after Jimmy turned five, Mildred decided to encourage his interest in the arts even more. Not only did she sign Jimmy up for violin lessons, she enrolled him in dance classes at the Marion College of Dance and Theatre Arts, a performance school on East Third Street owned by Zina Glad, a retired entertainer who had at one time performed in vaudeville with her parents. Not surprisingly, Mildred turned out to be a zealous stage mother. She was at Zina Glad's studio so much that she and Zina became close friends. Zina thought Mildred was an adoring and caring parent. She did not, however, form the same opinion of Winton. It didn't take her long to decide that Winton was a distant father. As much as Mildred was happy and outgoing in life, Winton was standoffish and reserved. The old adage about opposites attracting was certainly true with the Deans. Regardless of how his parents influenced him, Jimmy soon became good at dance. In fact, he mastered tap so quickly—in only a matter of weeks—that Zina Glad included him in the school's recital program for 1936, which took place on June 1.

As it happened, Jimmy spent little time studying at Zina Glad's school. Soon after Jimmy danced in his first recital, the Veterans Administration offered Winton a promotion to director of a dental laboratory in a veterans' hospital. The pay would be better, the position more prestigious. Normally Winton would have jumped at the opportunity, but there was just one problem. The job was at the Sawtelle Hospital in Los Angeles. If Winton accepted the assignment, the Deans would have to move to California, a state they had never even visited. Once Winton and Mildred thought the offer over, they decided it was too good to turn down. After all, they were still in their late twenties. They were young, ambitious, energetic. They had their entire lives ahead of them. So, in the summer of 1936, Winton, Mildred, and Jimmy said good-bye to their family and friends in Indiana and headed west, to Los Angeles.

*   *   *

The Deans moved into a small but pleasant duplex on Twenty-sixth Street, one-half block off Wilshire Boulevard in Santa Monica, then a quiet middle-class suburb of Los Angeles. With Winton's new position at the hospital, the Deans were coming up in the world. Their house, comfortable if not spacious, was still a definite improvement over their former one in Marion. In time, Mildred furnished the duplex attractively. As always, she took her role as homemaker seriously. When Jimmy was old enough for kindergarten, Mildred, as concerned a parent as ever, enrolled him in Brentwood Elementary School in West Los Angeles. He also started first grade there. Beginning on February 8, 1938, Mildred moved Jimmy to the McKinley Elementary School on Santa Monica Boulevard at about the same time the Deans moved from the duplex to a stylish, ranch-style house not far from the Pacific Coast Highway at 1422 Twenty-third Street, still in Santa Monica. At McKinley, Jimmy finished first grade, then stayed at the school for second and third. His third-grade year ended on June 21, 1940.

For the Deans, life in Los Angeles was comfortable and enjoyable. The weather was temperate year-round, so there were no frigid winters, a welcome change from Indiana. The city was large and sprawling, unlike Fairmount or Marion, so there was always something to do. It seemed the Deans' lives were full of promise in a way they never would have been back in Grant County. When Zina Glad visited California with her parents in 1939, she telephoned Mildred to ask if she could come by and see her and Jimmy. She ended up staying with the Deans for a week. Zina and Mildred sat around Mildred's kitchen drinking coffee and catching up on gossip. On numerous occasions, Zina had her picture taken outside with Jimmy. Then one afternoon Zina went swimming with the Deans at Lake Elsinore. That afternoon, Winton told a joke that supposedly explained how the lake, known for its high concentration of sulfur, got its name. A Mexican and a Spaniard were swimming in the lake one day when one said to the other, "It smells like hell, señor." And that's where the name came from, Winton said, chuckling. Zina could not help but think that the joke was less innocent than it sounded. Maybe she was just being too sensitive. After all, she was always bothered by jokes that appeared to make fun of a whole race of people.

Finally it was time for Zina to leave the Deans, who had come to represent to her the all-American family, Winton's personality notwithstanding. As she was going, Jimmy begged her to stay. Don't worry, Zina Glad said, I'll come back and visit you again. As it turned out, she never did. For around the time of Zina's visit, Mildred became sick, and the events that unfolded as a result of her illness would change the direction of Jimmy's life permanently.

2. It was the end of summer in Los Angeles and Mildred was looking forward to another Southern California autumn until, complaining of severe pain in her lower back, she went to her doctor, who put her in the hospital and operated on her. Surprisingly, Mildred neither asked her doctor the reason why she needed to be operated on nor pressed him to reveal to her the nature of her illness. The doctor did discuss these matters with Winton, who was selective about whom he shared the information with; apparently he never told Mildred what was wrong with her. After she recovered from the surgery, which had been on her reproductive organs, the doctor allowed Mildred to go home. Over the coming weeks, she failed to improve. She didn't even feel well enough to finish the course in cosmetology she was taking to become a beautician. Before long she didn't have enough energy to get out of bed. "She was in bed a lot," says Ruth Stegmoller, who in 1939 had moved out from Indiana to Los Angeles and was living with her sister. "One day she told me to go to the

Mildred Marie Wilson Dean

dresser drawers and get her rings and try them on. Then she said, 'When I'm done with those rings they're yours.' "

In the late winter and early spring, Mildred was deteriorating noticeably. Finally she and Winton decided to inform the family back in Indiana about her condition. By the time Winton wrote to his mother in late spring and described Mildred's physical state, Mildred had already become gravely ill. Though the doctor had diagnosed her illness and informed Winton of his prognosis, the doctor and Winton—both of them—avoided discussing Mildred's condition with her. In Fairmount, Emma Dean took her son's letter to her own doctor, who read Winton's description of Mildred's symptoms and explained to Emma Dean that Mildred most likely had eight weeks to live, maybe even less. To give Winton the assistance he needed, Grandma Dean took a train to Los Angeles; she also brought Mildred's other sister with her. At the time of their arrival, Grandma Dean had prepared herself for the worst. Now she had to prepare Winton—and Jimmy, if that was possible. It was not until Grandma Dean and Mildred's sister arrived that Ruth found out what was wrong with Mildred. "I knew she had surgery was all I knew," says Stegmoller. "The night before my sister and Ma Dean came out Winton came into the kitchen and asked me what I thought about Millie. And I said, 'She'll be all right. She'll get well.' And Winton turned around and walked out. My sister got there the next day and told me Millie had cancer. That was the first I heard of it."

Mildred's condition worsened quickly. Soon she was bedridden. Grandma Dean proved to be a great help around the house since sometimes Mildred demanded Winton's undivided attention. As the disease took over her body, Mildred endured excruciating pain. To take her mind off her illness, she liked to have the Bible read to her aloud. It made sense to Emma Dean that a gentle woman like Mildred would want to hear the Scriptures read to her as she approached death. On many occasions it was Jimmy who read to her. "Please call my Jimmy boy in," Mildred would say. Then Jimmy would go in, sit on a chair beside his mother's bed, and read aloud either a passage she requested or one he picked himself. Often he would read her the Twenty-third Psalm, his favorite passage in the Bible. *The Lord is my shepherd,* Jimmy would say in his soft boyish voice, *I shall not want. He maketh me to lie down in green pastures: he leadeth me beside the still waters. He restoreth my soul . . .*

After Grandma Dean had been in Los Angeles a few weeks, Mildred hemorrhaged. "They put her in the hospital and packed her," Stegmoller recalls. "In the hospital she said to my sister, 'I'm doing just like Momma, aren't I?' Evidently, she had some idea she had cancer, but I don't know for sure that anyone told her." In fact, it was cervical cancer, and by the time Mildred hemorrhaged the cancer was so advanced that she had only days to live. Eventually the doctors let her go home to die.

At night Jimmy checked on his mother before he went to bed. He would touch a finger lightly to her eyelid to make sure she was asleep. Then one afternoon what Jimmy did not want to imagine *could* happen happened: Jimmy's mother closed her eyes and she never opened them again. Jimmy was down the street playing with a friend when she died. "I went to get Jimmy," Stegmoller says. "The family told him. He took it pretty mature. He didn't get hysterical or anything like that. He was troubled. He was a very alert and intelligent child. He didn't start screaming or crying or anything."

To Jimmy, even if he did manage to hide his emotions, his mother's death was overwhelming. After all, his mother was the one who cared for him, the one who nurtured him, the one who *wanted* him. When Mildred Dean died on July 14, 1940, she was twenty-nine years old. On September 15, she would have been thirty. Had she lived two and a half weeks longer, she and Winton would have celebrated their tenth wedding anniversary. In February, Jimmy had turned nine. Normally these dates would have been important, but birthdays and anniversaries didn't mean much to Jimmy, now that his mother was gone.

Soon after Mildred's death, Grandma Dean made Winton a proposition. She sat him down in a chair and, as she would write some years later, put it to him straight. "Now Winton, I want you to think this over carefully," Emma Dean said that day. "If you see fit to let Jimmy come back to Fairmount, Ortense and Marcus would like to take him. They'll raise him, if you want." Obviously this proposition had been discussed in detail before Grandma Dean had left Indiana, once the doctor had concluded that Mildred's condition was fatal.

Winton, according to Grandma Dean, just sat there.

"It never occurred to me I might be separated from Jimmy," Winton finally said. Then he paused again to make his decision although, considering the gravity of his mother's proposal, he didn't seem to mull it over very long. "You can't find a finer man than Marcus Winslow," Winton said, "and so far as choosing between the way my sister would mother Jimmy and how some housekeeper would take care of him, there's just no question."

And that was that.

In a conversation that seems to have lasted less than a minute, Winton Dean gave up his son. In this context, his reference to Marcus Winslow is telling. It sounds as if he were looking for someone to whom he could give his son, and almost out of nowhere the answer presented itself: Marcus. If Jimmy had ever felt that his father did not want him, those fears must have been confirmed when he got the news of his father's decision. In the space of only a few weeks, Jimmy had gone from having a family that, from his point of view, had two parents (at least one of whom loved him deeply) to the prospect of having no parent in his life on a daily basis at all. His mother's death crushed Jimmy. Many close to him felt he never got over it. But on the heels of this catastrophic event he was then essentially abandoned by his father. In a sense Jimmy endured not one overwhelming loss but two. Nobody would ever be clear on who told Jimmy that he was not staying in California with his father. It's hard to imagine that Winton Dean had been the one.

Ironically, there was an alternative available to Winton besides hiring a housekeeper. "I told Winton that I would stay out there and take care of Jimmy," says Ruth Stegmoller. "I would have done it for the sake of Jimmy. But Winton and his mother had talked it over and that was the decision they wanted to make."

After a funeral service in Santa Monica, Mildred's body was shipped by train on July 16 back to Indiana where arrangements had been made for her to be buried in Grant Memorial Park in Marion. Jimmy and Grandma Dean accompanied the body on the train while Ruth and her sister went back to Indiana on the bus. In Salt Lake City, the coffin, covered with flowers, was removed from the train and placed on the station platform near Jimmy's window. "Oh, my mother! That's my mother!" Jimmy was supposed to have said. "I'm going out there. I'm going to stand right beside her." And, with the train's nurse by his side, that's what he did, until the coffin was moved back on board. Then Jimmy resumed his seat next to his grandmother.

Finally the train arrived in Marion and, the following day, Mildred's funeral and burial took place. On her tombstone the inscription would read "Mildred Marie Dean/September 15, 1910/July 14, 1940." Under those lines Winton had added the single word *Wife*. Surely Mildred Dean would have wanted him to include the words *And Mother*.

With his mother's death, Jimmy began to face the new life that lay ahead of him. Through the years, family and friends would justify Winton's decision to give up his son. Winton was drafted into the Army Medical Corps eighteen months later, they would point out, as if that could mend the emotional damage done to a nine-year-old boy who saw himself as deserted by his father. However, other people who

knew Jimmy were not so sympathetic to Winton. "I never could understand why his dad didn't keep Jimmy out there with him," Zina Glad
said years later. "I'll bet he regrets it now. I guess I just never had
much use for his dad after I found out he sent Jimmy back to
Fairmount to live."

3. In the weeks after his mother's funeral, Jimmy tried to adjust to his new home on the Winslows' farm. About three
miles north of town and a mile past the Back Creek Friends Church,
where the Winslows went to Sunday meetings and Ortense played the
piano for Sunday school, the farm spread out on the west side of the
narrow two-lane road. Built in 1904, the two-story white-framed farmhouse, which had thirteen rooms, was connected to the road by a
gravel-and-dirt driveway. On the L-shaped front porch, the most dramatic feature of the house, Marcus had hung, using chains bolted to
the ceiling, a swing on which Ortense liked to sit on warm afternoons
to feel the soft breezes blow in off the fields. The porch was shaded by
massive oaks and sycamores, much older than the house itself; on a
summer evening they gave off a cool fresh smell. Located near the
house was a large white barn in which Marcus stored hay for his cattle
and feed for his pigs. There was also a pond close to the barn. In the
summer it was possible to fish the pond, and many people did, sometimes coming over from as far away as Jonesboro and Gas City. When
the pond froze in the winter, one could skate on it too, especially after
Marcus strung up lights to illuminate the pond at night.

Aunt Ortense and Uncle Marcus, whom Jimmy would soon start to
call Mom and Dad, did all they could to help their nephew adjust to
living with them. They went so far as to give him their second-story
bedroom because he liked the furniture in it. A frail but iron-willed
farmer's wife, Ortense encouraged Jimmy to continue to draw, paint,

and work with clay. Also, Ortense and Marcus, a midwestern man as large and strapping as his wife was slight, urged Jimmy to play with their daughter, Joan, who was five years his senior. Still, the changes that had taken place in his life over the last few months were hard on Jimmy. One day about two weeks after he'd been on the Winslow farm, Jimmy suddenly broke down weeping. He was crying so hard his little body shook. "What's the matter?" Ortense wanted to know. "I was just thinking about my mother," Jimmy said as he cried. "Of course," Ortense would later observe, "he was upset when he came back, losing his mother. [But] the neighbor boys could come in and play with him. One of them had a pony. He even left it here a week or two for Jimmy to play with. Everyone kind of just felt sorry for him. We had no trouble. He cooperated just fine with us. Of course, we always had in the back of our heads he had lost his mother."

That fall, Jimmy was distracted considerably with the start of the school year. He signed up for fourth grade at West Ward Elementary, known around Fairmount as the Old Academy since at one time it had been run as a religious school. A small building located between town and the Back Creek Friends Church, it was one of Fairmount's two elementary schools. (The "town" children went to North Ward, located in town, while the "country" children, like Jimmy, attended West Ward.) At West Ward, Jimmy's main teacher was a colorful woman named India Nose. He also had Ivan Seward, who taught some of his classes, coached him on the basketball team, and sponsored him in the 4-H club. Jimmy felt uneasy about his new setting, but soon the other children, after poking fun at him at first, tried to make him feel at home. His teachers noticed that he was a "nice" boy, a bit more subdued and reserved than most boys are. Naturally they were mindful of the fact that his mother had recently died. "Jimmy was just like any other little boy," says Bertha Seward, Ivan's widow, who worked as a substitute teacher at West Ward when Jimmy was a student there. "He wasn't spectacular. He wasn't a bad boy. He wasn't trouble. He

Jimmy with elementary school friends

was kind of quiet, just a good little kid, although in years to come I think he felt terribly mistreated that he had to lose his mother. I don't believe he ever got over her death."

Before long, Jimmy fell into a routine. He would wake up early, eat the breakfast Ortense cooked for him, and take the school bus down to West Ward. Following a day of lessons and after-school sports, he returned to the farm, again on the bus, to do his homework and have an early supper, around five-thirty or six. As Jimmy got older, Marcus assigned him chores to do on the farm, which he performed either in the morning before he went to school or after he got home. At night, once his homework and chores were finished, he would spend his free time working on his art or listening to the radio. These were radio's glory days, when a person could hear dramatic programs like the *Lux Radio Theatre* or entertainment showcases based around personalities like Bob Hope, Red Skelton, and Jack Benny.

Some nights, as Jimmy listened to the voices drifting from the radio, he dreamed that some day he would *be* one of those voices. He knew in his heart that he could perform. Family and friends said he was just being like his Grandma Dean, who was known for her love of doing skits and, in her capacity as a member of the Eastern Star, dressing up in costumes. Still, most people didn't take Jimmy seriously. In no time he was saying that not only did he want to be on the radio, he wanted to be in the movies too. "When Jimmy'd be drying dishes for me," Ortense would recall, "he used to dream out loud about getting in the movies. 'Course, I didn't pay any attention—figured that'd be impossible for an Indiana farm boy. I mean, there wasn't anything very different about him—except that he had this strange ability to take you along with his feelings. When something would go wrong at school or on one of his ball teams, we'd all feel blue until he came out of it. And I remember a neighbor telling me once when he was about ten that he looked too fair for a boy, but I've never figured that out."

Though Ortense didn't understand what her friend meant by her comment that Jimmy was "too fair for a boy," it became clearer as he grew older. Jimmy remained almost too pretty to be a boy. The sandy hair, the cherubic face, the delicate body, all combined to give him an innocent sweetness not present in most boys. It didn't help that he spent so much time, when he wasn't listening to the radio, doing something artistic: painting, drawing, molding clay. In a town like Fairmount, children learn early on that most activities in life can be described by two sweeping terms: masculine and feminine. With his painting and his daydreams about acting, it seemed that Jimmy felt inclined to engage in activities that most Fairmount locals would have considered feminine.

Soon Jimmy became much more vocal about his wish to act. To this end, he began to take any opportunity he could to perform. At Back Creek Friends Church, which he attended with the Winslows on Sundays, various groups put on plays. Not yet a teenager, Jimmy got his first taste of the stage, such as it was, in these church plays. In one, *To Them That Sleep in Darkness,* he portrayed a blind boy who regains his vision. The vehicle may have been strictly amateurish, but Jimmy's performance was so deeply affecting that many years later audience members would still remember him in it. "My mother-in-law would talk about this one play Jimmy Dean was in at church," says Nancy Wood, a Fairmount resident. "She could remember him in it as plain as can be. It was a Christmas play and he played a little blind boy. He had been healed during the play. At the end of the play there was a star and the way you knew he had been healed was when he looked up at that star and said, 'Mother, look, I can see the star.'"

A good student, though by no means outstanding, Jimmy continued on at West Ward in the fifth and sixth grades. For Jimmy, these were quiet years, especially compared to what he had endured already in his life. In the world outside Indiana, though, events were anything but quiet.

Jimmy as a teenager

Three months into Jimmy's fifth-grade year, the United States entered World War II following the Japanese attack on Pearl Harbor. Like everyone else in Fairmount, Jimmy listened to reports about the war on the radio. Certainly he must have wondered if his father, who had been drafted into the army, would end up in the fighting, although maybe he didn't worry about this as much as one might think. With each passing month, Winton was becoming less of a real presence in his son's life.

In the fall of 1943, Jimmy started seventh grade, which meant moving from West Ward to Fairmount High School, located in town on Vine Street. This was a major change for Jimmy, but he seemed to weather it with few problems. That fall, Jimmy's life was altered in another way as well. On November 2, Ortense gave birth to a son, whom she and Marcus named Marcus Junior. Jimmy was thrilled with "Markie," as he was nicknamed. Because of their living arrangements and because of the nature of the relationship that developed between the two boys through the years, Jimmy did not think of Markie as a cousin but as a brother. Markie looked on Jimmy as a brother as well. In many ways Markie considered Jimmy more of a sibling than he did his own sister Joan, who married Myron Peacock around the time Markie was born and moved off the farm to live in a house of her own with her husband.

Over the next three years, as he attended the seventh, eighth, and ninth grades, Jimmy saw his life at Fairmount High and on the Winslow farm settle into an expected grind. There were eventful moments, like the day he fell out of the barn loft and knocked his front teeth out. As a result of this accident he had to wear a dental bridge for the rest of his life. On another occasion, he, his friend Bob Pully, and some other boys were playing in a field of dry grass when Jimmy got the idea to start striking matches. One match caught a patch of grass on fire and before the boys could put the fire out a huge section of the field had gone up in flames. The fire department had to be called in to put the fire out. But mostly Jimmy's day-to-day routine followed an established pattern. The longer he stayed in Indiana the more he felt himself turning into a farm boy. Memories of California were fading quickly from his mind, though he would tell one friend that he wished he could live there with his father, who had returned to Los Angeles at the end of World War II after he had completed his service in the army.

It's likely that Jimmy changed his mind about this—at least to some extent—on the day in 1945, some five years after his mother had died, that Jimmy's father married Ethel Case. If Jimmy ever had to identify an event that represented the moment when his father's abandonment of him was complete, Winton's remarriage would have been it. For no matter what hopes he harbored about any kind of future relationship with his father, Jimmy had to have assumed that Winton's marriage to Ethel signified Winton's effort to start a new life, one that would be separate from the life he had lived with Mildred and that would never include Jimmy in any meaningful way.

In the fall of his sophomore year, Jimmy took his first class from a teacher who, more than almost anyone else, would change fundamentally the direction of his life. Everyone who knew this woman—her name was Adeline Brookshire—had an opinion about her. Her supervisors thought she didn't enforce enough discipline in her classroom on occasion, but her students and their parents adored her. A native of Marion and a graduate of Marion College, where she took a bachelor's in English and French in 1929, she had taught in Chicago and worked as a society editor at the *Marion Leader-Tribune* before she ended up at Fairmount High in the early forties. There she became a mainstay of the faculty, teaching speech, Spanish, drama, and English. She also sponsored the Thespian Society and directed plays. In the fall of 1946 in Room 21, Jimmy took her beginning speech class. From the start, she was a revelation to him. For the first time in his

Dean played on his high school basketball team.

A high school dramatic production. Dean is seated, in black.

life, he was in the presence of someone who appreciated performance as much as he did. By now, after listening to the radio for years, he had come to love language and to understand how powerful a beautifully written theatrical piece could be when it is rendered by a good actor. Standing before him now in the person of Adeline Brookshire, a diminutive, articulate, energetic woman, was someone who could explain to him how to become one of those actors. Jimmy was drawn to her as if in some primal way. It also didn't hurt that she was just old enough to be his mother.

Though Jimmy had never taken a class from her before, he knew Brookshire. Two years earlier he had asked her to coach him on a recitation about the evils of liquor he was to make at a meeting of the Women's Christian Temperance Union, a group to which Aunt Ortense belonged. Happy to be asked to help, Brookshire met with Jimmy during her off periods and gave him suggestions about ways to develop the piece. However, it was the start of his formal speech training at Fairmount High that made him want to pursue the craft of acting more than he had in the past. To do this, he appeared during his sophomore year in two productions at the high school. He portrayed Herbert White in *The Monkey's Paw* and John Mugford in *Mooncalf Mugford,* the sophomore class play. For these two productions, he used the stage name Jim Dean.

Jimmy was involved in other extracurricular activities as well. Despite having eyesight so bad he could hardly see without his glasses, he joined the school's basketball team, known as the Quakers (he had to use specially made goggles for practice and games). Many days he would practice on the farm with a backboard and goal he rigged up inside the barn. On weekends he would spend hours shooting hoop after hoop. In Indiana, one of the rites of passage through which a young man must go is playing on his high school basketball team, if he's any good at the sport at all. So Jimmy just expected he would play. During his sophomore year he started out his basketball career by joining

Fairmount's second team, along with friends like Rex Bright. Much to their dismay, the team had a losing season that year, with seven wins and nine losses. At one point in the season, Jimmy decided to help them improve by organizing pick-up basketball games in the barn between his teammates and boys from nearby high schools. Eventually one of Jimmy's friends, a girl named Melba Reynolds, started playing with Jimmy's team. On one occasion, when a group of visiting boys didn't want to play because Jimmy's team had a girl on it, Jimmy told them that if Melba didn't play, his team didn't play. Melba played.

Jimmy had another passion—motorcycles. (In Fairmount, the word is always pronounced motor*sickle*.) When Jimmy was fifteen, Marcus went down to Carter Motors, a motorcycle shop owned by Marvin Carter located not far from the Winslow farm, and bought Jimmy his first motorcycle, a 1.5-horsepower Czech-made CZ. "Jim Dean was just like any other kid who grew up in this town," Marcus remembered. "He played basketball, he went to Sunday meeting at Back Creek Quaker Church, and he did his chores on the farm. [But he loved] to ride that little black cycle of his through the meadow. After a bit, we let him take it to school." Years later, Jimmy recalled the rides through the meadow. "I used to go out for the cows on the motorcycle," he would say. "Scared the hell out of them. They'd get to running and their udders would start swinging, and they'd lose a quart of milk."

The meadow was not the only place Jimmy rode his motorcycle. He drove it all over Fairmount, Jonesboro, even Gas City, and when he did he liked to ride as fast as it would go. He also had a habit of getting people to ride with him just so he could scare them. "I was walking home from school one afternoon and he came along on his motorcycle," remembers Jack Raup, a Fairmount resident who was several years younger than Jimmy. "He told me he'd take me home. I was scared but I did it. I got on the back and put my hands around his waist. He drove past my house and kept going. I said, 'Jimmy, where

Dean with some high school friends

At a high school football game. Curiously Dean
didn't date many girls in Fairmount.

are you going?' He said he felt like going for a little ride. I was really scared because he kept going faster and faster. I was holding on hard. Then I told him that I had to go home, so he finally went back. He held both of my hands in one of his while we rode back. I got home and my mother told him he better not take me on that thing again."

The motorcycle would also be the center of an episode that took place in Jonesboro, the hometown of Clyde William Smitson, one of Jimmy's friends whom he first met in grammar school when their schools played each other in baseball. Jimmy and Clyde would go on double dates with Jonesboro girls. Curiously Jimmy didn't date that many girls in Fairmount, and when he did the dates were seldom serious. The vast majority of the dates were actually the result of school functions, occasions on which he was required to bring a girl. In fact, throughout his pre–high school and high school years, Jimmy never had a steady girlfriend. He seemed much more interested in sports and the arts than he was in dating girls. His reluctance to have serious relationships with girls was one of the few traits that set him apart from the other high school boys, some of whom would become so involved with their girlfriends during high school that they ended up marrying them following graduation. But Clyde did get Jimmy to go on some dates, and one night up by Jonesboro High School's baseball park two girls dared Jimmy and Clyde to drive through town on Jimmy's motorcycle without wearing any clothes. "So we did," says Smitson. "And when we got back to the ball diamond they'd taken all of our clothes. We had to go down to my house to get some clothes."

On the surface, this scene sounds typical of the actions of a Hoosier farm boy growing up in the forties. The basketball, the motorcycle, the occasional double dates—these were badges that symbolized a healthy teenage boy's coming of age in the Midwest in the years after World War II. But some Fairmount townspeople believed that this image Jimmy projected with so much skill was just that—an image. They concluded that underneath the image lay a much different person. "Jimmy played basketball but he was very hung up on being part of the crowd," Raup says. "I know that for a fact. He worked hard at being a basketball player to prove himself to those people in Fairmount. He rode a motorcycle because he had to prove he was a man." To understand the dual nature of Jimmy's personality—and to understand why he never had a steady girlfriend in high school—one has to examine the relationship he developed at this time with a man old enough to be his father, but a man who in background and temperament could not have been any more unlike Winton Dean.

Besides Adeline Brookshire, the most influential adult in Jimmy's life during his high school years outside his family was James DeWeerd. Charismatic and handsome, DeWeerd, who was in his thirties, served as the minister of the Wesleyan church in Fairmount. This position was important, even if the town had significantly fewer Wesleyans than Quakers, because on the west edge of town stood a Wesleyan campground that the national church used every summer for its revival meetings. As a result DeWeerd enjoyed a place of status in the community. No one would have dreamed of speaking disparagingly of him even though in many ways he was completely out of step with the townspeople. DeWeerd pursued a quality of life different from that of most of the farmers. Unmarried when he knew Jimmy, he dined elegantly; he always used linen and silver. He appreciated classical music. He had traveled extensively, especially through Europe where he had lived for a while when he had done postgraduate work at Cambridge University in England and served as a chaplain in the army in World War II in France. He loved literature and art and often lectured his congregation on the beauty of poetry. (In this way his tastes coincided remarkably with Mildred Dean's.) In a town like Fairmount, where convention and tradition were celebrated, Reverend DeWeerd simply did not fit in. His predilections, had they belonged to almost anyone else, would have been found questionable because they were too refined. But he was a minister—and in essence above re-proach—so the people of Fairmount overlooked what might have been suspicious in someone else. In fact, instead of being ridiculed, DeWeerd enjoyed great respect. He was often asked to speak at civic functions, such as town meetings and graduation exercises. He even served on the high school's board of trustees.

Fairmount residents ignored another practice of Reverend De-Weerd's—entertaining teenage boys. If almost any other man in Fairmount had routinely taken teenage boys to the YMCA in Anderson, a town about twenty miles away, to watch them go skinny-dipping in the gym's swimming pool or had these same boys over to his home for candlelit dinners, he would have been considered highly suspect. However, these were ways in which DeWeerd often enter-tained teenage boys, including Jimmy, who had dinner with DeWeerd many nights alone. After the dinners, DeWeerd would sometimes show Jimmy films of bullfights, a spectacle made popular by Ernest Hemingway's romantic depictions of the sport in his novels. The films were for special occasions, though; most nights Jimmy and DeWeerd merely read or listened to music or talked. Years later DeWeerd would describe a typical scene from an evening. "Jimmy was usually happi-est stretched out on my library floor, reading Shakespeare or other books of his choosing. He loved good music playing softly in the back-ground. Tchaikovsky was his favorite." Jimmy stretched out on the floor, music playing softly in the background, DeWeerd looking on fondly, the image is vivid, sensual, erotic. "There was something funny about James DeWeerd and homosexuality," Raup says today. "He sounds gay to me. He was a small-town hick who was sort of in-tellectual. I know that he hung around all these boys and I have a funny feeling that he had sex with them. It's quite possible that he had sex with James Dean."

Actually, he did. In all probability, Jimmy lost his virginity to DeWeerd one of those nights after the two of them had watched a film of a bullfight. Indeed, over a number of years, DeWeerd and Jimmy had a romantic relationship that regularly included sex. In a real way Jimmy's affair with DeWeerd was the beginning of Jimmy's sexual life, and because of the nature of the affair and the person with whom he was having it, Jimmy was forced to remain silent on the subject. "Jimmy never mentioned our relationship nor did I," DeWeerd told a newspaper reporter years later when he finally admitted to the affair. "It would not have helped either of us."

On its most basic level, Jimmy's affair with DeWeerd was all but inevitable. Abandoned by his mother and rejected by his father, Jimmy would have logically sought out parental figures in his teenage years. If that relationship took on a sexual aspect, that was all right too. The psychology is not complicated. Jimmy wanted a male figure who loved him. He was also maturing as a man and exploring the limits of his own sexuality. With DeWeerd, he could enjoy the company of a man and experiment with his sexuality at the same time. Still, if the citizens of Fairmount had known that Reverend DeWeerd was having an affair with Jimmy Dean, one can imagine what the repercussions against DeWeerd—and Jimmy—would have been.

Had Jimmy been involved only with DeWeerd, one could dismiss their affair as an aberration. But Clyde William Smitson, Jimmy's friend in Jonesboro, offers the following: "I remember one time when I was standing out in front of the Webb's Drugstore in Jonesboro and Jimmy and this guy pulled up in this nice big New Yorker car. Jim asked me if I wanted to go over to the South Marion Fair—that's when they used to have these old street fairs over in South Marion. This guy was a master sergeant in the air force, so we went over there and anything Jimmy and I wanted he was taking care of it. When we got back, they left me off at my house on Main Street in Jonesboro. Then they went on alone. Well, the next night this guy came up in his Chrysler and wanted to know if I knew where this other buddy of mine lived. I said, 'Yeah.' He said, 'Well, come 'round here and drive me to his house.' Well, hell, here I was getting to drive this big Chrysler New Yorker—that was really something. So we start out and the next thing I know the guy's got ahold of my leg. He's a queer! I don't suppose we went three blocks, but that's when I unloaded that fellow right now. I don't like them kind of people. I got ahold of Jim Dean soon after that and cussed him out for putting that queer on to me. I don't know whether Jim knew he was a queer or not. He was from Fairmount. I never did know what his name was. Jim knew him and he introduced me to the guy, but I didn't pay any attention." ✶

4. In the summer of 1947, Jimmy went to Lake Oliver in northeast Indiana on a trip with the 4-H club, of which he was not only a member but also its reporter. Hugh Caughell, Jimmy's freshman biology teacher, accompanied the boys on the trip as the club sponsor. When they returned to Fairmount, Jimmy quickly forgot about the 4-H club and Lake Oliver, for no sooner had he started his junior year in the fall of 1947 than he landed the part of Otis Skinner in *Our Hearts Were Young and Gay,* which the junior class performed at the high school in October.

For the rest of the year, Jimmy continued to take courses and excel in extracurricular activities. He enjoyed Adeline Brookshire's Advanced Speech but barely squeaked by in her Spanish class. He played on the basketball team once again and showed considerable improvement as the season went on. In the yearbook under his basketball picture the caption would read: "Jim Dean, who made a fine showing on the second team last year and as guard this year on the first. Should be a regular next year." He even jumped high hurdles on the track team. Because he was on all of these teams, he was able to join the "F" Club, a fraternity for outstanding athletes at the high school. These afternoons of playing sports served as a counterpoint to the evenings he was spending at Reverend DeWeerd's where the night's activities were significantly different in tone and substance.

Then, after the long grind of schooling, it was finally here—his senior year. Jimmy had arrived at the brink of one of the pivotal points of his life and, coincidentally, circumstances arose that allowed him to describe in an essay what he was thinking. Fairmount High had just gotten a new principal, Roland Dubois, who wanted each student to write a brief essay about himself as a means of introduction. Jimmy produced a reflective piece of writing that hinted at past and present secrets and speculated about his future.

I, James Byron Dean was born February 8, 1931, Marion, Indiana. My parents, Winton Dean and Mildred Dean formerly Mildred Wilson, and myself existed in the state of Indiana until I was six years of age.

Dad's work with the government caused a change so Dad as a dental mechanic was transferred to California. There we lived until the fourth year. Mom became ill and passed out of my life at the age of nine. I never knew the reason for Mom's death, in fact it still preys on my mind.

I had always lived such a talented life. I studied violin, played in concerts, tapdanced on theatre stages but most of all I like art, to mount and create things with my hands.

I came back to Indiana to live with my uncle. I lost the dancing and violin, but not the art. I think my life will be devoted to art and dramatics. And there are so many different fields of art it would be hard to foul up. And if I did there are so many different things to do—farm, sports, science, geology, coaching, teaching, music. I got it, and I know that if I better myself there will be no match. A fellow must have confidence. . . .

My hobby, or what I do in my spare time, is motorcycle. I know a lot about them mechanically and I love to ride. I have

TOP: Dean dressed up

BOTTOM: Jimmy plays with his cousin Markie on the Winslow farm.

been in a few races and I have done well. I own a small cycle myself. When I'm not doing that I'm usually engaged in athletics, the heart of every American boy. As one strives to make a goal in a game there should be a goal in this crazy world for each of us. I hope I know where mine is, anyway, I'm after it.

I don't mind telling you, Mr. Dubois, this is the hardest subject to write about considering the information one knows of himself, I ever attempted.

A discussion of "the information one knows of himself" would have been revealing, but Jimmy did not pursue it.

In this year of reflection and anticipation, Adeline Brookshire came into her Advanced Speech class one day and announced the Indiana National Forensic League statewide tournament. After class, Jimmy went up to her and said, "If you want me to, I'll get a reading and enter that tournament." Mrs. Brookshire thought it was an excellent idea and told Jimmy she'd be happy to coach him. She was pleased several days later when he said that he wanted to perform "The Madman's Manuscript" from *The Pickwick Papers* by Charles Dickens. During the fall Jimmy was somewhat distracted by his work in a Halloween Carnival spoof called *Goon with the Wind* in which he hammed it up as the villain. The show was directed by Gurney Mattingly, Fairmount's art teacher, who from 1947 to 1949 coached the Thespian Society because, as Brookshire would later admit, "Jim was more than I could handle." Following the carnival, Jimmy got down to business, and with the help of Mrs. Brookshire, who seemed to deal with him better one-on-one than in a class, perfected his reading.

Around this time, Jimmy's difficult nature got him into trouble. In Mrs. Brookshire's class he was performing his monologue from "The Madman's Manuscript" for other students when David Fox, a classmate, began to make fun of him. After all, it was an over-the-top part and Jimmy was playing it to the hilt. But Fox broke Jimmy's concentration, which made Jimmy furious. Following class, the two boys got into a fight in the hallway at the foot of the stairs and, after the principal broke up the fight and determined that Jimmy was the one who had started it, Jimmy was suspended from school. As punishment, he was not allowed to play in the Fairmount-Sweetser basketball game. When he came to the school just to watch the game, he could not even buy a ticket to get into the gym because, he was told, he wasn't a Fairmount student. It was on this night that Jimmy was supposed to have sought solace at his mother's grave. "What do you expect me to do?" he said as he sat in the dark cemetery. "Do it all alone?"

Finally Jimmy returned to school and, this episode behind him, continued with his classes and his preparation for the tournament. In April 1949, he performed in his senior-class play, *You Can't Take It with You.* On Friday, April 8, the day after the second and final show of the senior play, Jimmy participated in the first round of the National Forensic League state tournament in Peru, Indiana. His chilling rendition left more than one person in the audience wondering if he really was mad. "He does a fine job," said Frieda Bedwell, that day's judge and a teacher from Terre Haute. "I was deeply moved. I was especially impressed with the eerie expression in his eyes. They actually looked glassy, and mad at times." When the league announced the results of the first round, Jimmy had won. There was only one problem, which Brookshire explained to him. All of his ad-libs, a tendency Jimmy had started to develop even at this young age, put his performance well over the ten-minute time limit. That was obviously not a problem with the first round, but it might be in the future. Still, Jimmy balked when Mrs. Brookshire advised him to trim his monologue. "But every part is necessary," he said belligerently.

In the final round the next day, he did his performance just the same. The audience was clearly startled by his vivid, original expression. The judges voted him state winner. This meant that he could compete in the Forensic League's national tournament at the end of the month in Longmont, Colorado. The school was ecstatic and, when the time came, gave Jimmy and Mrs. Brookshire a memorable send-off at the Marion train station. The event was even covered by the *Fairmount News,* in which Jimmy would be quoted as saying that he "will do his best for the Fairmount citizens, by speaking well." In Chicago, Jimmy and Brookshire transferred to the Denver Zephyr; in Denver, to a local train that got them into Longmont on the twenty-eighth.

The following day Jimmy competed against ninety-nine other students from twenty-four different states. In the first round, when Jimmy again ran long, the judge warned him that if she found another performer equally as good who fell within the allotted time frame she would pronounce that person the winner. "It might be splitting a hair," she said, "but I would have to use that against you." Brookshire never knew if Jimmy shortened his performance since she had to judge performances by other students. Odds were, he didn't. The next day, when the awards were posted after the final round, Jimmy had placed sixth. He felt crushed and angry that he hadn't won. Brookshire would blame the loss not on the time length but on the fact that Jimmy had gone out the night before the finals to have a good time. Even so, it seems likely that the judge who had warned him about running long had meant what she said. For Jimmy, this episode foreshadowed the way he would act throughout his life when he ran up against authority figures.

Following a week-long class trip to Washington, D.C., which the senior class paid for with the one thousand seven hundred and sixty-five dollars they had raised by having Penny Suppers at the high school during the school year, the class returned to Fairmount just in time for graduation. Their experiences in Washington (they saw the White House and the Washington Monument, took a cruise down the Potomac River, stayed at the Roosevelt Hotel) were still fresh in their minds when Sunday, May 15, arrived and all forty-seven of the Class of '49 went to their baccalaureate and commencement exercises. At commencement, held in the Wesleyan tabernacle, Jimmy offered the benediction. At baccalaureate, Reverend Xen Harvey gave the main speech. For his participation during his high school years, Jimmy was presented with awards for dramatics, art, and athletics. As they sat in the audience, Marcus and Ortense Winslow felt proud, proud as parents.

Over the last year, Jimmy had been considering what to do next in his life. Mrs. Brookshire had suggested that he go to college in Indiana, or at least in the Midwest, but Jimmy seemed to have another plan. His father, whom Jimmy had visited on three occasions in California and who had also come to Indiana to see his son on different trips, encouraged him to move to Los Angeles and sign up for pre-law classes at Santa Monica City College. After he weighed all the possibilities, Jimmy decided to try California. Besides filling out the papers for the school, Jimmy was prepared to be in Los Angeles by mid-July to start the classes that were required of students who had not been educated in the Los Angeles area. Before he left, Jimmy and Reverend DeWeerd went to the Indianapolis 500 on the last Saturday in May. DeWeerd's graduation present to Jimmy, the trip marked the first time Jimmy had seen a sports-car race in person. He was fascinated by the cars as they sped around the track, so much so that he began to wonder what it would be like to race one of those cars himself someday.

Then, on June 15, 1949, the Winslows took Jimmy to the train station in Marion. There they put him on a train, waved good-bye, and watched as he started on the journey that would take him to his father out west. A new life lay ahead for Jimmy. His life in Indiana was over. In years to come, he would remember many aspects of his youth in Indiana with fondness, especially the Winslows and the Deans. But he would also remember Fairmount as a place that had both inspired him to be what he wanted to be and stifled him when he tried. As Jimmy had lived on the farm and observed the Hoosier values, he could not help but feel a displeasure with the people of Fairmount. He came to see them as bigoted and hypocritical, for despite their quaint behavior and apparent goodwill the Fairmount locals could be unusually closed-minded in the way they looked at the world. This was reflected in the nature of the community itself. In Fairmount, there were no minorities—no blacks, no Hispanics, no Asians—and even though the town had many different kinds of churches in it, it did not have a Catholic church or a Jewish temple. The attitudes of the townspeople, mostly white working-class Christians and Quakers, were exceedingly rigid on numerous issues, such as male and female roles, family matters, and, of course, sexual orientation. For years the people of Fairmount would gossip about what Jimmy was supposed to have said when on February 8, 1949, his eighteenth birthday, he reported to the local draft board. Was there a reason why he shouldn't be drafted? one board official was said to have asked. Yes, there was, Jimmy answered. But his reason had nothing to do with his poor eyesight or his Quaker religion, either of which could have prevented him from being drafted. Jimmy had a different reason. "You can't draft me," he said. "I'm homosexual."

Despite his fondness for Indiana, Jimmy could not overlook the rigid attitudes of the people in Fairmount. No doubt these attitudes had much to do with the sexual ambivalence he felt during his youth, the same ambivalence he would try to deal with as he grew older. Talking to a friend several months later in California, Jimmy would say that he often felt "bad" about some of the things he did in his years in Fairmount. Without question Jimmy was indirectly referring to his affair with DeWeerd. "By 'bad,' I don't think he meant precisely 'evil,' " the friend said years afterward. "[A]t some point during his early Quaker background, he must have learned to associate 'bad' with those actions not conforming to the normal and accepted patterns of conduct." One day, once he had left Los Angeles and was living in

New York City, Jimmy would write a poem about the town in which he had spent so much of his youth. Devoid of the sentimentality he sometimes used when discussing the place, the poem, "My Town," reads like an indictment. In the poem, written in rhyming couplets, Dean says that Fairmount admires "industrial impotence" even as it fosters "dangerous bigotry" and commends a "sense of idolatry." It "believes" in God but "hates" Catholics and Jews. Finally, though, the town is no longer "what I am," Dean admits. "I am here."

Ten
Thousand
Horses
Singing

1. In all probability, some force much more basic than a desire to get a college education caused Jimmy to leave Indiana and head for the West Coast. If he only wanted to go to college, he could have stayed in Indiana and attended Earlham College where, with the help of Adeline Brookshire, he would surely have been admitted. There he would no doubt have become a valued member of the student body who was interested in the arts. And Earlham was by no means inferior to Santa Monica City College, the two-year junior college Jimmy was going to attend in California that was anything but outstanding. What brought Jimmy to Los Angeles in the summer of 1949 was not a thirst for knowledge but a compulsion to make one more effort to win the affection of his father. Over the past nine years, Jimmy had seen Winton infrequently. Ortense and Marcus—Mom and Dad to Jimmy—had been good to him. They had provided him with everything caring parents give to their children: moral training, financial support, and, most important of all, unqualified love. Yet in the end the Winslows were not Jimmy's parents, no matter what he called them. Winton was, even though up until now he had hardly acted like a parent. So Jimmy arrived at the train station in Los Angeles in the summer of 1949 hoping at last to form a relationship with the one man who had played such a hauntingly alluring, one might say disturbing, role in his life. There Jimmy was, then—standing on the train station platform in Los Angeles, most of his worldly possessions crammed into the beat-up brown suitcase sitting on the ground beside him. It was as if he were saying to his father who had come to pick him up, with nothing more than his mere presence on the platform, Will you finally love me? Will you help this lost boy find his way home?

At the time Jimmy arrived in California, Winton still lived in Santa Monica, although he and Ethel had moved from Winton's old house into a modest but pleasant house at 1527 Saltair Avenue, near the hospital where Winton worked. Even so, by moving back "home" with his father, Jimmy was being forced to confront memories from the most painful period of his life, the time when his mother died. It didn't help that Jimmy now had to deal with a stepmother, a woman who was threatened (perhaps understandably) by the sudden reappearance in her husband's life of a child from his first marriage. Over the years, conflicting stories would surface about the way Jimmy and Ethel got along. Some friends and family would feel that Ethel, an overbearing and unlikable person by nature (to these people), resented Jimmy's presence and did all she could to undermine whatever reconciliation Jimmy and Winton were trying to work out. Others believed she made a point of staying out of the way. In this scenario she even hoped that Winton and Jimmy would settle their differences. No matter what part Ethel played in the Deans' domestic arrangement, it was Winton who assumed the dominant role in Jimmy's life. During the past nine years, two male figures, Marcus and Reverend DeWeerd, had strongly influenced Jimmy. Marcus had given him fatherly love. DeWeerd had given him a semblance of fatherly love (because of their age difference, DeWeerd could not help but be a father figure to Jimmy), although that emotion got clouded by their becoming lovers. Now Jimmy was hopeful that Winton would come forward and become for him the true father he had never had.

In his way, Winton tried. He made Jimmy feel as comfortable as possible while he settled into his new home in Los Angeles. To get around the sprawling city, Winton bought Jimmy a 1939 Chevrolet. He encouraged Jimmy as he took the preparatory courses he needed to start college. Finally Winton offered Jimmy advice about the future. Though Winton probably didn't mean to, the advice he gave him and the way he gave it ultimately did more damage than good to their relationship. Winton wanted Jimmy, once he entered college in the fall, to study to become a basketball coach, a physical education teacher, or, best of all, a lawyer. Any one of these jobs would have allowed Jimmy to live his life relatively free of financial worry. Winton did *not* want him to pursue—under any circumstances—the one activity Jimmy seemed to love most in high school: acting. The vast majority of actors never make any money, Winton argued, and those who are lucky enough to get work don't know how long they'll have it or from where their next job will come. Anyway, Winton had lived in Los Angeles long enough to know that Hollywood was a corrupt business. For Jimmy to become successful as an actor, he would be forced to make compromises in his life Winton didn't want him to have to make.

Despite his father's objections, Jimmy was still interested in acting, and that summer he joined the Miller Playhouse Theatre Guild in Los Angeles in direct contradiction to what Winton wanted him to do. Even so, Jimmy was thrilled about working with the Miller Playhouse. His satisfaction surfaced in a letter he mailed to Ortense and Marcus. "I am now a full-fledged member of the Miller Playhouse Theatre Guild troop [sic]," he wrote. "I wasn't in time to be cast in any production but my knowledge of the stage and the ability to design and paint sets won me the place of head stage manager for the next production of four one-act plays." As it turned out, Jimmy *did* appear in one of Miller's summer stock productions. Using the name Byron James, he had a small part in *The Romance of Scarlet Gulch*.

With this move, Jimmy sent his father a clear signal. He might have come to California to try and establish a relationship with him, but if Winton thought he was going to kill Jimmy's drive to act, he was wrong. In Fairmount Jimmy had experienced the exhilaration of appearing onstage before a live audience. Now he was consumed with the desire to experience that feeling again. A father's pull on a son may be basic, but an art form's pull on an artist is hypnotic. Winton should have known what he was up against. Oddly enough, he didn't seem to realize just how single-minded Jimmy was about pursuing a career as an actor.

His summer courses completed, Jimmy enrolled in Santa Monica City College in the fall of 1949. The school was in the process of building new facilities, which had not yet been completed, so for the 1949–50 academic year the college held its classes in various rooms at Santa Monica High School. That first semester, Jimmy signed up for various courses related to a pre-law program (English, geology, physics, Spanish), a gesture that made his father happy. But he also decided to take History of the Theatre and Beginning Acting, two courses taught by Gene Nielsen Owen, who served as his counselor as well. Owen was quick to spot Jimmy's raw talent, yet at the same time she realized just how much his previous dramatic training, such as it was, had left him unprepared. "His articulation was poor, he mashed his words and he was somewhat difficult to understand," Owen would one day write. "In an interpretation class, someone pointed this out and blamed it on his Hoosier accent. Later, when we were alone in my office, Jimmy protested and removed the upper plate he wore across his hard palate for a dental problem"—the result of the accident when he fell out of the barn loft as a child. "To overcome his articulation problem, we launched a semester-long, extra-hour, oral interpretation of *Hamlet*. I told him if anything would clear up fuzzy speech it would be the demanding soliloquies of Shakespeare. And so we began, on a one-on-one basis, what was to be a fascinating and revealing study for both of us."

Owen would not forget their *Hamlet* sessions. "The job of reading a Shakespeare play," she says, "would have been too much for him. He could memorize letter perfect. I didn't want him to improvise Shakespeare, though. So I took him all the way through *Hamlet*. He didn't have any trouble with it at all, but I was helping him with the understanding. He would read alone and then he would memorize all of the soliloquies. That was a great event for Jimmy—to achieve that much that young in an academic field. I felt it was an encouragement to him. If Jimmy could have done Hamlet on Broadway someday, it would have been a revolutionary role. Oh, it would have been remarkable!"

On the whole, Jimmy did well during his first semester in college, although the grades he earned in his pre-law courses were not as strong as he—or Winton—would have hoped. While the highlight of the fall term was his work with Gene Owen, Jimmy also won a spot on the college basketball team, joined the Drama Club, and became a member of the Jazz Appreciation Club. By the spring semester, he was elected to the Opheleos Men's Honor Service Organization, a highly competitive group that consisted of the school's twenty-one most outstanding young men. Because he was a member of this group, Jimmy wore a royal blue blazer to class, a sort of symbol of prestige on campus.

During the spring Jimmy continued to be intensely interested in acting. He studied with Gene Owen, now taking classes in voice and diction and radio broadcasting from her, but that wasn't enough. As a part of the May Day activities at the college, he and another student organized and acted in a show called *She Was Only a Farmer's Daugh-*

ter. As busy as he was, the more time Jimmy spent at Santa Monica City College, the more he became consumed with a new idea. What he really wanted to do was transfer across town to the University of California at Los Angeles, a campus of the state university system located near Santa Monica in Westwood. He wanted to move there for one reason. At UCLA, he would have more opportunities to study the dramatic arts. When he talked to Gene Owen about his plans to transfer to UCLA for the fall term, she was adamant in her belief that she didn't feel Jimmy was ready to tackle the school's formidable academic demands. "I advised him against going to UCLA," Owen says. "I was a graduate of UCLA and I knew it was a very academic college for Jimmy. I knew he didn't have the background for that college. I wanted very much for him to stay with us an additional year and do more of the participation and maybe even select another college."

Yet Jimmy was obsessed. Something deep within his psyche—a creative impulse or a need to belong or maybe simply sheer ambition—made Jimmy ignore Owen's advice. The prospect of studying in one of the country's best theatre departments, a program that in the past had provided the Hollywood studio system with a steady stream of writers, directors, and actors, was too appealing for him to resist. If he stayed at Santa Monica, he had little chance of making the contacts he needed to get work in the entertainment business. At UCLA, his chances were much better. So Jimmy made up his mind. He would go to UCLA.

When he applied to the school for the fall semester of 1950, his grades were good enough that he was accepted right away. There was, of course, one major problem Jimmy had to deal with—his father. Like Gene Owen, Winton was opposed to Jimmy's transferring to UCLA. Winton realized that at UCLA, with its many opportunities for actors, Jimmy would lose interest altogether in the two career areas Winton continued to push—physical education and the law. Before Winton knew it, Jimmy would be a drama major. The prospect of that

happening made him cringe. On this issue, though, Jimmy wouldn't
give in to his father. He arranged to start school at UCLA in the fall
and, after spending the summer working as a counselor at a children's
camp, signed up for his classes as planned. To appease Winton,
Jimmy did select a pre-law program at UCLA. It did no good. Winton
was so furious that Jimmy would ignore him and change schools over
his objections that the two of them argued constantly, heated bitter
fights. Their confrontations soon became vengeful and mean-spirited.
Still, the more they fought the more Jimmy was determined to do what
he wanted. In a way Jimmy was saying to his father what he had
wanted to tell him for years: If you don't care anything about my feelings, then I don't care anything about yours either.

The friction between the two of them became so intense that Jimmy
could not continue living with Winton. Around this same time, Winton
and Ethel decided that they wanted to leave Santa Monica and buy a
house in Reseda, another Los Angeles suburb. After the Deans looked
for a while, they found a quaint house located at 7235 Yolanda Avenue. Since the family was relocating anyway, Jimmy used this as an
excuse to break away from his father and move onto campus at UCLA.
Once he had given some thought to where he wanted to live, Jimmy
decided to pledge a fraternity, Sigma Nu, and as soon as the term
started he moved into the fraternity house on Gayley Avenue. Despite
the falling-out with his father, Jimmy did not change his major from
pre-law. He may have made the selection in deference to Winton's
wishes, but people who got to know him during that semester believed
he was actually serious about a career in law. Maybe he *was* serious.
Even so, to hedge his bets—and to satisfy the drive that had gotten
him to UCLA in the first place—he signed up for theatre arts as a minor. This meant not only that he could take acting courses but that he
could put himself on an inside track to audition for upcoming theatrical productions at the college. One he had heard about, *Macbeth*, was
particularly appealing to him.

With college fraternity brothers. Dean is in
middle tier, on the left.

Jimmy was happy to be living away from home, but the rift etween him and his father created a serious problem he had not anticipated—a sudden lack of money. Besides allowing him to live at home rent free, Winton had helped Jimmy out financially. Now, that money had stopped more or less completely. Winton was not going to make Jimmy's life any easier, especially since he had defied him in such an obvious manner. Because of this, Jimmy was forced to take on part-time jobs at UCLA to pay for both his tuition and his room and board. At the start of the fall semester, he earned as much money as he could by working as a film projectionist in classes that required the use of visual aids. Even though the money was modest, Jimmy was at least able to work at a job he didn't hate.

That fall semester, while Jimmy attended his classes—Latin, geolMogy, American history, anthropology, and ROTC—he continued to think about acting. Finally, in early October, the theatre department announced that it would soon be holding tryouts for its production of *Macbeth*, scheduled to run on campus from November 29 to December 2. At the open auditions, Jimmy showed up, an unsure and relatively untrained novice who wanted to act as much as he wanted to do anything in his life. After he had read his lines onstage, out there in front of some of the toughest teachers in the business, he felt as if he had gotten into the part well enough to make an impression. Certainly all of the time he had spent studying *Hamlet* with Gene Owen in one-on-one tutoring sessions had helped him to become at ease with Shakespeare's language. In fact, he must have been more familiar with the language than most of the other students who had tried out, for once the auditions were over Jimmy learned that he had been cast in the role of Malcolm. To be directed by Walden Boyle, the production would be staged at UCLA in Royce Hall—without a doubt *the* most prestigious venue Jimmy had played so far. "God! It's a dream," he gushed when he found out he had won the part. "Don't let anyone wake me up." As he wrote to Aunt Ortense and Markie several days later, he was still ecstatic. "The biggest thrill of my life came three weeks ago," he said, "after grueling auditions for UCLA's four major theatrical productions, the major one being *Macbeth* which will be presented in Royce Hall (seats 160). After the auditioning of 1600 actors and actresses, I came up with a wonderful lead in *Macbeth*, the character being Malcolm (huge part)."

During the rehearsals for *Macbeth*, which began on October 12, Jimmy met a number of theatre people as he was introduced into a subculture he had not experienced at all in Indiana and only passingly at Santa Monica City College. In this world Jimmy began to encounter students and faculty members who shared his intense love for acting. At the same time, he would run across people who, although they adored acting, simply did not have the innate undeveloped talent he had been born with. Petty and jealous, these colleagues, usually fellow actors, looked down on Jimmy because of his humble background and his lack of expert professional training. They mocked his Hoosier accent. They made fun of his modest wardrobe. They ridiculed his unassuming Quaker demeanor. There were two students who overcame these prejudices to become friends with Jimmy: Jeanetta Lewis, a member of the crew on the *Macbeth* production, and William Bast, a theatre major who, like so many others at UCLA, was not impressed with Jimmy at first. "As I recall," Bast would later write about the occasion on which he was introduced to Jimmy in the Green Room at Royce Hall during a rehearsal for *Macbeth*, "he made no impression on me at all. He was quiet, almost sullen, and seemed to resent the fact that he had been asked to work in the show." This may have been Bast's initial impression, but over time, as he and Jimmy entered into a relationship that became increasingly complicated, Bill would have to admit that his first impression was considerably off the mark.

During the run of *Macbeth*, Jimmy turned in an inspired if flawed performance. His energy and inventiveness made up for his rough elocution and Hoosier accent. When the play's short run ended, Jimmy felt sad, but encouraged by what he had accomplished. "The play was very much a success," he wrote to the Winslows. "I was very much rewarded and proved myself a capable actor in the eyes of several hundred culture-minded individuals. Man, if I can keep this up, and nothing interferes with my progress, one of these days I might be able to contribute something to the world (theatrically)."

2. Jimmy had done it. He had come to Los Angeles, and in a little over a year he had acted in a play put on by one of America's most respected university theatre departments. He was so excited by the experience that he could almost ignore the one—bad— notice he received for his performance. "Malcolm made a hollow king," Harve Bennett Fischman wrote in a review that appeared in the campus publication *Spotlight.* Instead, Jimmy focused his attention on what was actually an important—and perhaps even improbable— development. Isabelle Draesemer, a highly regarded agent who owned her own firm, had come to a performance of *Macbeth* and, after watching Jimmy, felt convinced enough about his talent to sign him on as a client. Because Westwood was a short drive from the studios and major talent agencies, it was not unusual for people in the industry to stop by and see student theatrical productions at UCLA. What *was* unusual was for Jimmy to land an agent with his first show. Many students in the cast and the crew, some of whom were a lot older than Jimmy, had been in numerous productions—and still didn't have an agent to show for it. Jimmy may have been young and untrained, but his talent was obvious.

Jimmy was still excited about the success of *Macbeth* and Draesemer's signing him on when, much to his surprise, he was given his first paying job as an actor. One day Jim Bellah, a fellow student at UCLA and the son of the novelist James Warner Bellah, told Jimmy about a two-minute Pepsi television commercial in which he had been hired to act. In the commercial a group of young people were going to be riding on a merry-go-round in Griffith Park. Someone would pull Pepsis from an ice chest and hand them out to the teenagers, most of them girls, as they went past the camera on the merry-go-round. "They need a lot more young people," Bellah told Jimmy. "Come on along." So Jimmy did. And on the crisp winter day that the commercial was shot in Griffith Park—December 13, 1950—Jimmy had been on the set no time before the director spotted him and made him the star of the commercial. Jimmy played the young man who hands out the Pepsis to the teenagers on the merry-go-round, the one person who was on camera during the entire commercial. For the day's work Jimmy earned a modest fee—twenty-five dollars and a free box lunch—and met two other young actors with whom he knew he could be friends—Beverly Long and Nick Adams—but ultimately the validation he felt from this one marginal job was much more important than money or potential friendships. In the life of an artist, there comes a moment when he realizes that to pursue his talent he has to make a commitment to his art that he must honor, no matter what hardships he has to endure. In the fall of 1950, as a result of his work in *Macbeth* and his mundane job on a Pepsi commercial, Jimmy had reached the point where he was willing to make that commitment. He no doubt felt that he had already lost his father because of his love of acting, if he had ever truly *had* a father. What could he lose that would be worse than that?

Around this time, Jimmy had a run-in with a brother at the Sigma Nu fraternity house. He had never really fit in with the other brothers. Not one to embrace authority, Jimmy had trouble adhering to certain fraternity rules. He also didn't do his share of the chores around the house, a habit viewed by the brothers as indicative of his unwillingness to uphold his commitment to the fraternity. Jimmy participated as little as he did, however, not because he hated rules or was busy (and he was especially busy during the rehearsals for the play) but because he didn't like the Sigma Nu brothers. The situation came to a head on the day one of the brothers made fun of Jimmy because he was involved in drama. That could only mean, the brother implied, that Jimmy was homosexual. The last time someone had poked fun at him over being an actor—he would never forget David Fox mocking him that day in Mrs. Brookshire's class at Fairmount High—Jimmy had beat the boy up. On this occasion, at Sigma Nu, he did the same, laying into the fraternity brother with such fury that the boy couldn't even fight back. When Jimmy was through with him, the boy lay helpless on the floor, scared and bruised. As a result of the fight, the brothers met and, once they had discussed the confrontation, decided that it was Jimmy, not the brother who had provoked him, who was at fault. The brothers' verdict was harsh but simple: Jimmy was asked to leave Sigma Nu. In actuality, Jimmy had not intended to live in the fraternity house much longer anyway. With his recent successes, he was even thinking about quitting college altogether so that he could devote all of his time and energy to trying to make it as an actor. After all, he was already getting work, and he had an agent eager to send him out on auditions. The brother's comment about his being homosexual and the fight that ensued were simply what he needed to force him to move on.

It's ironic that the incident at the fraternity had to do with Jimmy's sexuality. Recently, Jimmy had been casually dating Jeanetta Lewis, though the one important ongoing relationship he had had in his life so far was with James DeWeerd. Yet despite this affair and his apparent lack of serious heterosexual relationships, Jimmy felt compelled to defend his honor when a fraternity brother questioned his sexuality. Of course, Jimmy's affair with DeWeerd had been a secret that he and DeWeerd intended to keep from the people of Fairmount (or anyone else, for that matter). Now, apparently, Jimmy had made up his mind that, to the outside world anyway, he would continue to create the facade that he was heterosexual. If he had to, he would go so far as to fight someone who accused him of being otherwise. In reality he felt something else entirely. As Jimmy looked around him, he grew more certain that he *was* sexually attracted to men, not women. To be precise, he wanted to be with younger men, boys about his age. Boys, in fact, like Bill Bast.

It was a typical night in Los Angeles—pleasant, cool, peaceful. In the year and a half he had lived in California, Jimmy had grown to love the climate. It was so much more agreeable than the weather he had lived through in Indiana. If he had been in Fairmount right now, it would have been the dead of winter, which brought with it snow and frigid temperatures and stiff biting winds that swept down off the flat fields. Tonight, as he sat on a bus in the seat next to Bill, Jimmy wasn't thinking about the Indiana weather, necessarily. He was thinking about Bill. Jimmy had known him for only several weeks, ever since they met at one of the rehearsals for *Macbeth,* but in that short time the two of them had formed a close, comfortable friendship. There were several reasons why. They were dating friends. The actress who played Lady Macduff in *Macbeth,* a young woman named Joanne, Bill's date on and off, was friends with Jeanette, Jimmy's occasional date. The two couples had gone on double dates together, once even traveling to Mexico. What's more, Jimmy and Bill were both from the Midwest. Born in Milwaukee in 1931, Bill had spent time on a farm in Wisconsin when he was growing up and had attended the University of Wisconsin for two years before transferring to UCLA as a junior. Even more important, each was working hard at breaking into the entertainment business in some way. Jimmy wanted to be an actor, Bill an actor or a writer. For weeks Bill had been trying to get a job at CBS. He had already been a member of a radio workshop there, but now he hoped to work for the company full-time. Just this afternoon, Bill had taken Jimmy over to CBS to show him around and introduce him to a few of the people he had met so far. While they sat beside each other on the bus on their way back to campus, Jimmy was happy that Bill had taken him to CBS, even if the trip had not been *that* productive since Bill had not yet made any influential contacts. The trip told Jimmy something about Bill. Maybe Bill wasn't going to be jealous like so many of the other students in the UCLA theatre department. Maybe he was going to *help* Jimmy instead.

Bill and Jimmy may have had these external similarities, the kind that often play a role in two people's becoming friends, but there was something else about their relationship, something so ephemeral, so unspoken, that Jimmy himself had trouble putting his feelings about it into words. He sensed an energy between them, a sort of force pulling the two of them together. Jimmy had never felt this attraction with a woman before. He *had* felt it with Reverend DeWeerd; however, because DeWeerd was so much older than he, Jimmy often could not separate the sexual desires he had for DeWeerd from the fatherly love DeWeerd gave him. With Bill, there was no age difference. When Jimmy looked at Bill, in many ways it was as if he was looking at himself. Bright and energetic, Bill seemed absolutely determined to get what he wanted in life; even so, he was a sensitive, caring person who went out of his way not to hurt people. *And* he was handsome. His black hair and sharp facial features combined to give him a dark, seductive look that appealed to Jimmy. Still, he was soft too—not effeminate, a trait Jimmy had come to hate in a man, but gentle, open.

Jimmy had never lived with a boy his own age before, so he didn't know how he was going to approach Bill with the idea he had come up with. Now that he had been asked to leave the fraternity house, Jimmy planned to move off campus into an apartment, but he needed a roommate to share the expenses, which he could not afford alone. After he had thought it over, Jimmy decided that he wanted Bill to be his roommate. *That* was his idea. Bringing up the subject wasn't as easy as it might have seemed, mostly because of the way Jimmy was starting to feel about Bill. Even though they were both dating girls, Jimmy was beginning to sense more strongly his attraction to Bill—a palpable sexual longing. He could not help but wonder if Bill felt the same way about him. Sitting on the bus, Jimmy finally decided to come right out and tell Bill what was on his mind.

"You know," Jimmy said as the bus roared on, "you and I would make a good team."

At first Bill didn't answer. He just sat there.

"I said," Jimmy repeated, "I think we'd make a good team."

While Jimmy waited for Bill to speak, the bus ground on down Sunset Boulevard, passing the Beverly Hills Hotel.

"Team?" Bill said eventually.

"Yeah," Jimmy said. "We sort of complement each other. You're a pretty smart guy. I mean, you know a lot of things I should know. And there's a lot I could help you with, I suppose. I guess what I'm driving at is, well, if we stuck together—you know, combined forces—it might make for easier going."

On one level Jimmy was talking about combining forces to help each other pursue their careers. To show Bill he was willing to share whatever professional contacts he had made so far, he offered to introduce him to Isabelle Draesemer. Jimmy's gesture was important since Bill did not have an agent but needed one desperately.

Still, Bill did not respond. Jimmy was about to decide that his hunches about Bill were all wrong, that he shouldn't have even brought up the subject.

"You know," Jimmy said, "the other night at a beer bust at the house, they started riding us. I said I didn't like the stuff they wanted me to do for initiation. They started on me about being a theatre arts major and all. I guess I can't take a riding. It happened once before in high school. At the beer bust I slugged a guy."

For some reason this confession seemed to do it. Always one to question authority and conformity, Bill had come over to the fraternity house, at Jimmy's suggestion, to see if he wanted to rush Sigma Nu. Bill had hated the place, especially the Sigma Nu brothers. Later Bill told Jimmy in no uncertain terms his feelings about the house. Now Jimmy was letting him know that he too had had his fill of all their Greek phoniness. Finally Jimmy told Bill that the brothers had asked him to move out, that he was looking for an apartment, and that he thought he and Bill should move in together.

There was another long pause.

"You know, Jimmy," Bill said, his comment taking on more than one level of meaning, "you're probably right. Maybe we would make a good team."

With this, Jimmy felt a flood of emotions: reassurance, relief, acceptance, hope. In some basic way Jimmy believed that he and Bill had formed a connection much deeper than their fledgling friendship might have warranted, for even though Jimmy had known Bill for only a matter of weeks, he sensed they were building a substantive relationship. Jimmy had met the first person in his life with whom he wanted to live, and that person had agreed to live with him, regardless of Jimmy's limitations. As they rode on the bus, Jimmy could no longer control his emotions and found himself, before he knew it, confessing to Bill in a long but passionate monologue his most private dreams and aspirations.

"I've never told this to anyone else," Jimmy began. "I guess I always thought people would say I was crazy, if they heard it, so I just never told anyone."

Then Jimmy launched into his speech. "Have you ever had the feeling that it's not in your hands? I mean, do you ever just know you've got something to do and you have no control over it? All I know is I've got to do something. I don't exactly know what it is yet. But when the time comes, I'll know. I've got to keep trying until I hit the right thing. See what I mean?"

Bill said nothing, but let Jimmy go on.

"It's like, I know I want to be an actor, but that isn't it. . . . Just being an actor or a director, even a good one, isn't enough. . . .

"I figure there's nothing you can't do, if you put everything into it. The only thing that stops people from getting what they want is themselves. They put too many barriers in their paths. It's like they're afraid to succeed. In a way, I guess I know why. There's a terrific amount of responsibility that goes with success, and the greater the success, the greater the responsibility. . . .

"But I think, if you're not afraid, if you take everything you are, everything worthwhile in you, and direct it at one goal, one ultimate mark, you've got to get there. If you start accepting the world, letting things happen to you, around you, things will happen like you never dreamed they'd happen.

"That's why I'm going to stick to this thing. I don't want to be just a good actor. I don't even want to be just the best. I want to grow and grow, grow so tall nobody can reach me. Not to prove anything, but just to go where you ought to go when you devote your whole life and all you are to one thing."

Finally Jimmy got to the heart of what was on his mind. "Maybe this sounds crazy or egocentric or something to you, but I think there's only one true form of greatness for a man. If a man can bridge the gap between life and death, I mean, if he can live on after he's died, then maybe he was a great man. When they talk about success, they talk about reaching the top. Well, there is no top. You've got to go on and on, never stop at any point. To me the only success, the only greatness for a man, is in immortality. To have your work remembered in history, to leave something in this world that will last for centuries—that's greatness.

"I want to grow away from all the petty little world we exist in. I want to leave it all behind, all the petty little thoughts about unimportant little things, things that'll be forgotten a hundred years from now anyway. There's a level somewhere where everything is solid and important. I'm going to try to reach up there and find a place I know is pretty close to perfect, a place where this whole messy world should be, could be, if it'd just take the time to learn."

At last Jimmy stopped. "Well, then-there-now," he said. "I shot my wad. Now you know what a nut I am."

As Jimmy and Bill sat looking at each other, the bus moved on through the night, toward Westwood.

Once they had made up their minds to live together, they had to face the immediate problem of finding a suitable apartment. Rents were high, and their combined income, two college students living on whatever money they could scrape together working part-time jobs, was not sizable. Modest incomes or not, they had to locate a place, so one day they set out on their search by looking at a number of apartments in Santa Monica. (It's curious to note that when, for the first time in his life, Jimmy had the opportunity to rent an apartment of his own, in whatever section of Los Angeles he chose, he picked the one in which he had last lived with his mother.) Each of the countless apartments they saw proved to be unsuitable; usually they were way too expensive. Jimmy and Bill were about to give up apartment-hunting for the day when they spotted a FOR RENT sign on the street and decided to stop by one last place. The landlady, an eccentric older woman, showed them a tiny bachelor apartment. They hated it, but as they were leaving the woman took pity on them. Let me show you, she said, what my husband and I call Our Penthouse.

To reach the apartment, which was located upstairs in a building behind the main house, the three of them had to climb an outside set of stairs covered with fronds hanging from a palm tree growing beside the building. The instant Jimmy and Bill walked through the front door of the three-room apartment they were taken with its Mexican decor and warm, comfortable feel. The living room featured a beamed ceiling and original paintings depicting Mexican landscapes. The

kitchen had a quaint bar that connected it to the living room; cute red-
wood stools sat at the bar. There was one bedroom, but it was so small
it could hold nothing more than a bed. This meant that for Jimmy and
Bill to sleep comfortably one would have to sleep in the living room,
which also contained a bed. That arrangement didn't matter. The
apartment had such charm and style that the two boys fell in love with
it immediately. There was only one drawback—the price. The landlady's husband had set the rent at seventy dollars a month. The price
was also non-negotiable, since the couple was not in any rush to rent
the place out and the landlady, who had decorated the apartment herself, considered it her pet project. When Jimmy and Bill took everything into consideration, though, the price seemed worth it. "This was
just too perfect a place to start our lives of dedication to let a little
thing like money stand in the way," Bill eventually wrote. Judging
from his actions, Jimmy felt the same way. "We'll take it," he said
happily to the landlady when she came back from telling her husband
about their potential renters. "If it's okay with your husband."

Since it was okay with her husband, the apartment was theirs. With
more than a little trepidation about where the money would come from
to pay for the place, Bill and Jimmy handed over cash for the first
month's rent to the landlady, who wished the boys well before she left
them by themselves in their new home. Neither of them could have
known it at the time, but for the next five years their lives would be
deeply intertwined. More than anyone else Jimmy would ever meet,
Bill would become the stabilizing force for him, the one person he
could always come back to. They would have their arguments, they
would break up and get back together, Jimmy would wander off and
become involved with someone else, yet Bill was always there for
Jimmy when he needed him, from this day in early 1951 when they
rented their first apartment together until the day Jimmy died. "I felt
strangely right about what I had just done," Bill later said about his
and Jimmy's decision to rent The Penthouse, as Jimmy immediately

named the apartment. Even so, Bill, like Jimmy, could not have predicted the mix of emotions—the happiness and the anguish, the joy and the sorrow—the two would experience with each other as they lived their lives, mostly together, over the next handful of years.

After moving into the apartment on a Friday, Jimmy and Bill did their best to settle into their new living arrangement and get to know each other better. In those early days Jimmy spent a lot of time alone painting with oil on canvas. Over the last year or so, as he had lived first with his father and then at Sigma Nu, he had not felt comfortable enough with his surroundings to develop all of his artistic interests, not like he did now. At night, when Jimmy and Bill spent time alone, they often read aloud from works of literature. Besides Henry Miller and Kenneth Patchen, two of Bill's favorite writers, they read Stanislavsky, the Russian director and drama teacher who had invented the Method. Naturally Jimmy had studied the Method, on a very basic level, at Santa Monica City College and UCLA, but this chance to discuss the acting approach with Bill, someone whom he was growing to respect for his intellectual abilities, was invaluable to him. As they read passages together—Bill usually read to Jimmy because Jimmy seemed to have a great deal of trouble reading himself, a problem he had had since childhood—Jimmy would ask Bill to define words he didn't know and to explain concepts he didn't understand. Jimmy had formed a pattern in his life of seeking out people who were more knowledgeable than he and then doing all he could to learn from them. It was as if he always had to have around him a person who played the role of teacher, the way DeWeerd had. What's more, these relationships sometimes took on qualities that had nothing to do with the intellectual pursuits that had brought Jimmy and his "teacher" together in the first place.

While they were getting to know each other better at home, Jimmy and Bill were both trying to advance their careers. After trying to land a job at CBS for months, Bill was finally offered a part-time usher position not long after he and Jimmy moved in together, a development he attributed to the new apartment's bringing him luck. Jimmy was out looking for work as well. Through Draesemer, he got several auditions and cold readings, all of which he went to with the same enthusiasm and high level of expectation he had brought to any other part he had pursued. But as Jimmy moved from person to person, from casting director to director to producer, he began to see one basic fact about Hollywood. Frequently, a person in power *knew* he had power, and, more often than not, he would not help a young actor advance his career unless he agreed to provide certain favors.

The myth of the Hollywood casting couch is not a myth, and by no means are women the only ones who end up on that couch. In the fifties, within its power structure, Hollywood had a network of homosexual men who held influential positions in all of the studios and in the entertainment-related companies outside the studios. This network of homosexual men worked together during the day and socialized with each other at night. If a young actor gained access into this group, his professional contacts multiplied since these men made a habit of getting their friends, or friends of friends, jobs. The group was closed and secretive to an extent—although everyone within the industry knew about it—because homosexuality was still looked on by the general public with disdain. It was, according to a biography of Hart Crane published around this time, "abnormal," "a physical or mental aberration." Many medical doctors, even psychiatrists, considered homosexuality a mental disorder that could be treated under the proper conditions. It was definitely not thought of as a personality trait someone was born with or a lifestyle choice someone made. As Jimmy began to go on the audition rounds in early 1951, he picked up on the unspoken—and sometimes spoken—messages that the people audi-

tioning him sent his way. At first he noted the advances but didn't acknowledge them. He was not desperate. He would make it in this industry on his talent—and nothing else.

Soon Jimmy discovered that this network of homosexual men contained a number of actors, none of whom was open about his homosexuality. There was good reason. The American public had always been
highly sensitive about the way Hollywood stars handled their private
lives, especially when it involved sex. Should the public decide a
star's conduct was inappropriate, it would show its disapproval by not
seeing that star's pictures. This meant, of course, the end of the star's
career. Years earlier, for example, as soon as the first newspaper reports appeared about the death of a starlet named Virginia Rappe—
she died of a punctured bladder after being violently raped by Fatty
Arbuckle during a drunken orgy in a San Francisco hotel room—
Arbuckle, even though he was one of the most popular comedians at
the time, saw his career destroyed. In the coming years Arbuckle
would direct a few pictures under the name William B. Goodrich, but
the public never forgave him—and he never starred in a picture
again. Then in 1949 there was Ingrid Bergman's extramarital affair
with Roberto Rossellini, which resulted in the birth of their illegiti-
mate son Robertino. The moment the affair made the newspapers, no
studio would hire Bergman, who didn't work in another American-
produced film until 1956. Just as disastrous as these cases of indis-
cretion was any suggestion that an actor might be homosexual. When
a *Chicago Tribune* editorial writer called into question Rudolph
Valentino's masculinity by suggesting that he used powder on his
cheeks, applied with a pink puff, Valentino became so furious—and
terrified that the public might doubt his heterosexuality—that he is-
sued a challenge in the *Chicago Herald-Examiner* to fight the *Tribune*
writer in a boxing match. The writer never answered the challenge,
but Valentino had made his point. It somehow seemed inconsequen-
tial that both of the women Valentino had married turned out to be les-

bians and that at least one of the marriages—maybe both—was never consummated.

By the early fifties, Hollywood—a community that would soon play a part in one of the country's most profound disgraces when Joseph McCarthy began his hunt for Communists in America—had not changed the way it handled its stars' private lives. Hollywood was a place unusually conscious of its own activities—closed, closed-mouthed, and more than a little paranoid.

3. One day not long after the boys had settled into The Penthouse, Bill approached Jimmy with some exciting news. Bill had come up with an idea that was so good he could hardly believe he had pulled it off. What was it? Jimmy wanted to know. So Bill began.

He didn't have to remind Jimmy that for some time now he had wanted to take an acting class that would be much more intense than any he had signed up for at the University of Wisconsin or UCLA. Nor did he have to remind Jimmy of the long discussions they had had about the Method. In America, the organization that best taught the Method was the Actors Studio in New York City, a place Jimmy and Bill had often talked about with respect and admiration. Founded by Elia Kazan in 1947 and featuring such teachers as Lee Strasberg, the Studio was America's premier acting workshop. Jimmy and Bill both dreamed about studying there, and, by chance, Bill knew James Whitmore, a young actor who had studied at the Studio, had appeared on Broadway in *Command Decision,* and had been nominated for a supporting actor Academy Award for his part in *Battleground.* Bill had approached Whitmore with the prospect of conducting an acting class in Los Angeles in the tradition of the Actors Studio, and, much to Bill's surprise, Whitmore had agreed to teach the class. He named three conditions: Bill had to find ten good students; Bill had to locate a suitable place to hold the class; and he—Whitmore—would teach the class once a week as long as he wasn't paid. (Living in Los Angeles so he could do film work, Whitmore missed studying at the Studio; even so, he didn't want the added pressure that would be brought on by accepting payment for teaching the classes.) Ecstatic, Bill found a location, a meeting room over the Brentwood Country Mart on San Vicente Boulevard at Twenty-sixth Street in Brentwood. He was now lining up the ten students. Which was why he was talking to Jimmy: He wanted Jimmy to be a member of the class. Overjoyed at the prospect of studying with a teacher as accomplished as Whitmore and indebted to Bill for asking him, Jimmy gladly accepted. Neither could wait for the first class to begin.

When it did, within the next week or so, Jimmy felt nervous as he walked into the drab meeting room in the Brentwood Country Mart. Still, he was thrilled. Up until now almost all of his acting training and experience had come in a school setting where most of the students (and sometimes some of the teachers) neither had his talent nor shared his enthusiasm for the craft. Studying with Whitmore would be different, or so Jimmy hoped. In his opening remarks, Whitmore proved Jimmy right. With his credits and his commitment to the profession, he was conducting these classes, Whitmore said, only because he loved acting. As the students listened, Whitmore then delivered a speech that set the tone not only for that class but for the classes he would teach in the future.

"Learning to act is no child's game," Whitmore said, standing in front of the students, "so forget the romance part. Acting is a craft, a serious profession. And to learn any craft you have to apply yourself. It takes time, study, practice, patience. Most of all it takes hard work. And sweat. If it's glory you're after, you won't find it learning to act. You may not even find it in acting. But if it's a sense of fulfillment, a sense of personal gratification you want, there is no other profession in the world that can give you more. At least, that's the way I feel about it.

"If you are dedicated to your craft, you work until you're ready to drop, and then go on and work some more. By the time you're ready to call yourself an actor, you'll be so dead tired you probably won't even care about the applause. But you'll feel good, like you feel after a workout, when you ache all over and you're aware of every inflated muscle in your body. It'll hurt, but it'll hurt good.

"We're going to work here. That's what we're here for. I'm not qualified to teach you, but I can pass on to you what I've learned. I'll try to explain it the way I see it. Maybe it'll make sense, maybe it won't. That's partly up to me and partly up to you. If we're lucky, we might accomplish something."

Inspired by Whitmore and excited about his chances of making it in the entertainment business, Jimmy became more and more disillusioned with going to the classes he had signed up for that spring at UCLA. Boring and academic, the classes paled in comparison to the experience he was picking up from making the audition rounds. The fact that he now lived off campus in an apartment with a roommate only made him feel less connected to the university. The final blow came when Jimmy auditioned for the lead part in *Dark of the Moon*, to be put on in a major campus production at UCLA, and was turned down for the play outright. The best way to keep an up-and-coming actor with obvious talent from becoming conceited is to bring him down by telling him he's not as good as he thinks he is. Whether or not this was the theatre faculty's intention in Jimmy's case, the end result was that Jimmy, crushed and angry over being rejected for the play, decided he'd had enough not just of UCLA but of college in general. A few weeks into the spring term, he stopped going to classes, effectively dropping out of school. In his senior year and near graduation, Bill continued to work toward his degree. Jimmy saw no reason to. For him, something more important awaited—the industry.

*   *   *

Almost as a kind of vindication for himself (and an indisputable sign that he had made the right decision), Jimmy got a call at this time from Isabelle Draesemer, who had good news. Jerry Fairbanks, the producer of the Pepsi commercial in which Jimmy had appeared, was putting together a religious-theme-based television movie to be aired on Easter Sunday called "Hill Number One" and he had been so impressed with Jimmy's good looks and remarkable camera presence that he wanted him to play the part of John the Baptist in the special. The program, starring Roddy McDowall, would be shot in February and shown on Easter—March 25, 1951—on *Father Peyton's Family Theatre*, a recurring series of specials filmed under the supervision of Father Patrick Peyton, a local religious figure in Los Angeles.

Jimmy was excited over the job, for which he was to be paid one hundred and fifty dollars, and began to prepare for it immediately. He was doing well with his preparation until it was almost time to shoot the show. Several days before the taping, he became moody and withdrawn, as if the enormity of the event—it would be the first time Jimmy appeared in a real acting role on television—weighed on him with such force that he could almost not talk about it. Even so, on the day of the taping, he turned in an excellent performance. Wearing a togalike outfit and sandals, he delivered his lines with precision and sureness, although during his preparation process he had developed a British accent, which made his lines sound somewhat stilted. In the end the slightly conceited quality of the portrayal didn't matter. What viewers saw when the show aired on Easter Sunday night was the actor playing the part. And Dean was something to see. Stunningly youthful, he made the viewer watch him with nothing more than the way he moved his body or spoke his lines. True Hollywood stars are not made—they are born—since they must have the one character trait that can't be taught: an ability to look better on film than in real life. This goes beyond being photogenic. It involves what Marilyn Monroe called "making love to the camera." Dean had this quality, and it showed through even in the small part he played on "Hill Number One."

There was one group of viewers in particular who could hardly control their enthusiasm. After the show aired, a number of girls at Immaculate Heart Catholic School in Los Angeles were so taken with Jimmy's performance that they formed the Immaculate Heart James Dean Appreciation Society. Once the girls, who had watched the show as a class assignment, had organized the club—Dean's first fan club—they wrote him a letter to tell him about their meetings and to ask him to attend one. Intrigued by the idea, Jimmy couldn't resist. Still, when the date arrived, he took Bill along for protection. At the meeting the girls fawned over Jimmy. Soaking up the adulation, he gave a talk and signed autographs. It was a moment of pride for Jimmy, modest as it was. For the last few years he had dreamed about becoming a successful actor. The attention he'd received after *Macbeth* only made him want more, and now, to some small extent, he was getting it. His television acting debut, his first fan club, his first autograph-signing session—this was heady stuff for a young actor. Best of all, with these tokens of success to his credit, Jimmy could look at his father and know how wrong he had been when he'd miscalculated Jimmy's chances of making it in the entertainment business.

Unfortunately, as Jimmy went on audition after audition over the next several months, more than hopeful that his impressive performance on "Hill Number One" would get him work, he was turned down for every part he read for. In show business, rejection is the only constant. For actors, getting used to it is the hardest part of the job. But, single-mindedly ambitious, Jimmy didn't cope well with rejection. While the list of casting directors who wouldn't hire him grew longer, he started to suffer from bouts of depression. If achieved ambition—success—works like a stimulant on the psyche, then rejection is a depressant. There were many days when Bill simply couldn't deal with him. Gloomy and angry, Jimmy would sit around The Penthouse in a dark funk, waiting to explode if Bill happened to make the wrong comment to him. Finally Jimmy became more than depressed over his inability to find work. He got desperate. There was no doubt in the mind of anyone who knew him well, Bill among them, that it was only a matter of time before Jimmy would do anything for a part.

In the spring of 1951, Bill introduced Jimmy to a young woman who, for several months at least, played an important role in his life. Through his contacts in Hollywood, Bill happened to know Beverly Wills. A regular on the radio show "Junior Miss," Wills was the daughter of Joan Davis, one of the most popular comediennes on television. Bill had introduced Jimmy to Beverly on a blind date, a picnic at the shore. During the picnic, Jimmy, who was sullen and reserved as he often was these days, would barely speak. Then Beverly brought up the subject of acting and Jimmy perked up noticeably. When their discussion turned to Stanislavsky, about whom Whitmore had been lecturing in class, Jimmy decided to demonstrate the Method by pretending to be a palm tree in a storm. So there he was on the beach with Beverly Wills watching him: His arms outstretched, his head tilted down, he let his whole body sway with the imaginary wind. Following his demonstration, Jimmy was much more sociable for the rest of the evening. Still, in some metaphorical way, Jimmy himself must have felt like a palm tree in a storm, out on the shore as he was with all of these spoiled Hollywood children, one of whom was the daughter of a famous comedienne.

As the weeks passed and Jimmy continued to go on auditions only to be turned down time and again, he felt a new level of frustration. He also realized that when a person is trying to break in in Hollywood, he has to play by the rules of the game if he wants to get work, no matter how talented he is or how good his looks might be. In addition, many men in key positions in Hollywood had made clear the rules of the game. Occasionally the price of getting cast in a part was having sex with the person who was offering the part. Some people were subtle in the ways they used their power. They created social situations in which the actors felt compelled to have sex with them. Others were less subtle. These producers or directors, even casting agents or actors with clout in the business, would explain to an actor in no uncertain terms that in exchange for their favors and influence they wanted sex.

Eventually Jimmy buckled under the pressure of failure. If he had to sleep with people to get work, then that's what he would do. So while he made the audition rounds, he started to hit the Hollywood party circuit, usually as the date of one of these influential men in the industry he met on auditions. At the same time he also had a series of short affairs or one-night stands with a number of men. One man to whom Jimmy became extremely close was Clifton Webb, an accomplished and socially connected actor who wielded significant power within both the homosexual clique and the greater Hollywood community. For instance, Webb was good friends with Hedda Hopper, Hollywood's most feared gossip columnist. "[I know] the rumors were rife," William Redfield, an actor who later worked with Dean, would say, "that he was Clifton Webb's protégé. Which always struck me as odd, because Jimmy in his manner in my presence didn't strike me as at all a homosexual. But of course that often happens. . . . And what exactly went on between Webb and him I don't know, though I imagine it took a sexual form." While he dated Webb, Jimmy also had brief affairs with other men who had connections in Hollywood. One was Alfredo de la Vega, the scion of a wealthy California family. Another was a man who was known throughout Hollywood for his penchant for directing commercial pictures and for his love of beautiful young men. It was inevitable that the beautiful young James Dean would end up "auditioning" for this director. The encounter would be so memorable for Jimmy that, months later, he would describe it to a friend in vivid detail.

It was a breezy summer night and the director had invited Jimmy out to his house in Malibu. As Jimmy sat in the living room and sipped the drink a butler had brought him, he could see firsthand the spoils of a successful career as a Hollywood director—expensive furniture, original paintings, fine crystal ornaments. This man's home life was an exercise in good taste and elegance, vaguely reminiscent of the lifestyle to which Jimmy had been exposed back in Indiana through Reverend DeWeerd, although on a much grander scale here. While they sipped their drinks, Jimmy and the director chatted idly about music, art, literature, and, of course, show business.

Later, once they had finished their drinks, the two men went outside to the deck, where the butler, a black man dressed in a tuxedo, served them the dinner the cook had prepared. As the waves crashed onto the beach below and a brisk breeze blew in off the Pacific Ocean, Jimmy ate heartily. The meal was so much better than the ones he and Bill had had lately. In fact, the only time recently that he had eaten a meal this good had been dinner with Beverly at Joan Davis's house. Finally, after Jimmy had finished dessert, the director made the move that was the point of the evening.

"You know," he said, "before I can really audition a young actor for a part in one of my pictures"—what Jimmy wanted more than anything—"I really have to get to know him better."

Here was the moment Jimmy knew was coming. Recently he had reached this moment with several men. Jimmy had a choice. He could make it obvious that he was not interested in getting to know the man better—which would end the evening, as well as any chance he had of auditioning for a picture he was directing—or he could play along. By now, Jimmy more than knew the rules.

"I know you do," Jimmy said. "I would like that."

"I'm glad."

And when they went into the bedroom and closed the door, Jimmy pretended that he liked what happened next. Or maybe he wasn't pretending at all. He certainly could have kept it from happening, and didn't. Then again, if he had, he knew what that meant: an even slimmer chance of having a career in Hollywood.

4. Jimmy continued to see Beverly Wills although, of course, he never mentioned anything about the other people he was dating besides her. So far in his life, Jimmy had made a point of talking about his sexuality to a mere handful of people. Naturally Beverly wasn't one of them. Jimmy told her so little about what was going on in his personal life that years later Beverly would actually say that at this time she and Jimmy "talked about getting married." While he was closed-mouthed about his sexuality, he did discuss with her some of the reasons casting agents gave him for turning him down for parts. He was either too short or not attractive enough—or at least that's what the casting agents told him, he said. The first reason had some merit (even as an adult, Dean was only five feet eight inches tall and one hundred and thirty-five pounds), but the second one is hard to believe. The producers who had hired him so far had not missed his boyish good looks. Regardless, Jimmy always responded the same way every time he was rejected: he got furious, indignant. Right from the start, Joan Davis noticed this unpleasant side of Jimmy's personality, one of the main factors in her concluding that she didn't like him. She told Beverly this too. For his part, Jimmy wasn't particularly fond of Joan Davis either. Before long he treated her with open disrespect. Distressed over the situation, Beverly decided that Jimmy was jealous of her mother's professional and financial success. More probably

Jimmy saw her as pretentious and condescending, the very type of person who was keeping him from achieving what he wanted to in the business. *She* was what was wrong with Hollywood. Whatever the reason for their conflict, Joan Davis soon made no secret about the fact that she didn't like Jimmy. Rude and unkempt, he wasn't worthy of her daughter, she said. Anyway, she had started hearing rumors about Jimmy, rumors that bothered her a lot. Jimmy's secret affairs were not yet common knowledge, but word was getting around. How could it not? While he was dating Joan Davis's daughter, he was also, as he would one day tell a friend, having his cock "sucked by five of the big names in Hollywood."

Unfortunately, Jimmy wasn't just having problems with his career and his relationship with Beverly. He was also having trouble with Bill. At this time, Bill was still an usher at CBS. Even so, his salary was not large enough to cover his and Jimmy's living expenses. Because Jimmy wasn't making any money, they were always tight on cash; often they had to borrow money from friends just to get by. Their financial situation became so bad that Bill finally pulled strings at CBS and got Jimmy a job as a part-time usher. On their two incomes, they would've been able to survive, but just barely. However, Jimmy's attitude was so poor—he didn't like his superiors and resented having to wear "a monkey suit," as he called it—that in a rare move CBS fired him. Humiliated by Jimmy's behavior and angry at himself for jeopardizing his own position at CBS by getting Jimmy a job, Bill blamed Jimmy for the debacle. Naturally this disagreement further strained their relationship.

Summer wore on. Jimmy's life didn't get much better. Neither did his relationship with Bill. Soon their problems centered around more than money. Years later Bast described one of their key areas of conflict. "The thing I resent most," Bast would say, "is that Jim was never honest with himself. He put down the games that one had to play in

Hollywood in order to succeed. He felt that he was above having to kiss anyone's ass in order to get a part, and whenever he saw his friends in this situation, he put them down for it, said he lost respect for them. The truth, though, is that Dean kissed a lot of asses, and he hated this about himself. That's why he took it out on others." Bill could remember specific comments Jimmy would make. "What a pile of hogwash," Jimmy had once told him, referring to what young actors like himself had to do to get work in Hollywood. "They've got in their heads they're gods. This town is full of them. They've got these poor lads—saps like me—and make them perform. You know, run around like lost goats and charming the pants off important people. I thought it might pay off. But it doesn't take long to find out it won't. And if I can't make it on my talent I don't want to make it at all."

Obviously, still unable to get work, Jimmy was starting to hate himself for giving in to the desires of the men he was dating. But instead of taking out his anger on himself, he took it out on the people close to him, specifically Bill. In time, Jimmy and Bill were having to cope with a variety of pressures: pressure over finances, over Jimmy's displeasure about having (as some would call it) to prostitute himself, over their own relationship, which by now had become extremely complicated. For years, Bill, who would one day be somewhat open about his homosexuality, would not publicly confirm that he and Jimmy had had a sexual relationship. Yet other friends would speculate that they *were* lovers and that they had become lovers as soon as they moved into The Penthouse. Given what's known of Jimmy's sexual experiences, it would be hard to believe that Jimmy and Bill maintained a platonic relationship while they lived in The Penthouse. More likely, the two of them began to have sex soon after they moved in with each other. In the end, neither sex nor any of the emotional, spiritual, and intellectual ties Jimmy and Bill had formed was strong enough to hold them together. At the end of the summer of 1951, the tension between the two of them became so strong that Jimmy moved out, leaving Bill to deal with the financial responsibilities of The Penthouse alone.

Jimmy moved into the Gower Plaza hotel in Hollywood, not far from CBS. He now needed money just to pay the rent, so he had to find a job right away. To keep meeting people in the entertainment business, he decided to look for work near CBS (naturally, no one *at* CBS would hire him). With this in mind, Jimmy got a job parking cars at a lot close to the CBS Radio Studios at 6121 Sunset Boulevard. As luck would have it, one day not too long after he had started working, Jimmy ran into a handsome, distinguished-looking older man who attracted his attention immediately. What's your name? Jimmy said. Rogers Brackett, the man answered. Jimmy would find out, if he did not already know, that Brackett was a radio director with Foote, Cone and Belding, an advertising agency whose programs were broadcast over CBS. In radio and television in the early fifties, advertising agencies played a pivotal role in the creative process. Many radio programs were completely produced by the advertising agency, from the writing of the script to the casting of the actors to the recording of the show. The network merely broadcast the final product. Because of his job at the advertising agency, then, Rogers was a potentially important contact for Jimmy. In fact, as Jimmy and Rogers chatted briefly in the parking lot that first day, Jimmy realized that Rogers was exactly what he needed at the moment. Successful and well-connected in the business, he could support Jimmy financially *and* introduce him to the people he needed to meet. What's more, he was attractive, much more so than DeWeerd. Before Rogers left, Jimmy made plans for the two of them to see each other. Several days later over coffee, they got to know one another better. Before long they were going out—to dinner, to parties, to private studio screenings. Jimmy seemed more than willing to let a relationship develop. If nothing else, it meant that he could quit his job at the parking lot, which he did, and move in with Rogers. There was only one problem: Jimmy was still dating Beverly Wills, no matter how superficially.

"It was a question of marrying Joan Davis's daughter or going off to live with a studio director," Isabelle Draesemer would remember. "In any case, the next thing they were living together"—*they* meaning Jimmy and Rogers Brackett. As it turned out, Jimmy's situation with Beverly was not difficult for him to resolve. He simply stopped seeing her. He was able to do this in large part because Beverly, who had just graduated from high school, spent much of the summer of 1951 out of Los Angeles with her father in Paradise Cove. (Beverly's parents were divorced.) Meanwhile, as he separated from Beverly and Bill, Jimmy settled into his new life with Rogers in his apartment on Sunset Plaza Drive off the Sunset Strip in Hollywood. Still going to college and struggling to make ends meet, Bill Bast could hardly control the jealousy he felt over Jimmy's living arrangements. "A new boredom set in," Bast later wrote, a faint bitchiness creeping into his tone. "Through some of his newly acquired friends"—that would be Rogers—"Jimmy was introduced to the plush life on Sunset Strip." All Jimmy seemed to do, Bast complained, was sit around the Sunset Plaza's swimming pool and "make clever talk with the 'Strip Set.' "

Actually, Jimmy wasn't bored at all. With his contacts, Rogers had finally gotten Jimmy some work. The parts were brief appearances on three radio programs—"Alias Jane Doe," "Hallmark Playhouse," and "Stars Over Hollywood"—but at least they were jobs. Soon, again through Rogers, Jimmy was getting extra or bit-player work in pictures. In no time, he did small roles in the Jerry Lewis–Dean Martin comedy *Sailor Beware,* the first time Dean appeared on-screen in a film; the Rock Hudson vehicle *Has Anybody Seen My Gal?;* and *Fixed Bayonets,* a war picture. Rogers provided for Jimmy in other ways too. He gave him books to read, especially works by Camus and Colette. He took him on trips to Mexicali and Tijuana. He indulged him with expensive dinners, usually at trendy restaurants like LaRue. On some level, Jimmy was impressed by all of this. "Finished *Moulin Rouge* last night," Jimmy once told Bill Bast, whom he was still seeing even though they had broken off their friendship. "The end! You've got to read it. It's the novel about Lautrec's life. Rogers flipped over it, too. So we picked up the phone and called [Pierre] La Mure, the guy who wrote it." On a more visceral level, however, Jimmy was repulsed by the phoniness of the Sunset Strip scene. "The other day we were sitting by the pool," Jimmy told Bill on another occasion, "and I made a bet with Rogers that the names of LaRue or the Mocambo would be dropped at least fifteen times within the next hour. We kept count, and I won. What a pile of hogwash!"

As the weeks passed, Jimmy became discontent with Rogers—who later disclosed to a journalist that their father-son relationship was in fact "incestuous"—and the empty Hollywood scene Rogers came to represent. Just when he was most confused about what to do with his life, Jimmy got a walk-on part on *The Alan Young Show,* a half-hour television variety program. Ralph Levy, the show's director, formed an instant rapport with Jimmy. During the week they worked together, they became so comfortable with each other that Levy found himself offering Jimmy career advice even though Jimmy had not asked for it. "I suggested to Jimmy that Hollywood was not the place to get started," Levy remembers, "that he should go to the stage in New York and let Hollywood say, 'We can use him.'"

Jimmy was working at last, but the bit parts and walk-ons were not the substantial roles he wanted. As he thought about Levy's advice, he remembered a brief exchange he had had one night following class with James Whitmore.

"Mr. Whitmore, how do you get to be an actor?" Jimmy had asked.

"There's only one way, Jimmy. Stop dissipating your energy and talent. Go to New York. There you will find out whether you can take the uncertainty of an actor's life. Get to know yourself. Learn to have the actor's disdain for convention. Learn to study. Learn to act—above all, act."

"Is there any place I can go to learn?" Jimmy said. "What's the best place?"

"Go see Elia Kazan at the Actors Studio. I don't know if they'll take you, but you can't do better."

5. Taking the advice he had been given by Whitmore and Levy, Jimmy concluded it was time to leave Los Angeles and go to New York. Actually, he could do this by simply following Rogers. Foote, Cone and Belding had decided to send Rogers to Chicago to do some work for the company and then to relocate him permanently to New York. Jimmy could go with Rogers to Chicago, stay as long as he wanted, and proceed to New York. After he was finished with his work, Rogers would meet Jimmy there. In New York, Jimmy hoped to get his break on Broadway. Maybe his luck would be better in the theatre district than it had been in Hollywood; it certainly couldn't be much worse.

So in October 1951 Jimmy traveled from Los Angeles to Chicago to be with Rogers, who had gone on just ahead of him. In Chicago, Jimmy stayed with Rogers for a week at the Ambassador hotel. Then he took a brief trip to Fairmount where he told his family and friends about his plans to move to New York and make it on Broadway. He even went down to Indianapolis to see James DeWeerd, now the minister of a large tabernacle in the city. DeWeerd stunned Jimmy by giving him two hundred dollars to help pay his way in New York. Rogers had also offered to give him money—and of course Jimmy and Rogers would be living together in New York when Rogers wrapped up his work in Chicago—but because Jimmy would need all the cash he could get, he took DeWeerd's money. After the relationships he had had with older men in Hollywood, Jimmy better understood the dynamics of his and DeWeerd's affair. Perhaps Jimmy, somewhat more mercenary about these things now, even felt that DeWeerd owed him the money since DeWeerd had never really compensated Jimmy for the sexual favors he had provided in the past, except for giving Jimmy friendship and guidance. Regardless, fortified with some cash and plenty of emotional support, Jimmy felt he was ready to head for New York.

With the money he had been given by DeWeerd and Brackett, plus money he had left over from his extra work in Hollywood and an additional sum he got from selling his 1939 Chevy, Jimmy was not broke when he arrived in New York. Because of this, he bypassed the flea-bag hotels and rented a room at the Iroquois. Located on West Forty-fourth Street a few doors down from the Algonquin, one of the most famous hotels in the city, the Iroquois had reasonably priced rooms that were functional if not elegant. Actually it had been Rogers who arranged for Jimmy to stay at the Iroquois. One of his best friends, Alec Wilder, the well-known song composer, lived at the Algonquin. When Brackett contacted him, Wilder suggested that Jimmy try the Iroquois. As it turned out, in those early days Jimmy was in New York he needed a decent hotel room. "For the first few weeks I only strayed a couple of blocks from my hotel off Times Square," Jimmy one day wrote. "I would see three movies a day in an attempt to escape from my loneliness and depression. I spent a hundred and fifty of my limited funds just on seeing movies." While the sum may have been exaggerated, there's no doubt that in those first weeks Jimmy saw *a lot* of movies.

After a while, Jimmy got up the nerve to stray from the safety of his hotel room and the movie theatre. When he finally started to explore

New York, he fell in love with the city. Downtown, he wandered through the narrow, meandering streets of Greenwich Village where he discovered quaint haunts like the Minetta Tavern, a bar in which he felt at home the first time he walked through the door. Uptown, on the West Side in the Sixties and Seventies, he especially liked the charming neighborhood bars, the stores on Broadway, and the brownstones that lined street after street. Many days he would end up in Central Park, the green landscape reminding him of the Indiana countryside. But in those early days he felt most comfortable in midtown. There he hung out in Cromwell's Pharmacy on the ground floor of 30 Rockefeller Plaza, the building in which NBC was located. He often ate at Hector's, off Times Square, and Jerry's Bar and Restaurant, close to Fifty-fourth Street on Sixth Avenue. Mostly, though, he adored the theatre district. Strolling the streets, he saw one theatre after another and a blur of marquees for the shows that were playing. *South Pacific, A Tree Grows in Brooklyn, The King and I*—if only he had the money to see them all. In this part of town, he had also found the Actors Studio, then located near Fifty-third Street at 1697 Broadway. Naturally this was one of the first places Jimmy had looked for. He had made up his mind that he was going to apply to the Studio for admission as soon as he thought he was ready.

What Dean could not see as he walked through these various neighborhoods, what he would not learn until he had lived in New York for a while, was the tone of the city's political climate at the time. As a strident group of left-wing creative artists had formed to embrace a liberal social and cultural agenda in America, the government clamped down hard on anyone who was considered suspect, especially if that person seemed to endorse Marxist ideals. In the fifties there was an actual list—recorded on paper so it could easily be referred to—of actors, writers, and directors who could not be hired to work on television, Broadway, and film because they were thought to be communists. It was an impressive list of names—Lee Grant, Arthur Miller, Zero Mostel, Dashiel Hammett, Lillian Hellman, Ring Lardner, Jr., Edward Dymtryk, to name just a few—but if an artist found himself on it, his career was seriously damaged, if not ended. Many artists, especially young ones starting out in the business, were caught in a dilemma: How much could someone rebel, which on some basic level is the essential nature of a creative artist, without going so far as to be censored? On the surface the American social climate in the fifties seemed calm and staid. Underneath, there was a ground-swell of discontent. Nowhere was this more evident than in New York, once a person had lived there long enough to recognize it.

Before long, Jimmy began to worry about money. In his first weeks in New York, he had spent about half of his cash, mostly on all those movies. Since he had no real prospect of landing any acting work, he decided to take a job washing dishes at a bar on Forty-fifth Street. Also, to cut down on his rent, he moved from the Iroquois to a room at the West Side YMCA, located just off Central Park on West Sixty-third Street. Still, Jimmy was hopeful about his future in New York. For judging from the superficial contact he had had with people in the city so far, as he chatted with other struggling actors at Cromwell's or met industry types at Hector's or talked to one person or the other he had bumped into in the lobby of the Algonquin where he went to meet Alec Wilder, Jimmy was certain that the entertainment community in New York was much different from the one in Los Angeles. "I've dis-covered a whole new world here, a whole new way of thinking," Jimmy later told Bill Bast. "This town's the end. It's talent that counts here. You've got to stay with it or get lost. I like it."

Soon Jimmy began to pursue the few contacts he had in New York. Ralph Levy, for whom he worked on *The Alan Young Show,* had talked about Jimmy with James Sheldon, a friend of Levy's who was a televi-sion director in New York. When Jimmy called him, Sheldon set up an appointment to meet with him right away. An articulate and intelligent gentleman (and he was a gentleman in the truest sense of the word,

)

which shocked Jimmy since he was used to the Hollywood crowd), Sheldon was taken with Jimmy from the moment they first met in his office. At the time, Sheldon had stopped directing to work for an advertising agency. But he knew that the producers of one of the agency's shows, *Mama*, the CBS comedy-drama based on the Broadway play *I Remember Mama*, was about to start auditioning young men in their early twenties to replace Dick Van Patten, who had been drafted into the army. Van Patten's character, Nels, the younger brother on the show, seemed perfect for Jimmy, so Sheldon arranged for the producers to audition him. At the reading Jimmy was stunning—so good that the producers offered him the job immediately. Naturally Jimmy was beside himself with joy. He had been in New York no time at all and he had already landed his first job. Not just any job either, but a significant part in a popular show inspired by a hit Broadway play. Imagine what they would say about him back in Fairmount.

Then disaster struck, or at least it was a disaster for Jimmy. Unexpectedly the army gave Van Patten a 4-F deferment. This meant, of course, that Van Patten didn't have to go into the army. It also meant that Van Patten wouldn't have to leave the show and that Jimmy couldn't have his part. Jimmy was despondent. He had gotten so close only to come up short. Still, in a strange way, he felt reassured. At least he had not had to sleep with anyone to get the part. In Hollywood he would have probably had to go to bed with someone just to get an audition. Maybe New York really *was* different from Hollywood.

Jimmy did get a job in November 1951. It was a letdown from a lead role on a CBS television show, but still it was a job—and he needed one. He had heard that the game show *Beat the Clock* was looking for someone to pretest the stunts and warm up the audience, so he stopped by the studio, applied for the job, and got it. He started work at once. There was certainly no career advancement involved here—on some days the experience was actually humiliating—but it was money, although, at five dollars an hour, not much. Even so,

Jimmy was desperate for work. About the only income he had coming in was a small trickle of gifts from Uncle Marcus and Aunt Ortense. "We would send him money," Marcus Winslow would say later. "I smoke and when I'd buy a carton of cigarettes, I'd buy one for him and mail it to him." A check here, a carton of cigarettes there—Jimmy was grateful for what he could get.

Sheldon's first lead had come so close to paying off that Jimmy went back to him for more advice. Again, Sheldon had a good suggestion. What Jimmy needed, he said, was an agent. To this end, Sheldon sent him over to see his agent, Jane Deacy, at the Louis Shurr Agency. As soon as Jimmy and Deacy sat down in her office and started to chat, they hit it off. From the start, Deacy, who was by nature gentle and maternal, handled Jimmy the way he responded best: She mothered him. Because of this, Jimmy was drawn to her, almost instinctively. At the same time, Deacy recognized Jimmy's raw—and as yet still untapped—talent. Since they liked each other, they decided to start working together. Jimmy was so committed to their professional partnership that he even moved with Deacy, whom he started calling Mom, when she left Shurr to set up her own agency at 60 East Forty-second Street. Jimmy's name would be just one on an impressive list of Deacy clients, which came to include artists as diverse as Marge and Gower Champion, Martin Landau, and George C. Scott.

With his professional life looking up, Jimmy became friends at this time with a young woman named Elizabeth Sheridan (everyone called her Dizzy) whom he had met one night at the Rehearsal Club, a private all-girls residence. The daughter of Frank Sheridan, a classical pianist, Dizzy felt a kinship with Jimmy. They spent hours together, regularly hanging out in neighborhood bars. But as the weeks passed Jimmy became less interested in his private life than in his career, which was still developing too slowly for his satisfaction.

On February 8, 1952, Jimmy turned twenty-one years old. His struggle to break into acting remained formidable although, now that he had Jane Deacy in his life, he believed his chances were much better. Before Deacy had left Shurr, another agent at the company had gotten Jimmy a small part in *The Web*, a mystery television series. Then Jimmy didn't work again (he did get fired from *Martin Kane*, a television series about a private investigator, because he was too hard to work with) until he landed a job as an extra on a science-fiction show called *Tales of Tomorrow* and the tiny part of a bellhop on a *Studio One* episode entitled "Ten Thousand Horses Singing." In that show, based on a short story by Robert Carson, "You Gotta Stay Happy," Jimmy had to dress up in a bellhop outfit and appear, speaking no lines, in a quick scene with John Forsythe. To Jimmy, that seemed to sum up the absurdity of his career so far. It was as absurd as ten thousand horses singing. Nevertheless, Jimmy had hope and Jane Deacy and an indefatigable drive to make it in the entertainment business at whatever the cost, whatever the pain and sacrifice.

Dean, the dapper gangster, on the set of the television
show "A Long Time Till Dawn"

Broadway
and the
Motorola

1. It was 1952. A decade earlier the United States had been preparing to enter World War II, the war that should have accomplished what World War I—"the war to end all wars"—hadn't: end warfare. Only seven years had passed since the conclusion of World War II and already America was involved in a political and military conflict in a country on the other side of the world—Korea. The Communists were trying to take over the country in a conquest that many Americans viewed as central to their ultimate goal of dominating the world. When it became apparent that young United States soldiers would have to go to Korea and risk being killed—that is to say, when it became apparent just how badly *two* world wars had failed to eliminate warfare—a cynicism began to emerge in America, especially among the country's youth. Like no other time in history, American teenagers were ready to rebel against the older generation. If World War II had not brought about permanent world peace, what chance would another war have? One could even argue that World War II had made the world *less* safe. After all, it had given society Albert Einstein's toy, the atomic bomb, and consequently a whole new mind-numbing worry to obsess about: nuclear holocaust.

As this happened, a large segment of the American youth was developing a different—and alarming, their parents would say—attitude about sex. Because of the population explosion, for the first time sex could be seen not as a method by which a society replenishes itself (there were too many people already) but as a means to an end in itself. The only reason a person needed to have sex was because he or she wanted to. As the youth became more alienated from their parents' generation, they began to ignore that generation's beliefs and dictates. The youth would have sex. They would fuck whenever, or however, they wanted. They would, or they would not, be open about it. It didn't matter. Although the power of the sexual revolution would not become obvious until the sixties, the youth of the early fifties were the first in America to fuck in the backseats of cars in the parking lots of drive-in movies for no better reason than to experience the pleasure of doing it.

This new climate of defiance also allowed subgroups in society, like the homosexual community, to become more bold in the advancement of their agendas. To traditional Americans, homosexuals were as bad as Communists since both were destroying what the conservatives proudly referred to as the "American way of life." Even so, in the early fifties the homosexual community tried to forge changes. In Los Angeles, for example, a group of homosexual men founded a publication called *One—The Homosexual Magazine.* In a cover letter written to a long list of potential contributors, the editors explained that they hoped *One* "might help . . . to dispel public ignorance and hostility on the subject [of homosexuality]." While a worthy notion, it was not likely that the founding of a single magazine on the topic would accomplish such a lofty goal. Yet the magazine's mere existence underscored the fact that the social landscape in America was about to go through fundamental changes.

For Jimmy, exploring his sexuality meant breaking away, though maybe just temporarily, from the types of sexual partners he had had until now, dominant older men or submissive men his own age. In New York in the early fifties, Jimmy would push the boundaries of his sexuality in ways he never had before. With one young man who was a dancer, Jimmy had a wild, passionate sex life that was defined by a total lack of restraint. Jimmy's friend, beautiful, blue-eyed, blond-haired, had, of course, the slender yet delicately muscular body of a dancer. With this boy, Jimmy liked to be fucked slowly but forcefully. What's more, when Jimmy was in a certain mood, he wanted to stand naked in the doorway to his friend's walk-up apartment—the door wide open and Jimmy facing out so that he might be caught if someone happened to walk up the stairs—and have his friend fuck him there. His arms lifted above his head as they were having sex, Jimmy steadied himself by holding on to each side of the door frame. Eventually, he would let go with one hand and play with his own cock, which was, Jimmy had decided after being with so many men, long and thick for someone who had a body as diminutive as his. And if Jimmy masturbated while his friend fucked him, he would come violently, his sperm shooting out onto the landing.

During the months Jimmy knew the dancer, their relationship never became romantic, although Jimmy saw him fairly often; instead, the purpose of their getting together was to have sex. Because of this, just about every time Jimmy stopped by his friend's apartment, he wanted to have sex. What's more, the dancer wouldn't be the only boy with whom Jimmy went to bed at this time. In New York, Jimmy would be more sexually active than he ever had been before. If there was any sex act that could be performed (almost always, it had to be a homosexual act), Jimmy wanted to try it. He was so promiscuous at this time that a journalist would one day describe him as "an instant hit with the fist-fuck set" because it's said he would try anything during sex, and Kenneth Anger would say this about him in his sequel to

Hollywood Babylon: "[Jimmy liked] sex assorted with beatings, boots, belts, and bondage—spiced with knowing cigarette burns (which gave Jimmy his underground nickname: The Human Ashtray)." It now appears that while Dean was certainly promiscuous during these years in New York, he probably overstated his involvement in violent sexual activity to his friends and acquaintances. Still, the rumors do attest to the fact that Jimmy was more than willing to experiment with sex. As it happened, during these same years, Jimmy matured as an artist. He was probably not aware of it at the time—and maybe he never was— but it seems more than coincidental that as he explored his sexuality, he also began to realize the fathomless potential of his creative talent.

In early 1952, Rogers Brackett finally joined Jimmy in New York. Once Rogers had finished his work in Chicago, Foote, Cone and Belding transferred him as planned to its New York office, then on Madison Avenue. As soon as Brackett got to New York, he rented a roomy, attractive apartment on Fifth Avenue at West Thirty-eighth Street, a neighborhood not as posh as upper Fifth Avenue but definitely upscale. Without a doubt, the apartment was an improvement over the place in which Jimmy had been living. So, in March 1952, as a kind of last fling with the older crowd before he settled down for good to date young men like the dancer who fucked him in the doorway, Jimmy moved in with Rogers and the two of them resumed the affair they had started in Los Angeles.

The move was not an easy one for Jimmy to make. Jimmy was now looking to have relationships with boys his own age; to him, Rogers almost represented a step backward. Still, Jimmy couldn't resist the way of life that Rogers had to offer. In no time they were living as stylishly as they had in California. They ate at expensive restaurants. They would go out at night to the ballet or the theatre. When Jimmy could get Rogers to, they would drop in on trendy nightclubs. One of Rogers's favorite outings was to go to the Algonquin and socialize with his friends. Rogers and Alec Wilder could sit in the lobby of the Algonquin for an hour or more, just sipping drinks and chatting with whomever happened to be killing time there. Jimmy didn't enjoy hanging out in the lobby of the Algonquin, but he did it because Rogers wanted him to. Indeed, almost from the beginning, Jimmy seemed unhappy about his living arrangements with Rogers, a reflection of the apprehension he felt over moving in with him in the first place. Jimmy loved the life they lived—the dinners, the plays, the nightlife—but he felt resentful at the same time. After all, he was being kept by Rogers. There was no other way to describe their relationship. It's one thing to explore your sexuality; it's something else altogether to feel as if you're being used. Unfortunately, as Jimmy and Rogers lived together in New York, that's exactly how Jimmy began to feel. As a result, Jimmy was often surly and withdrawn, more so than he ever had been in the past. His behavior became so bad that occasionally Rogers's friends simply didn't want to be around Jimmy. Wilder reached the point where he hated to be in the same room with him. Before long, it seemed Rogers was the only person who *could* get along with Jimmy, a fact that mystified Rogers's friends as well as others who knew the couple.

"James Dean was the type of guy you wouldn't like," says Tony Cichiello, an employee of the Algonquin who knew Jimmy. "He was always walking behind Brackett, not with him. And he would sit in a corner if Wilder and Brackett were at a table in the lobby. This guy would sit in a corner by himself. He always had that snarl, that sneer. That wasn't acting. That was James Dean. If he didn't like you, he would insult you all night. He would sit there muttering little epitaphs at you, saying 'You-son-of-a-bitch.' The surliness, the aloneness—this kid was alone in a crowd. I never saw the guy smile. He never laughed. He always seemed to want to be by himself. Only Brackett got along with him, but he got along with him terrifically. Brackett kept him. I don't want to say the word *lover*, but they were *very* close."

Jimmy's arrangement with Rogers in New York was short-lived, surely much more short lived than Rogers would have hoped. It might have lasted longer, however, if Bill Bast had not moved from Los Angeles to New York after he graduated from UCLA in May 1952. With the two of them living in the same city again, Jimmy couldn't resist sharing an apartment with Bill. In making this decision, Jimmy compared his options. If he stayed with Rogers, Rogers would continue to provide for him financially and introduce him to influential people in the business. Jimmy was constantly meeting show business people through either Rogers or one of Rogers's friends. This was important to Jimmy because little else mattered to him besides acting. But Jimmy knew that to grow as an actor he had to mature as a person; Rogers could simply no longer be the catalyst for that growth. As soon as Bast got to New York, Jimmy moved out of Rogers's apartment so that he and Bill could take a room together at the Iroquois Hotel. It was a sentimental choice for Jimmy since the Iroquois had been the hotel he had lived in when he first moved to New York. For a single room with two beds and a private bath—their room number was 82—Jimmy and Bill paid ninety dollars a month, more than they had spent for The Penthouse in Santa Monica. That was Santa Monica, though; now they were in Manhattan.

From the start, Bill noticed that Jimmy had gone through some major changes. Needy and uncertain in the past, he was now resolved, sure of himself, independent. He took charge of a situation, told a person what he wanted, something he had never been able to do before. "During the course of [our] first week [together]," Bast later wrote, "one thing became increasingly clear to me: our relationship had made a complete about-face. No longer was I the one with my feet planted firmly on the ground, or perhaps in the mire of false confidence. No longer was it Jimmy who turned to me for the answers, as it had been in the beginning. Now I was following Jimmy's lead, and

I didn't like it." Bast could even identify particular ways in which Jimmy had changed. In the past Jimmy might have "held within him some of the answers," but now he "radiated the undeniable truth that he did know some of the answers, if only a choice handful." Jimmy had "an aura of contained excitement," as if he were "a child . . . guarding a special surprise." Then, over the first couple of weeks they lived at the Iroquois, Jimmy slowly began to be more open with Bill. "He seemed to be trying to tell me," Bast eventually wrote, "that there could be, among people, a stronger tie, a permanent link of love and compassion, which could only be possible when they would put aside all the extraneous, complex trivialities, the mountain of unnecessary and petty thoughts that now kept them apart. It was, perhaps, the concept of being in harmony with a single unifying power."

In time Jimmy revealed to Bill one key source of his newly acquired knowledge. While they were alone in their room one day, Jimmy walked over to the dresser, picked up a slender book, and handed it to Bill, who was lying on the bed. Jimmy handled the volume—*The Little Prince* by Antoine de Saint-Exupéry—as if he had in his possession a rare ancient treasure. He did not tell Bill that it had been Rogers who introduced him to *The Little Prince*. Jimmy had always gone out of his way to keep his friends from meeting each other. By doing so, he could often take credit for knowing information without disclosing where he learned it. That day he simply told Bill that he should look at *The Little Prince*. If Bill was lucky, Jimmy said, he would learn something from it the first time he read it. If he wasn't lucky, he should read the book again. And again. Jimmy had.

As he read, Bill discovered that *The Little Prince* was a fable about a man who, stranded in the Sahara when the plane he is flying goes down, meets an extraordinary tiny person, the little prince. Originally from a planet the size of a house where he owned three volcanoes, the little prince set out on the interplanetary journey that had brought him to Earth. Here, after an arduous search, he learns, on the day he finds himself having a long conversation with a fox, the secret of what is most important in life. As he told the little prince good-bye, the fox had said, "And now here is my secret, a very simple secret: it is only with the heart that one can see rightly; what is essential is invisible to the eye." When the little prince tells this to the man stranded in the desert, it changes the way the man looks at the world. At that moment he comes to realize that physical appearances and material objects pale in importance compared to love, friendship, spirituality. Finally, at the end of the book, the little prince returns to his planet and the man escapes from the desert. Over the years, the man would be haunted by memories of the little prince. On the next-to-last page of the book, the narrator, who is the man haunted by the little prince, has drawn a picture of an empty desert with a single star in the sky. "This is, to me," he says, "the loveliest and saddest landscape in the world. . . . It is here that the little prince appeared on Earth, and disappeared. . . . Look at it carefully so that you will be sure to recognize it in case you travel some day to the African desert. And, if you should come upon this spot, please do not hurry on. Wait for a time, exactly under the star. Then, if a little man appears who laughs, who has golden hair and who refuses to answer questions, you will know who he is. If this should happen, please comfort me. Send me word that he has come back." When Bill closed the book the first time he read it, he felt deeply moved by the story. He too was haunted by the secret revealed by the fox—*What is essential is invisible to the eye*—and by the beautiful golden-haired little prince who appears on Earth just briefly and is gone.

While Jimmy and Bill were striving to reach a deeper level of understanding in their spiritual life, it is likely they were bonding more deeply in another way as well. During the months the two of them spent in New York, Jimmy and Bill would begin to consider themselves more of a couple. Most likely, because he was now so much more confident and aggressive, Jimmy had pressed the issue of having a sexual relationship as soon as the two of them moved in together at the Iroquois. After all, at the same time Jimmy pursued his inner journey of self-awareness and enlightenment, which he did in part by reading *The Little Prince* over and over, he was continuing to explore his sexuality. Naturally, the longer Jimmy and Bill lived together at the Iroquois the more Rogers came to believe that he had lost Jimmy. Even if he felt this, Rogers kept reaching out to Jimmy by suggesting him for jobs and sending him around to meet people in the industry. Of course Jimmy was thrilled with Rogers's efforts. For Rogers, though, there seemed to be an implied contract between them. Should he be able to get Jimmy what he wanted—work as an actor—Jimmy would come back to him.

Actually, the favors Rogers did for Jimmy were considerable. On May 21, Jimmy appeared in "Prologue to Glory," an episode of *Kraft Television Theatre*. Five days later he had a small but pivotal part on a *Studio One* episode about Abraham Lincoln. Though it's unclear how Rogers pulled strings to get Jimmy these jobs, his involvement in lining him up another part, this one on the June 2 episode of *Hallmark Hall of Fame* called "Forgotten Children," is obvious. Through his advertising agency, Rogers was directly connected with the production. Even with these acting jobs, Jimmy needed a steady income. To help him out yet again, Rogers made some telephone calls and got Jimmy a job as a production assistant at NBC for July and August. Slowly, Jimmy was starting to accumulate a handful of impressive television acting credits, small parts that indicated he could handle larger ones. Finally, in the summer of 1952, he was ready to try to achieve something much more substantial than appearing in small parts on more television shows. Before Jimmy had come to New York, James Whitmore had suggested that he contact Lee Strasberg and apply for admission to the Actors Studio. That summer, Jimmy felt that he had learned enough about himself—and the art and craft of acting—to take a chance and audition for the Studio.

*   *   *

"We were best friends. We said this to each other. We identified, and we understood it. We wanted a sense of belonging. The only thing that mattered to us was the arts. But we had no experience. We were like two little mudlarks splashing around on the street. We just decided what we were going to do and we did it. On a more personal level, Jimmy was careful not to annoy me like he did a lot of his friends. He didn't want to upset that really fine opinion I had of him. If he liked someone he was going to act as grand as he could. If he didn't like you, though. . . . There was this spring in him that would turn off or leap over you as if to say, 'You don't see me. You don't understand me. You don't know what's going on inside me, what's really important to me.' "

This is how Christine White remembers James Dean, an opinion she formed after years of reflection on a period of her life that was as challenging as it was creative. She and Jimmy were young. They were also arrogant and talented. They wanted to settle for nothing short of the ultimate they could achieve in both their private lives and their careers. In the end one of them *would* achieve the ultimate (in his career, at least) and make a contribution to the art of acting that would easily outlast the lives of his friends, much less his own. But that would come later. In the summer of 1952, Jimmy and Chris, as he would call her, couldn't think about the future. They were having too much trouble concentrating on the present. They knew their hopes and their dreams. They knew what they *wanted*. They wanted to be actors and, to accomplish this, they wanted to be members of the Actors Studio. After they had known each other for a while, it became obvious that there was a logical pattern to the narrative of their lives. Not at the beginning, though. Their first meeting was accidental, purely by chance.

They met one day during lunch hour in Jane Deacy's office. Jimmy had come there to waste some time when he noticed a young woman sitting at a desk where a secretary usually worked. She wore a red jumper and a red baseball cap. Pretty and petite, she had a soft, wistful quality about her. At the moment she seemed completely absorbed in what she was doing—typing a manuscript. The longer Jimmy looked at her—how many people wore a red baseball cap in an office in New York City?—the more intrigued he became. Slowly, almost hesitantly, he walked up to her. "Hi," he said in his most innocent tone, "who are you?" Suddenly the young woman glanced up from her typing. "Can't you see I'm busy?" she snapped. She was so rude that Jimmy felt stunned. All he was trying to do was be friendly. Turning away, Jimmy walked to a sofa and sat down. After a while the girl must have realized that she had hurt his feelings. Once she had finished her typing, she approached him, told him her name, and apologized. To smooth things over she suggested that the two of them go out for coffee.

At the Blue Ribbon Cafe, an actors' hangout not far from Jane Deacy's office, they warmed up to each other, at least enough to chat. As they sipped their coffee, Chris, who was an actress represented by Deacy, told Jimmy that what she was typing was a dramatic scene she had written called "Ripping Off Layers to Find Roots." She was rude to Jimmy because she was in an enormous rush since she had to finish typing her manuscript before the secretary whose desk she was borrowing came back from lunch. What's more, she added, she intended to use her dramatic scene to audition for the Actors Studio. Coincidentally, the scene called for a couple, a young man and a young woman. When Jimmy asked her if she needed a scene partner for her audition—he was an actor too, he said, and had come to New York to try to get into the Studio—Chris was so elated by the idea that she made plans for them to start rehearsing right away.

They rehearsed everywhere—in Central Park, in the back of taxis, in Jimmy's room at the Iroquois. They worked hard on the piece, a scene that detailed the lives of a rich southern girl and a brilliant young homeless man by depicting the encounters they have at night on a beach over several weeks. As they spent day after day rehearsing, Jimmy and Chris completely reworked the original manuscript. Finally the morning arrived when they were scheduled to audition at the Actors Studio, along with one hundred and fifty other hopeful actors, out of whom just fifteen would be accepted. But only moments before Jimmy and Chris were getting ready to walk onstage in front of the judges, one of whom was Lee Strasberg, Jimmy became so terrified that he told Chris he couldn't go through with the audition. It didn't help matters that, since the part called for him not to wear his glasses, he couldn't even see where he was walking. "I'm not going out there," Jimmy said. "We're not ready yet." Chris didn't mince words when she answered him. "Listen, you little wretch," she said, "you're not going to louse up my audition. We're here now, and we're going through with it. Now get out there!"

Reluctantly, Jimmy did. And as they enacted the scene the judges were so impressed with Chris and Jimmy's performance that they did not stop them when their allotted time ran out. (Even as a semiprofessional Jimmy had trouble adhering to rules for an audition, just as he had back in high school when he was performing in speech tournaments.) The judges' favorable response was even more unusual considering the fact that the Studio strongly urged students not to audition with original material because its quality was normally inferior to established texts. The purpose of an audition, Studio personnel pointed out, was to evaluate an actor's ability to act, not his ability to write. The Studio was an *actor's* studio, not a writer's workshop. Jimmy and Chris didn't appear to know this. All they knew was that, once they had finished, they had made a profound impression on the judges. "It seemed simple, easy, believable," Strasberg later said about their work. "[It had a] wonderful quality. Very much what we would like to see from people when they come to us."

As soon as Jimmy and Chris walked offstage, Jimmy was relieved.

He felt even better a few days later when he found out that both he and Chris had been invited to join the Studio. At twenty-one, Jimmy was probably the youngest member in the Studio's history. He was so pleased with himself he could hardly control his joy. "I have made great strides in my craft," he wrote to Aunt Ortense and Uncle Marcus back in Indiana. "After months of auditioning, I am very proud to announce that I am a member of The Actors Studio. The greatest school of the theatre. It houses great people like Marlon Brando, Julie Harris, Arthur Kennedy, Elia Kazan, Mildred Dunnock, Kevin McCarthy, Monty Clift, June Havoc, and on and on and on. Very few get into it, and it is absolutely free. It is the best thing that can happen to an actor. I am one of the youngest to belong. If I can keep this up and nothing interferes with my progress, one of these days I might be able to contribute something to the world."

By getting into the Actors Studio, Jimmy had made a significant step forward in his career. Now, he hoped, he might finally be on his way. In a sense, over the last several months, he had been ripping off the layers of his own personality to find *his* roots. The Little Prince, as he now referred to himself, was on the verge of better self-understanding. This, he decided, was what he had needed to do to improve his art, more than anything else.

As he attended his first few classes at the Studio, Jimmy could almost feel his love of acting growing. In the early weeks he learned by observing other actors do their scenes. He also became friends with a number of Studio members, among them Roddy McDowall, Lonny Chapman, Vivian Nathan, and David Stewart. He felt inspired simply by being in the same room with legendary figures in the theatre like Strasberg and Elia Kazan. He had certainly come a long way from the modest little theatre back in Fairmount High School where he had dressed up like Frankenstein for *Goon with the Wind*.

Still, Jimmy wasn't happy just watching scene work. He wanted to act. Naturally he was worried about doing his first piece in front of the Studio, but in time he got up enough nerve to prepare a scene himself. Initially he had intended to present an original piece he and Christine had written called "Abroad," a short dialogue that centered around two young people planning a trip to Europe. But several days before he and Christine were scheduled to perform, an actor at the Studio talked them out of doing the piece. This was an actor's studio, he reminded them, not a writer's workshop. So in its place Jimmy adapted a monologue from the novel *Matador* by Barnaby Conrad, a piece that traced the thoughts of a matador preparing for his last bullfight. On the morning of the day Jimmy was scheduled to do his scene, he completely reworked the monologue. Then, only hours later, he performed the piece at the Studio before an audience that included Strasberg. But no sooner had he gotten into the monologue than he began to feel uneasy about the material, so much so that he didn't even finish it but quit halfway through. Something told him the scene simply wasn't working. He was right too. Strasberg hated it. He also hated Jimmy's performance. The moment Jimmy sat down in the audience Strasberg launched into a vicious criticism of almost every area of Jimmy's piece: his motivation, his delivery, his characterization. Strasberg's attack was so harsh that, as Kazan later described the event, "[Dean sat] in a sort of poutish mess in the front row and scowled."

Some members who were there that day would remember that Jimmy finally threw his bullfighter's cape, a prop, over his shoulder and stalked out of the theatre in a huff. Others would remember Jimmy's pain. "I don't recall the criticism but I do recall it was really pretty rough," says Vivian Nathan, an original member of the Studio who was in the audience for Jimmy's performance. "Sometimes Lee was rather tough, especially if you were talented. He could tolerate mediocrity. He could even praise it because he didn't care. But if you had talent he was wicked. He wanted to pull out of you that which he knew was there. So he took no nonsense. He really was mean with

Jimmy. David Stewart, another original member, saw that Jimmy was suffering. It was like his skin was being pulled off. He shriveled. David asked Jimmy to come home to his house for lunch and we all went—my husband, David, Jimmy, and I. At the house David and Jimmy were like kids trying to figure out this Rubik's cube–like puzzle that David had. What was interesting to see was the terrific concentration Jimmy could have if he wanted something done. What struck me hard was that he had the kind of concentration it takes to be a good actor, because you really have to zero in on what you're doing. Anyway, once they had figured it out, Jimmy said to David's wife, 'Let's go to the movies.' They didn't even wait for lunch. They just went out to the movies. Somehow the fact that he had worked something out—whatever it was, whether it was with his hands or what—released him in some way. Onstage he didn't have that. As it turned out, on film he did."

That—Jimmy's work on film—was some time off. First Jimmy had to learn his craft. He could not do that in Hollywood. He had tried, but the people in the business out there seemed to care more about getting him in bed than helping him learn to act. Apparently he wasn't going to be able to get much out of the Actors Studio either. Instead, Jimmy would have to learn his craft by working in the theatre and on television—on Broadway and the Motorola, as it were.

It could be argued that Dean was the first postmodern actor. That is to say, he was the first actor who consciously tried to shatter the classical style of acting popular at the time, a style practiced by actors as diverse as John Wayne and Laurence Olivier. To break away from the classical mode, which demanded that an actor be more mindful of his whole performance than its isolated moments, Dean would *focus* on those individual moments. To Dean's way of thinking, an actor should try to achieve the ultimate in a performance every moment he is on the stage or the screen. Marlon Brando and (especially) Montgomery Clift did this, but they didn't seem to be aware of it. Dean *wanted* to be aware of what he was doing even if the audience never was. The Method had opened the door for Dean to formulate the new style of acting he was attempting to develop. Finally, though, with its emphasis on sense memory and motivation, the Method never really addressed the concept of building a performance through perfecting individual moments. On one level Dean and Strasberg clashed as violently as they did because the Method did not address this issue. A devout disciple of Stanislavsky, Strasberg didn't understand what Dean was doing, and if he did he didn't approve. At this time, perhaps Dean himself may not have been able to describe completely what he was trying to achieve in his acting, but he did know this: He had no choice but to fight vehemently any destructive analysis of his acting even if that analysis came from someone as famous and respected in the field of drama as Strasberg. "I don't know what's inside me," he told Bill Bast, explaining his response to Strasberg's attack. "I don't know what happens when I act . . . but if I let them dissect me like a rabbit in a clinical research laboratory or something, then I might not be able to produce again. They might sterilize me. That man"—Strasberg—"had no right to tear me down like that. You keep knocking a guy down and you take the guts away from him. And what's an actor without guts?"

After Strasberg attacked him, Dean was never as enthusiastic about the Actors Studio. For a while, he stopped going there altogether. Finally, in 1953, Jimmy was performing in a production of *The Scarecrow* directed by Frank Corsaro at the Theatre de Lys when Corsaro, another Studio member, talked him into coming back. Following that, Jimmy worked on some improvisations directed by Corsaro. He played a small role in *End as a Man* while it was being developed at the Studio, again in 1953. He performed in *The Sea Gull,* turning out work that Strasberg called "lovely." But when Jimmy acted in Edna

St. Vincent Millay's *Aria Da Capo*—he was Pierrot—Strasberg suggested that he play things closer to himself. In the end Dean's relationship with Strasberg was extremely complicated. Dean admired Strasberg for the position he had achieved in the industry yet he resented him for what he perceived to be his attacks on his acting. Finally, even though he was unusually good at spotting talent, Strasberg may have misread Dean since Dean was working in a way no other actor was working at the time.

During the months Jimmy had spent in New York so far, he had tried to diversify his interests in the arts by developing his talents in music, dance, and literature. He took dance lessons from Eartha Kitt and Katherine Dunham. He became fascinated with the bongo drums, often sitting alone in the corner of his room banging away for hours. He got interested in the piano and started taking lessons from Leonard Rosenman, a musician and composer he met through a mutual friend. "I felt he was gifted and sensitive," Rosenman would say, "but didn't have the patience or the rigor to practice. He never was able to figure out why he couldn't sit down and simply play Beethoven sonatas without learning something about music." On the surface Dean may have seemed to be a prima donna dabbling in different art forms, yet in reality he was further developing his new approach to acting. To Dean, anything he learned about any art form fed directly into what he was trying to accomplish as an actor. In other words, his acting was the product not only of everything he learned from living his day-to-day life but of the knowledge he acquired from studying literature, art, music, dance. Dean's ultimate goal was to achieve a deeper level of acting moment to moment, a purely postmodern concept. His total performance could only be as good as this series of individual moments. Those moments would be made powerful when they resonated with the full range of what he had gained from his personal, intellectual, and artistic pursuits.

*   *   *

During 1952, as Jimmy made the auditioning rounds in New York, he met a number of people who were in the same position as he was. One afternoon at a cattle call at the Mansfield Theatre, Tommy Tompkins, an acquaintance of his, introduced him to another young actor who was busy making the auditioning rounds. Tall, dark-haired, and uniquely handsome, Martin Landau had grown up on the other side of the East River in Queens, where his family still lived. Almost instantly Jimmy and Marty, as his friends called him, struck up a conversation, which, following the cattle call, continued over coffee. Since neither of them had gotten the part he was auditioning for, both complained about having their talent ignored for one more day. Beyond that, Jimmy and Marty talked about a variety of other subjects as well: acting, the arts, New York City.

At this same time, Jimmy and Dizzy Sheridan were becoming closer, mostly because Dizzy had gotten to be friends with Bill after he and Jimmy started living together at the Iroquois. Dizzy worked as an usher at the Paris Theatre, the movie house next to the Plaza hotel. That job just paid the rent, though; what she really wanted to be was an actress or a dancer. While Dizzy and Jimmy's friendship was intense, it never became anything more than a friendship. In fact, once Bill moved to New York and he and Jimmy became involved again, Dizzy seemed content to play the role of Bill's confidante, the person he could talk to about his relationship with Jimmy. Witty and fun-loving, Dizzy would maintain an important place in Jimmy's life for the time she knew him, even if their friendship never took on the qualities of a traditional romantic relationship.

During the fall of 1952, a relationship in Jimmy's life that had been anything but platonic—his and Rogers's—may have cooled from a love affair to a friendship, but it was Rogers who helped Jimmy get the break he had wanted for so long. Rogers had been instrumental in landing Jimmy many jobs in the past. Apparently he was not going to stop now; he probably still saw this as a way to lure Jimmy away from Bill. If Jimmy felt indebted enough to Rogers, Rogers seemed to be thinking, then maybe he would leave Bill and come back to him. It really didn't matter to Jimmy what Rogers's motivations were; he was just happy that Rogers continued to do him favors. Rogers had started to line up a particular professional contact, the one that would lead to Jimmy's break, back in the summer. At that time he had taken Jimmy out one weekend to meet his friends Lemuel and Shirley Ayers, who owned a large estate on the Hudson River north of New York City. Jimmy had had a pleasant time with the Ayerses, especially Lemuel. Naturally it did not escape his attention that Lemuel was a highly successful Broadway producer, a man who could, by himself, launch Jimmy's stage-acting career.

That weekend in the early summer was the first of several weekends Jimmy spent at the Ayerses'. After a while he started to go out and spend time with the Ayerses alone, without Rogers. Finally, in late August, Lemuel asked Jimmy to go with him and his wife on a ten-day yacht cruise from New York to Cape Cod. Jimmy eagerly accepted his offer. When he told his friends about the trip, Jimmy announced that he was going on the cruise to work on the yacht's crew and earn some extra money. Seemingly none of Jimmy's friends questioned him about why the Ayerses would hire him for this job when he had absolutely no training at working on a yacht, when, in fact, he had never even been *on* a boat. Actually, after the trip, some of Jimmy's friends suspected that on the cruise Jimmy had had a brief affair with Lemuel. In the past Jimmy had never been shy about exchanging sexual favors for the chance to further his career, although he was repulsed by the fact that he felt he *had* to do this to get somewhere. In Hollywood, he may not have approved of swapping sex for jobs, but if that was what he had to do he would do it. In this case maybe the sex was just sex, with no strings attached. Whatever happened on the yacht, for whatever reason it happened, Lemuel Ayers knew that

Jimmy Dean was a young actor desperate for a part on Broadway. More than almost anyone Jimmy had met, Ayers was in a position to give him that part, should he decide to.

While Jimmy was away on the yacht trip, Bill moved them into an apartment he had arranged to sublet from a couple they had known at UCLA. Shortly after Jimmy got back from the trip, the couple returned to New York, earlier than Bill had expected, so Bill and Jimmy were forced to move again. This time they ended up in a much smaller apartment. They still had not gotten used to living in the new place on the night Jimmy and Bill were having dinner with Dizzy at a midtown diner and Jimmy came up with one of his ideas: He wanted to go see the farm in Indiana, and he wanted to go right away.

"You'd both love it," Jimmy told Bill and Dizzy. "It's all clean and fresh, lots of trees and open fields. Tons of good food, chicken, steak, all that jazz. We've got cows, pigs, the whole bit."

"They got horses?" asked Dizzy, who was known for her love of horses.

"Yes," Jimmy said.

"Let's go now," she said.

And that, to an extent, was what they did. For after they had solved the problems of how Bill would explain missing work at the job at CBS he had had for several months now (it was decided that someone in New York would call in sick for him every day he was gone) and how they would pay for the three of them to travel the eight hundred miles from New York City to Fairmount (they would hitchhike), they were almost ready to go. "Three of us hitch eight hundred miles to Indiana and eight hundred miles back?" Bill said, somewhat apprehensive. "That's a laugh. Nobody would pick us up. All we've got is about ten dollars between us. What if we got stranded someplace?"

The question was legitimate. Despite that, the next morning, Jimmy, Bill, and Dizzy boarded a bus that took them out of Manhattan as far as the New Jersey Turnpike. There they didn't have to stand on the side of the highway any time at all before they were picked up by someone driving west. By ten o'clock that night, once the first driver had dropped them off and a second one had picked them up, they had only gotten as far as the end of the Pennsylvania Turnpike, still a long way from Fairmount. Luckily, a man driving a Nash Rambler stopped to give them a lift. As they drove along, the man explained to them who he was—Clyde McCullough, a catcher for the Pittsburgh Pirates—and where he was going—to Iowa to play in an exhibition game. He could take them as far as Des Moines, he said. That would leave them a relatively short distance from Indiana. Before he dropped them off, Clyde treated the three of them to dinner at a roadside café. Then, when he did leave them on the side of the highway after they had been driving for hours, Jimmy, Bill, and Dizzy felt as if they had made a new friend in Clyde McCullough; it was with some emotion that they all said good-bye. From Des Moines, Jimmy and his friends hitched a ride to Fairmount without much trouble. As soon as they got out of the car in front of the Winslow farm, Jimmy seemed to be completely in his element. He appeared content, pleased, happy to be back in Fairmount.

Over the next few days, Jimmy enjoyed being home on the farm. He rode his old motorcycle through the pastures and on the local roads, impressing Bill and Dizzy with his riding ability. He had long conversations with Aunt Ortense and Uncle Marcus as they sat around the dining room table after supper. He went out of his way to play with Markie, who was now old enough—almost nine—to be interested in drawing and watercolors, much to Jimmy's approval. One morning Jimmy stopped by Fairmount High to see Mrs. Brookshire, who was so happy to see him that she let him teach her drama class. But mostly, during the time they spent in Fairmount, Jimmy and his friends simply relished the pleasures of country life. They ate home-cooked meals. They slept more soundly than they ever could in the city. They whiled away hour after hour wandering around out-of-doors in the most beautiful season to be in Indiana, the fall. The three of them would have probably stayed on longer too, but the chance for Jimmy's break came in the form of a telephone call from Jane Deacy in New York City. Lemuel Ayers was casting a Broadway show called *See the Jaguar* and he wanted Jimmy to read for a part. Whatever had taken place on the yacht in late August was now beginning to pay off in early October. Jimmy couldn't turn down the audition, so, rested and well fed, he, Bill, and Dizzy set out hitchhiking the eight hundred miles back to New York.

As soon as he got to the city, Jimmy began studying *See the Jaguar*. An exotic story set in the rural South, the play written by N. Richard Nash centers around Wally Wilkins, a seventeen-year-old boy who is dominated by an eccentric mother. She is so paranoid about her son's being hurt by society that she refuses to let him leave the farm. At one point she even locks him in an icehouse to keep him from leaving her. When she dies, Wally is clueless about how to conduct his life. Soon he wanders into a nearby town only to be taken in by a young couple, Janna and Dave. Janna's father owns a roadside zoo that features animals such as a weasel and a jaguar. The play ends after Wally accidentally kills the jaguar and, in revenge, Janna's father locks him in the jaguar's cage. SEE THE JAGUAR, reads the sign posted on the side of the cage that contains Wally. On the day that Jimmy auditioned for Wally, one of the most emotionally crippled characters an actor could play, he felt as if he had gotten to the essence of the boy. It was disturbing how convincingly he could play the part of this damaged child. Ayers and Michael Gordon, the show's director, agreed. They were so delighted with Jimmy's audition that a few days later they called Jane Deacy to tell her that Jimmy was being offered the part.

On November 13, following a short rehearsal period, *See the Jaguar* began its out-of-town tryouts in New Haven, Connecticut, at the Parsons Theatre. Besides mastering the difficult role of the naive

Dean, locked in a cage, in *See the Jaguar*, his Broadway debut

farmboy, Jimmy also had to sing "Green Briar, Blue Fire," a song written for the show by Alec Wilder, who was also a close friend of
Ayers's. After three try-out performances in New Haven, *See the
Jaguar* opened on Broadway at the Cort Theatre on December 3,
1952. The reviews were devastating. *The New York Times* dismissed
the play as "verbose," one that "says nothing." The *New York Post* described it as "full of sound and fury, signifying nothing." The *New
York Journal American* quipped, "[I]f you want to see *See the
Jaguar*—you had better hurry." While they destroyed the play itself,
the critics dealt with Dean much more favorably. The *Post* said Dean
"achieves the feat of making the childish young fugitive believable
and unembarrassing" while the *New York Herald Tribune* called his
performance "extraordinary . . . in an almost impossible role." With
such damaging notices, *See the Jaguar* closed on December 6, with
only five official performances to its credit.

Around this time Jimmy suffered other professional disappoint-
ments. During the New Haven tryouts for *See the Jaguar,* he had
asked John Stix, a graduate of the Yale theatre department, a member
of the Actors Studio since 1950, and a friend of his, to come see the
show. "I didn't know what he was doing onstage," Stix recalls, "but I
saw enough to call him in for an audition for a play I was directing, *In
the Summer House* by Jane Bowles. Bowles had spent ten years writing
this play. It was flawed but brilliant. There were two young troubled
characters—Molly and Lionel. Jimmy seemed perfect for Lionel. Jane
was in the auditorium with me for the audition, and we both went ape
over him. It was hand-in-glove casting. But the producer said he
wanted 'no Actors Studio shit.' This was my first Broadway play and
I didn't know any better so we missed the opportunity to reveal Dean's
talent to a wider public for the first time." Still, even though *See the
Jaguar* closed and he was continuing to lose some of the parts he
wanted, Jimmy was gradually reaching the career goal he had

dreamed about for so long: He was on the verge of being taken seriously as an actor.

Other actors realized this about Jimmy too. "I was sitting in Cromwell's one day," says Sylvia Miles, who herself was starting out in the entertainment business in the mid-fifties. "I was talking to my girlfriend when I smelled something funny. I turned around and Jimmy Dean was standing there with a cigarette and it was burning a hole in my coat. He was talking to someone and didn't realize he was burning a hole in the collar of my brand-new Borgano coat. I said, 'You ruined my Borgano coat. What am I gonna do?' And he said, 'Well, I'm not going to buy you a new one. Cut off the collar.' So I did. Anyway, this was around the time he did *See the Jaguar*. Even then, I knew he was going to be a great actor. I knew this because he was so self-absorbed. Any actor that self-absorbed had to end up being great."

In the spring of 1953, while he fought to make it in show business, Jimmy would meet a young man with whom he could have had a passionate and fulfilling relationship had the circumstances of their lives been different than they finally were. Nineteen, slender, blond, the young man had a face so boyishly innocent that Jimmy felt attracted to him the moment he first saw him. There were few boys who were as attractive as Jimmy was himself. One of them was Jonathan Gilmore.

2. It was a typical spring day in New York—gray, chilly, windy. A young man named Ray had called Jimmy to see if he would hang out with him that afternoon. Jimmy and Ray were friends, though not close friends. They had first met in Los Angeles on the set of a picture; Jimmy had had a walk-on part and Ray had been an extra. Recently, Jimmy had run into Ray in New York where he was

Jonathan Gilmore

now working as a small-time drug dealer. Ray charged fifteen dollars for a Prince Albert tobacco can full of pot—a bargain, really, for New York.

One of the places Ray wanted to stop by that afternoon was a drugstore in the West Forties. He needed to go there because that particular drugstore had a pay telephone that, if he inserted an open bobby pin in the coin slot just right, he could use for free. There was another pay telephone he could rig this way at the Museum of Modern Art, but Ray didn't want to go all the way over to Fifth Avenue and Fifty-third Street. No sooner had they walked through the front door of the drugstore than Jimmy spotted a young man sitting in the small restaurant section at the counter by himself. How could he have missed him? With that face and body, he had to be a model or an actor, or maybe a dancer. He was even Jimmy's physical type—young, cute, almost pretty.

As luck would have it, Ray knew the boy. So he and Jimmy walked over to the counter and sat down next to him. Jimmy made sure to leave an empty stool between the boy and himself since he didn't want to appear too forward. Naturally Ray introduced them—the boy's name was Jonathan—and, after that, Jonathan and Ray began to talk. Mostly they swapped Hollywood gossip. As Jimmy had thought, Jonathan *was* an actor and had done a good amount of work recently on television and in film. Just as Jimmy had, Jonathan had met Ray originally in Los Angeles on the set of a picture. While Jonathan and Ray chatted, Jimmy sat in silence, except when he ordered a muffin and a cup of coffee from the waitress. Sitting there, Jimmy couldn't help but notice what Jonathan was reading—a book on bullfighting. Finally Ray went to use the telephone, leaving Jonathan and Jimmy alone. At first Jimmy didn't know what to say. Then he decided to make a comment about the eyeglasses Jonathan was wearing.

"Are you nearsighted or farsighted?"

"Farsighted," Jonathan said. "I just need them to read."

"You're really lucky," Jimmy said. "I can't see a thing without my glasses. I wish I was farsighted, instead of being as nearsighted as I am."

Jonathan said nothing.

"Do you speak Spanish?" Jimmy asked, motioning to the book on bullfighting. "Can I see it?"

Jonathan slid the book across the counter. Jimmy picked up the book and began to thumb through its pages, glancing at the pictures. Next he sipped the coffee and cut in half the muffin the waitress had brought him. Before he ate the muffin, he spread his butter on it. Then he reached over, took Jonathan's butter—without asking him if he could have it—and spread that butter on his muffin too. When Jimmy looked up to see that Jonathan had noticed that he had taken the butter without asking, Jimmy just smiled.

Eventually Jimmy ate the muffin, Ray came back, and he and Jimmy left. Over the next few days, Jimmy found himself thinking a lot about Jonathan, this beautiful boy who was interested in bullfighting, not unlike himself.

In the coming weeks, Jimmy kept running into Jonathan, usually in the drugstore or on Forty-fifth Street near the studio where Jimmy was taking private dance lessons from Eartha Kitt. A cabaret singer and a dancer, Kitt was just beginning to enjoy some minor fame. "Jamie"—Kitt's nickname for Jimmy—"and I were like brother and sister," Kitt later wrote. "He told me, in fact, that he thought of me as a sister. Our relationship was strictly platonic and spiritual; we had wonderful times together. He was a consummate artist, always striving to improve himself. He wasn't satisfied to schlepp across stage; he wanted to move, to learn body language so that his movement, too, would communicate."

One day Jimmy was leaving Kitt's dance class—he still had on his low-cut scooped-neck shirt under his jacket—when he met Jonathan

In a dance class with Eartha Kitt

on the sidewalk. As they talked, Jimmy mentioned that *A Place in the Sun* had recently opened at a theatre on Forty-second Street. He had heard that Montgomery Clift was wonderful in the picture. Did Jonathan want to go see it? Sure, Jonathan said.

Sitting in the theatre, Jimmy ate candy and popcorn as he stared at the screen. He simply couldn't take his eyes off Montgomery Clift who loomed before him, his luminous face sometimes filling up the whole screen. Of the actors whose work he respected, Clift came closest, or so Jimmy said, to doing what *he*, Jimmy, wanted to do. When the picture was over and the full impact of Clift's performance had sunk in, Jimmy felt overwhelmed. He had loved Clift before; now he adored him. Jimmy was so swept away that he insisted on watching the picture a second time. He was halfway through watching it a third time before he could make himself leave the theatre. Unfortunately Jonathan didn't share Jimmy's obsession with Clift. Jimmy noticed that Jonathan dozed off at least once, maybe twice, during the two and a half times they sat through *A Place in the Sun*.

Later, Jimmy and Jonathan had coffee at a cafeteria not far from the theatre. As they sat at the table, Jimmy couldn't stop talking about Clift's performance. Jimmy told Jonathan that for some time now he had been formulating the theory that an actor should combine all he has learned form his personal life with his knowledge about various art forms (dance, literature, music, painting) and channel that information through the instrument of his body to create an inspired moment of acting. In that moment on the stage or on film the actor should be able to combine everything he has experienced in life—a brilliant, impassioned moment. An outstanding performance was nothing more than a series of these inspired moments. Jimmy believed Clift had succeeded in producing these moments in *A Place in the Sun*. He also believed that George Stevens, the director of the picture, had made a similar breakthrough. While Jimmy and Jonathan talked, Jimmy began to feel that he and Jonathan were communicating with each other on some significant level. Unlike many of Jimmy's friends, Jonathan seemed to understand what Jimmy was talking about. Eartha Kitt, to name one friend, thought that Jimmy was crazy when he started rambling on and on about these "moments of acting." There was something else about Jonathan. Though he and Jimmy had not spent much time together, Jimmy could sense that Jonathan was becoming as intrigued by him as he was by Jonathan. Jimmy had been with enough men to know when one was approachable. Jonathan, he concluded, was approachable.

A few days passed before Jimmy and Jonathan saw each other again. Jonathan had told Jimmy about his motorcycle—a Norton he had bought in Astoria, Queens, after he spotted it while he was there on a modeling assignment once—and Jimmy wanted to look at it. For several months now, Jimmy had owned a motorcycle, which he used to get around New York. So one night Jimmy stopped by Jonathan's apartment building at Forty-seventh Street and Eighth Avenue and searched around until he found the Norton chained to a rain pipe attached to the side of the building. Studying the motorcycle, Jimmy couldn't resist tinkering with the motor. Then, his hands covered with grease, he decided to go upstairs and see Jonathan even though it was well past midnight and Jonathan was possibly asleep. (Throughout his life, Jimmy regularly disturbed his friends in the middle of the night either by calling them on the telephone or stopping by in person.) When Jimmy knocked on Jonathan's apartment door, it took Jonathan some time to answer it. Sure enough, he had been asleep.

"Can I come in and wash my hands?" Jimmy said. "I've been trying to fix your carburetor."

"Of course," Jonathan said. "Come on in."

After he washed his hands, Jimmy walked into the living room and sat down. Jonathan was now wide awake. Soon the two of them started to talk about a painting Jonathan was working on, a scene of the street in front of his apartment building. In the unfinished painting Jonathan had not yet added people. When he asked Jimmy if he should put people in, Jimmy answered emphatically—*"No."*

Eventually Jimmy brought up another reason why he had come to see Jonathan: He wanted to talk about bullfighting. Excited by the subject as well, Jonathan showed Jimmy some photographs he had of bullfighters in the ring. Then Jimmy told him that he had once been on the set of a picture about bullfighting starring Anthony Quinn and Mel Ferrer when he met Sidney Franklin, the famous bullfighter who had been hired as the picture's technical adviser. Franklin had given Jimmy a cape with dried blood on it, blood from bullfights. (This was the cape Jimmy had used as a prop when he did his *Matador* monologue at the Studio.) From a discussion of the cape, Jimmy moved on to another topic that seemed to fascinate him, goring. "Have you ever thought about what it would be like to be gored by a bull?" Jimmy asked Jonathan, who, Jimmy had decided, was just odd enough to play along with a conversation like this one. "How deep would the horn go? Where would it enter the body? Why would it always enter in the area of the crotch? What would the pain be like? Would you go unconscious because of the loss of blood?" From these questions, Jimmy mentioned other acts that interested him—death by hanging, execution, and specific aspects of dying, like what it feels like when a bullet enters the body. Finally Jimmy began to recite poetry to Jonathan in Spanish, translating it as he went along. As he did this, the evening started to take on an almost romantic tone. Actually, that was exactly what Jimmy wanted. For while Jimmy's actions *appeared* to be haphazard, they were not. He was methodically pulling Jonathan under his influence through a subtle, purposeful seduction. At this point in his life, after he had been unable to control so much of what happened to him over the years, after he had been dominated by older men like James DeWeerd and Rogers Brackett, Jimmy wanted to be in charge. If he couldn't control what happened to him in his professional life, then at least he would control what happened in his private life. Or he would try.

The better part of a week passed before Jimmy ended up at Jonathan's apartment once again. He'd had a terrible day and just wanted to go out and have dinner, but neither he nor Jonathan had enough money. So Jimmy called James Sheldon, for whom he had recently worked on a television show, to see if he wanted to have dinner at a French restaurant near Jonathan's. Jimmy knew Sheldon would pick up the check. When Jimmy called, Sheldon agreed to go. While the three of them talked during dinner, mostly about acting and Jimmy's and Jonathan's careers, Jimmy got drunk. This was not hard for Jimmy to do since he had an unusually low tolerance for alcohol. Jimmy became so tipsy that at one point he picked up a crêpe suzette and squeezed it in such a way that the jelly oozed out one end. It was a childish act, if suggestive, but Jimmy thought it was hilarious. Laughing, he looked over at Jonathan and began to flirt. Then later, when the three of them were having after-dinner drinks, Jimmy stuck his hand down the front of his pants and grabbed his cock. It was another not-so-subtle gesture he made to force Jonathan to pay attention to him. Finally Jimmy was ready to go. Sheldon paid for dinner and they all said good night outside on the sidewalk before Sheldon got into a taxi to take him uptown and the two boys started walking toward Jonathan's.

In the apartment Jimmy and Jonathan fell into a long discussion about men being sexually attracted to each other. Jimmy wanted to know what Jonathan's feelings were on the subject. Jimmy had suspected that Jonathan had had homosexual experiences in the past, and he was right. Jonathan told him that he used to fuck a relative of his in the ass and that that same relative also liked to suck him off.

"Did you ever suck him off?" Jimmy asked.

"Yes," Jonathan said, "but I didn't do it until he shot in my mouth. But he would."

Then Jonathan told Jimmy about someone named Bill, a young actor who was a friend of his. Jonathan and Bill had once shared a room at the Ojai Country Club when, right before they were going to bed one night, Bill came into the bedroom, pulled down his pajama bottoms to show Jonathan he had a hard-on, and asked Jonathan if he fooled around. No, Jonathan had said. So Bill got into his bed alone and jacked off.

"Why didn't anything happen?" Jimmy asked Jonathan.

"Because I felt scared."

"Why?" Jimmy said. "Because his cock was so big?"

"Not necessarily," Jonathan said. "The situation just scared me."

"Be honest with me, Jonathan, be honest with me as all the days. What did you really feel about Bill's cock because it obviously stands out in your mind as very important."

"I can't say more than I have about it."

Jimmy paused for a moment. "Have you ever tasted jizz? Do you know how it tastes?"

"I've tasted my own on my finger," Jonathan said. "Sure I know what it tastes like."

"Well, do you like the taste of it?" Jimmy asked.

They both burst out laughing.

"No," Jonathan said. "I have to spit it out."

"Is that why you're scared of Bill's dick? Because you don't want to have that stuff in your mouth?"

"I don't know." Jonathan paused before he put Jimmy on the spot. "What about you?" he said, meaning had Jimmy ever tasted jizz.

Jimmy waited. Then he started to giggle.

"I'm not active," he said. "I'm passive."

When Jonathan asked him to explain the idea of being active and passive, Jimmy told him that if you fuck someone you're being active and the other person is being passive, but if you get your cock sucked you're being passive and the other person is being active.

"It all depends on how it happens to come about," Jimmy said, as if they were wrapping up a set of sensitive negotiations.

A few days later, on yet another night in Jonathan's apartment, Jimmy put his first real move on Jonathan. He was lying on the bed as Jonathan sat near him on the floor. The score to *A Streetcar Named Desire* was playing on the phonograph. The soft sensual music filled the room, which was lit only by a huge drip candle that Jonathan had used so much the bottle was completely covered with wax. Close to the bed, a large Japanese paper fish hung from string attached to the ceiling. Sudden movements in the room made the fish sway slightly. After they had talked for a while, Jimmy got up the nerve to ask Jonathan to touch his face. Jonathan reached over and rested the palm of his hand on Jimmy's warm cheek. Then Jimmy rolled over on the bed so that he could extend one hand and run his fingers across Jonathan's lips. As he did he pushed a finger through Jonathan's lips and rubbed his lower teeth with the tip of his finger. "Your teeth are good," Jimmy said, "but they're small."

Jonathan didn't answer. Jimmy sensed he was apprehensive but willing to see what might happen next.

"Why don't you kiss me," Jimmy said.

Jonathan thought it over. "Okay."

Still sitting on the floor, he scooted over next to the bed, leaned into Jimmy, and kissed him on the lips, tentatively.

"No," Jimmy said, pulling back. "Kiss me like you were kissing a girl."

So Jonathan kissed him much more fully, opening his mouth to let Jimmy's tongue in. Though he was aroused, Jonathan also felt strange, awkward.

They stopped kissing. "Can I fuck you?" Jimmy said suddenly.

"Jesus," Jonathan said. "I don't know."

"Can we try?" Jimmy said. "Let's just try."

"Well, I guess."

In the dim light of the room Jimmy and Jonathan undressed. When Jonathan was naked, Jimmy could not stop looking at his smooth slim body. Jimmy's erection was huge, he wanted Jonathan so badly.

Next, Jimmy had Jonathan lie down on his stomach on the bed. His pale skin looked even whiter in the room's near-darkness. Carefully Jimmy positioned himself on top of Jonathan. Jimmy spit in the palm of his hand before he rubbed the saliva on his cock. Gently he wedged his cock between the cheeks of Jonathan's ass and placed the tip of his cock to Jonathan's tiny hole. When he pushed the cock head just inside, Jonathan's body tensed up in pain. If Jonathan wasn't a virgin, he sure hadn't done this a lot. Jimmy tried to force his cock deeper but it was useless. He was hurting Jonathan too much. Finally Jimmy pulled his cock out and sat back on the bed. Jonathan could tell that Jimmy was disappointed.

"Will you go down on me, then?" Jimmy said.

After he thought about it for a moment, Jonathan did what Jimmy wanted. He took as much of Jimmy's cock in his mouth as he could. Even doing this, though, Jonathan felt uncomfortable, as if their actions were somehow forbidden. He had had his own cock sucked in the past, even by some of the same men in Hollywood whom Jimmy had dated, yet somehow what he was doing with Jimmy didn't feel the same. They were dealing with each other on equal terms. It was not a game where an older man was calling the shots or a younger friend was being submissive. In some way Jonathan felt threatened by what Jimmy was doing to him, what Jimmy was having him do. Finally Jimmy pulled Jonathan's face away from his cock and the two boys lay down next to each other on the bed and embraced. Eventually Jimmy took Jonathan's cock in his hand, had Jonathan take *his* cock in *his* hand, and they jacked each other off. When Jimmy came, his whole body went limp. Then he rolled over into Jonathan so that Jonathan could put his arms around him. Jonathan held Jimmy like that, like he was holding a child, for a very long time. The music on the phonograph had stopped. The room was so quiet the two boys could hear each other breathing.

"So what are we going to do now?" Jonathan said after a while, ending the silence.

Jimmy paused.

"Do you want to try and let me fuck you again?"

Jonathan was still scared, but to please Jimmy he told him he could try.

Again, Jonathan lay down on the bed on his stomach. Jimmy rolled on top of him and attempted to insert his cock into Jonathan. Just like before, the pain was so severe that Jimmy stopped and lay down quietly on the bed. After a while Jimmy got up, put on his clothes, told Jonathan good-bye, and left.

If only Jonathan had been able to be more responsive, he and Jimmy could have had an affair that would have rivaled any Jimmy would ever have. Jimmy tried to force the issue with Jonathan not only because he was so sexually drawn to Jonathan but because he believed Jonathan *wanted* to be doing what they were doing. Ultimately, though, Jimmy was more comfortable with homosexuality than Jonathan was. If Jonathan would have let him, Jimmy would have made love to him. Sadly, that's probably what Jonathan wanted Jimmy to do. Yet because of his own inexperience, Jimmy had not learned how to introduce other young men into homosexual sex, the way DeWeerd had introduced him.

After that last night in Jonathan's apartment, Jimmy saw Jonathan a few more times. Nothing sexual happened, but Jimmy still sensed a tension between them. One night, the two of them went to a party, which they both enjoyed. On another night, Jimmy invited Jonathan to stop by Jerry's Tavern and meet Barbara Glenn, a friend he had made around the time he acted in *See the Jaguar*. Normally Jimmy didn't let his friends meet each other—he usually went to great lengths to ensure that they didn't—but tonight was different. He wanted Jonathan to meet Barbara. It was almost as though by introducing Barbara to Jonathan, Jimmy was trying to make Jonathan jealous. Whatever his true motivation, Jimmy succeeded in creating friction between Barbara and Jonathan at the table. With Jimmy sitting between them, Barbara kept looking at Jonathan on and off the whole night, trying to figure out what kind of relationship he and Jimmy had. Nothing was ever resolved of course, if there *was* anything to resolve.

The event the two boys would remember most, however, was the night Jimmy took Jonathan up to his apartment to look at his photographs of Marlon Brando. In the tiny one-room studio at 19 West Sixty-eighth Street, into which Jimmy had recently moved now that he and Bill were more or less separating yet again, Jimmy told Jonathan that Brando himself had once rented the place. To prove this, Jimmy showed him a picture of Brando. In the picture Brando is standing in an apartment in front of a porthole window, one just like the porthole window in Jimmy's studio but also just like the the porthole windows in countless apartments all over Manhattan. Still, Jimmy was convinced Brando had rented the apartment. He was certain, he said, because a friend of his at his neighborhood gym had told him about Brando's living there. The friend claimed he was in a position to know too, since he bragged that he had been intimate with Brando. That seemed to be the point of Jimmy's story to Jonathan: that even Brando had been involved with men. Still, details about Brando's sex life, true or invented, had little effect on Jonathan. Nothing happened between Jimmy and Jonathan that night in Jimmy's studio. Mostly what Jonathan thought about was the photograph of Brando that hung in the window of Mario's, one of Jimmy's favorite Italian restaurants. Earlier in the evening, Jimmy had taken Jonathan to see the photograph. On it, Brando had written a phrase that stuck in Jonathan's memory.

"With zenith of gusto," Brando scrawled in a handwriting that looked like scribble.

In November 1953, Bill Bast, who still saw Jimmy even though they were no longer living together, called Jonathan to ask if he would meet him at Jerry's Tavern for a drink. In the past the only time Bill and Jonathan had met was at a party given by a casting director in an industrial space in the West Forties. The party had been memorable if for no other reason than because, at some point late in the evening, Jimmy had approached a young black man who had been enjoying the jazz music the band was playing and asked him if he could suck his cock, right there in front of everybody. The young man had said yes, so Jimmy knelt down on the floor as the black man unzipped his pants. Then Jimmy took the man's cock in his mouth and began to suck. It was a strange, surreal moment, one nobody at the party would forget.

Bill Bast hadn't, nor had Jonathan. They agreed to meet. At the restaurant, as Gilmore would recall, no sooner had they sat down at a table than Bill got to the point.

"I am leaving New York," he said, "but I want to know what's the deal between you and Jimmy."

"What do you mean?" Jonathan said. "And why is it your business?"

From Bill's actions and words, Jonathan came to believe, if he had not already known for sure, that Bill and Jimmy had been lovers.

"Jimmy has put me through the mill," Bill said. "He's just an impossible person. He's been destructive to me and his friends. We all feel that you are encouraging him to behave this way to other people. I want to know why."

Jonathan told Bill he didn't know what he was talking about.

"Jimmy is hurting people's feelings all the time. You bend over backwards to be his friend and then he'll just dump you or not be interested in you anymore. The more sincere you try to be with him the more destructive he is."

Jonathan still said nothing.

Finally Bill got exasperated. "You can have the debris with my blessings," Gilmore remembers him saying. Then he stopped. "So are you two carrying on?"

Now Jonathan answered immediately. "Who are you to ask that?"

"If you are," Bill said, "everything is understandable. It's understandable that other people are being hurt." He paused. "Well," he said. "I'm washing my hands of this."

It was then—as Bill Bast got up to leave—that Jonathan realized just how distraught, how completely disgusted, Bill was with Jimmy and—apparently—how little Jimmy cared about that.

Soon everybody got on with their lives. Bill returned to Los Angeles. Jimmy and Jonathan drifted apart. In time, Jimmy and Jonathan would see a lot of each other again, once they both moved back to California (at separate times), but by then Jimmy was busy with work and distracted by an affair he was having with yet another young man. As a result Jimmy and Jonathan's relationship in California only progressed so far, about as far as it had in New York. Over the years, Jonathan Gilmore would remember his "intense sporadic friendship" with James Dean with a mixture of fondness and regret. When he thinks back on that time in his life, Gilmore reflects on what brought the two of them together, what held them together for a while, and what finally pushed them apart.

"We talked a lot about the subject of the mother," Gilmore says. "He used to ask me a lot about my feelings about my mother because we didn't have a close relationship. My mother had been an actress and a party girl. She wanted to party and booze it up instead of being a mother. I told him my remembrances of her were the smell of her fur coat and her blurry eyes and the scent of liquor and her telling me how much she loved me and how we were going to be together. And yet we never were together. Promise to conceal delivery. She moved into a place two blocks away from where I was being raised by my grandmother. My father got remarried again and lived in an apartment behind my grandmother. I never knew really what was going on.

"I think Jimmy felt a connection with me. He would ask me about my feelings to see how his feelings would be. He wanted to know if I resented the fact that she withheld something from me. And how did my resentment affect her feelings about me? Interestingly Jimmy never mentioned his father. Then again, I never knew Jimmy was from Indiana because what he did tell me about was Santa Monica. He'd talk about games he played as a kid but he didn't talk about Indiana. I always thought he was born in California. The games he played were with his mother—and they were imaginary. They would walk through the house and she would say, 'We are now in a train station and you can feel a big train going by.'

"In the end Jimmy looked at me as a crazy mixed-up kid. He was attracted to me in part because I was so beautiful—he liked that, certainly—but I wasn't just a pretty boy. I was a difficult problem person. He was intrigued by that. For me, whatever the attraction was didn't translate into a physical place. I was more straight. I had been used by a lot of people in Hollywood and he had certainly been used by a lot of people. Still, Jimmy had a powerful effect on my life. I remember that night with Barbara Glenn in the restaurant. I didn't know about her but she knew about me. There was this tension between us. And I remember very distinctly that Jimmy and I shared a look, just a look, that said, 'If one of us were a girl, we would have been able to have a romance.' "

Dean holds Ronald Reagan at gunpoint on the set of the television show "The Dark, Dark Hour."

3. *See the Jaguar* may have closed after five performances, but more than any other previous project Dean had worked on it launched his career. Mostly on the strength of the good write-ups her client received in *See the Jaguar*'s otherwise disastrous reviews, Jane Deacy was able to get Dean a number of key roles on television shows. As one job led to another, he ended up being offered so much work that he stayed busy for almost all of 1953. On February 8, he co-starred in "The Capture of Jesse James," an episode of *You Are There*. In the show, directed by Sidney Lumet, Dean played Bob Ford, the man who killed Jesse James. Dean didn't work in March, but in April he acted in "No Room," an episode of *Danger* (on the fourteenth) and "The Case of the Sawed-off Shotgun," an episode of *Treasury Men in Action* (on the sixteenth).

In May and June, Dean worked in the Actors Studio production of *End as a Man,* directed by Jack Garfein. The play was only performed at the Studio three times, but backers felt confident enough about the show to open it off-Broadway although Dean did not appear in that production. As it turned out, he would not have had time for an off-Broadway show anyway since Deacy continued to line up work for him on television. During the last eight months of 1953, Dean co-starred in "The Evil Within," an episode of *Tales of Tomorrow,* on May 1; "Something for an Empty Briefcase," an episode of *Campbell Soundstage,* on July 17; "Death Is My Neighbor," an episode of CBS's *Danger,* on August 25; *The Big Story* on NBC on September 11; "Glory in the Flower," an episode of *Omnibus,* on October 4; "Keep Our Honor Bright," an episode of *Kraft Television Theatre,* on October 14; and "Life Sentence," an episode of *Campbell Soundstage,* on October 16. In November, Dean turned in his most important performances on television so far. On the eleventh, on "A Long Time Till Dawn," an episode of *Kraft Television Theatre* written by Rod Serling, he appeared in his first starring role. Then on the Monday before Thanksgiving he had a good part in the Thanksgiving episode of *Rob-*

ert Montgomery Presents entitled "Harvest," a show directed by James Sheldon that starred Ed Begley, Dorothy Gish, and Vaughn Taylor.

As Dean performed on these television shows, he became more and more sure of himself as an actor. When Dean breaks down weeping on "A Long Time Till Dawn," a program in which he played a delinquent trying to straighten out his life, there is no trace of artifice to his style. He actually appears to be crying; the tears and the emotions are real. With each show he did in 1953, Dean made a concerted effort to be realistic as an actor, particularly as a craftsman. Ironically many of his fellow actors did not realize the commitment he had to his art and his craft. Because of his unconventional mechanics, they believed he was either a novice or a scene-stealer. In actuality, he was perfecting his technique of moment-to-moment acting.

In this phenomenally busy year, Dean did get rejected for some parts. He shot a screen test for a part in *Battle Cry*, but lost out to Tab Hunter. He auditioned for a role on *Life with Father*, a CBS television series based on the articles written by Clarence Day, Jr., that appeared regularly in *The New Yorker*, but he lost that job too. It's just as well that Dean didn't get the role on the series, for if he had he would not have been available for a play in which he desperately wanted to appear. Billy Rose and Herman Sheulan had hired Ruth and Augustus Goetz to adapt André Gide's autobiographical novel *The Immoralist* into a Broadway play. To be directed by Herman Shumlin, the drama dealt openly with the issue of homosexuality. Because of this, it was sure to cause a controversy when it opened in early 1954. Jimmy could identify with the story on more than one level. Set at the turn of the century in France, it is about a young archaeologist, Michel, who tries to fight his homosexuality by marrying a woman, Marceline. On their honeymoon in Biskra, Algeria, Michel is seduced by Bachir, the houseboy who works in the villa in which Michel and Marceline are staying. When Bachir taunts Michel about his inability to have sex with his wife (in two months the couple has yet to consummate their marriage), Michel gets drunk and sleeps with Marceline, who becomes pregnant. The play ends in France with the couple resolved to the idea of staying together although, if they do, they will probably be unhappy and despondent for the rest of their lives.

In Billy Rose's office over the Ziegfeld Theatre, Dean read for the part of the homosexual Arab houseboy with such flair and confidence, with such a complete understanding of the part, that Rose and the Goetzes were ready to offer him the job on the spot. In a way Dean had been preparing for the role since he had first started trying to break into show business in Hollywood. After all, the motive of the houseboy is to seduce the older man so that he can get what he wants. Shortly after the audition Dean was offered the part, for which he had started studying intensely by the time rehearsals began at the Ziegfeld on December 18. Under Shumlin's direction, the company, which included Louis Jourdan as the husband and Geraldine Page as his wife, worked hard to bring the play to life. From the start, though, there were problems. Dean's and Jourdan's acting styles could not have been more different. Classically trained and rigid in his delivery, Jourdan acted his part with studied restraint. A member of the "old" school, which demanded that an actor hit his mark and deliver his line the same way every time, he believed that interpretation should consist of little more than slightly varying the delivery of a line. On the other hand, Dean was now firmly committed to his theory that the actor should strive to create unpredictable, spontaneous moments in his performance. According to this line of thinking, no two performances of a role should ever be the same. Naturally Dean and Jourdan clashed as soon as rehearsals began. Though the tension produced by their disagreement was appropriate for the two characters in the play, the conflict that developed between the two real people became a source of distraction. Unfortunately Shumlin did not handle the situation with as much care and diplomacy as he should have and the problem soon became serious.

During rehearsals, the company took off long enough to celebrate Christmas. Jimmy used this break as an opportunity to make a quick trip home to Fairmount. Following Christmas, rehearsals resumed. Then in early January 1954 the company moved from New York to Philadelphia to start a week-long run of tryouts, which began on the ninth. In Philadelphia, the show played at the Forrest Theatre on Walnut Street near the St. James Hotel, where the cast and the crew stayed, and the Hickory House, a restaurant at which Jimmy often ate. The rehearsals had been difficult in New York (the antagonism between Jimmy and Jourdan had grown to the point where it was affecting the quality of the play), but in Philadelphia the situation got even worse. Finally, with opening day approaching and the prospect of his production falling into disarray, Rose fired Shumlin and replaced him with Daniel Mann. While Jourdan got along with the new director much better, Jimmy could hardly abide him. In some ways, because he saw Mann as siding with Jourdan in rehearsals, Jimmy felt betrayed. Even more damaging to their relationship, Jimmy and Mann disagreed completely on the way the character of Bachir should be played. Mann wanted him to be subdued and conventional. Jimmy saw him as being flighty, fey, over the top. As the discord between Jimmy and Mann intensified, Jimmy became more confused. Sometimes he felt paralyzed while he tried to develop Bachir and work through his differences with the director. The rift turned so ugly that Rose even thought about replacing Jimmy, but it was too late. Rose had to stand back and watch as Jimmy fumbled his way through the tryouts. In all of this time, the only real ally Jimmy had in the production was Geraldine Page, who became an important person to him during this battle—and another in the succession of mother figures he would have in his life.

On February 1, the production moved back to New York to begin previews. Jimmy's performances remained erratic, but Rose decided that the production would somehow have to endure his weak perfor-

With Geraldine Page in *The Immoralist*

With Louis Jourdan in *The Immoralist*

mance despite his part's importance to the play. Then on opening night at the Royale Theatre—February 8, Jimmy's birthday—Dean turned in a performance that was so stunning, so breathtakingly brilliant in its originality, that both the audience and his fellow actors were left speechless. In the final analysis Dean was the consummate professional. On the night the critics showed up at the theatre, he showed up too. One particular sequence, what came to be known as the Scissors Dance, was soon legendary. Wearing a dresslike nightgown and a pair of slippers, Dean flitted across the stage as if he were the most effeminate yet seductive ballet dancer Jourdan's character had ever seen. All the while he danced, Dean snipped at the air with a pair of shiny silver scissors. The visual effect was startling, unforgettable. Dean explained the significance of the dance to Jonathan Gilmore. "Jimmy said," according to Gilmore, who saw the show twice, "that what he was doing with the scissors—he was seducing the character played by Jourdan. 'Every time I snipped the scissors,' he said, 'I was cutting a string loose from the guy and bringing him more into the web.' When he cut with the scissors he was cutting Louis Jourdan away from the straight life he was leading. He was taking him into the homosexual world."

In February, as he was working in *The Immoralist*, Jimmy became friends with Arlene Lorca, a young actress trying to make it in New York. After they had met at a party, they struck up a friendship. One day on a whim, Arlene took Jimmy around to see a friend of hers, Roy Schatt. A talented photographer, he often shot young actors and actresses, many times for their portfolios but also for magazines. That first day in Roy's apartment, a small but cozy studio in Murray Hill, Jimmy and Roy got along well. With Roy and Arlene as his audience, Jimmy even did the Scissors Dance from *The Immoralist*. Jimmy liked Roy so much that a few days later he got Arlene and Roy tickets to the play. Backstage after the show, Roy told Jimmy how much he loved his work. Jimmy appreciated Roy's comments as well as Roy's apparent fondness for him. Because of this mutual respect, Jimmy often stopped by Roy's apartment over the coming days for what they called photography lessons although Jimmy never paid Roy for his efforts. More than once Jimmy brought with him two friends to serve as subjects for his pictures: Marty Landau, with whom Jimmy had become good friends, and Billy Gunn, his understudy for *The Immoralist*.

Occasionally Jimmy's behavior bordered on the strange. One time Jimmy showed up at Roy's front door completely nude. When Roy pulled him inside so none of his neighbors would see him, especially the two old ladies who lived upstairs, Jimmy, as Roy later wrote, "stretch[ed] out like one of those Western paintings that hung over saloon bars, one hand over his crotch, the other across his breast, . . . giggling like a virgin with pursed lips and fluttering eyes." Because of exhibitions like this, Roy came to question Jimmy's sexuality. "Jimmy gay? Or bisexual?" Schatt would write. "Well, maybe. His nuttiness and constant attempts at breaking from the humdrum could have led him into it." On this subject Jimmy had revealed something of himself to Arlene as well, although when it was recorded years later by a journalist a significantly different slant was placed on the information. "Jimmy's big problem during his early days in New York was learning how to adjust to what he saw about him without losing his self-respect," the journalist wrote. "Because he was an attractive, almost beautiful boy, he was sought by homosexuals. They sent him gifts and offered him entrées for jobs. . . . 'What is it about me that attracts them?' he asked Arlene. 'I'm a man, but if they don't let up soon, I'm going to begin to doubt myself!' " If this is an accurate representation of what Dean actually said to Arlene, all one can assume is that he was not dealing with his friends honestly about his sexuality, not that all of them were ready for him to do so.

On the subject of his sex life, Jimmy could in fact be coy with his friends. Late one afternoon around this time, Jimmy was having coffee

Performing the scissors dance in *The Immoralist*

in a café on the West Side with Geraldine Page and William Fox, a friend of his who was a figurative artist and sculptor. When Jimmy had written to Fox originally, back in September 1952, he had wanted him to make a sculpture of him. Oddly, the sculpture was supposed to be an ashtray. Jimmy would be in a sitting position, himself smoking a cigarette, his legs wrapped around the bowl of the ashtray. Interestingly, in his letter to Fox, Jimmy had told him that he "will send [Fox] all of the photographs you need—even nude shots." Jimmy had underlined the word *nude* twice. No doubt Jimmy was referring to a set of nude photographs he had had taken of himself sometime between the date he arrived in New York in the fall of 1951 and September 1952, the month he wrote Fox. Years later, one particular shot would become infamous. Sitting in the branches of a tree, Jimmy, totally nude, plays with his cock, which is fully erect. Fox never used the nude photographs, nor did he ever sculpt the ashtray. Instead, one night he went over to Dean's studio on West Sixty-eighth Street and did a series of ten freehand drawings of Jimmy wearing only a pair of underwear. After that night, Jimmy and Bill became friends, even if Fox would never find the time to do the ashtray Jimmy wanted.

Bill discovered that sometimes it wasn't so easy to be friends with Jimmy either, like that day in the café with Geraldine Page, for example. At some point Jimmy looked over at Geraldine and Bill and said, "I'm going to get myself burned." When Geraldine acted like she didn't understand what he meant, Jimmy explained that at certain bars on the West Side people would put out their cigarettes on your body if you wanted them to. Geraldine was embarrassed; so was Bill. "He never went to leather bars on the West Side," Fox says. "That's ridiculous. Jimmy was just joshing. He liked to shock people. I saw no burns on his body when I sketched him and he was naked except for his briefs."

On the opening night of *The Immoralist,* after he had turned in the extraordinary performance of which Billy Rose knew he was capable,

Dean came backstage, searched out Rose, and gave him his two-week notice of resignation. The producers, the cast, the crew—everyone was shocked. Just when Jimmy had broken through and given his best performance since the audition he had done in Rose's office, he quit. What no one knew, what would not become public knowledge until later, was that Jimmy was not dropping out of the production because of any disagreement he had with anyone involved in the show but because Elia Kazan had offered him a leading role in the film adaptation of John Steinbeck's novel *East of Eden* he was doing for Warner Bros. Kazan had not yet received the go-ahead from the studio, but he felt confident enough about his clout with Warner Bros. to promise Jimmy the part anyway. Kazan and Jimmy would both be heading to California soon to begin shooting. It would be Jimmy's first role in a picture, and he would be one of the stars. So when he resigned from *The Immoralist*—the scene backstage with Rose gave him a certain pleasure, to be sure—he knew he had to drop out of the show in order to make his next important career move.

Four days before he fulfilled one last obligation—performing along with Anne Jackson and Eli Wallach in a staged reading of Ezra Pound's translation of Sophocles' *Trachiniae*, which took place on the night of February 27 at The New School for Social Research in Manhattan—Jimmy had ended his run in *The Immoralist* on February 23. Then, early on the morning of March 8, Kazan picked up Jimmy at his apartment. When he emerged from the brownstone on West Sixty-eighth Street, Jimmy was carrying all his essential belongings in two paper bags tied shut with string. Excited but nervous, he got into the backseat of the limousine with Kazan. At the airport, with Kazan by his side, Jimmy boarded an airplane for the first time in his life and took his seat. Before he knew it, the plane taxied onto a runway, lunged forward with a jolting rate of speed, and took off, heading for California.

James
Dean

1. As the airplane descended onto Los Angeles and he looked at the miles and miles of buildings stretching out below, Jimmy felt as if he were coming back to the city a completely different person than he was when he had left it two and a half years ago. He was too. At the time he went to New York from Los Angeles, he was still involved with Rogers Brackett, a man who was in essence keeping him. Now Jimmy was flying back to the city (in a first-class seat paid for by Warner Bros., no less) in the company of Elia Kazan.

In a way it had all happened so quickly. In early 1954 Kazan was in New York directing *Tea and Sympathy* on Broadway and working on editing *On the Waterfront*, his latest picture, when he started to think about adapting *East of Eden*. At that point in his career, Kazan was the most bankable director in the business. Over the last few years he had directed Montgomery Clift in *The Skin of Our Teeth* and Marlon Brando in *A Streetcar Named Desire* on Broadway, won Tony awards for *All My Sons* in 1947 and *Death of a Salesman* in 1949, and won an Academy Award for *Gentleman's Agreement* in 1947. He was so highly regarded as a director that when he told Jack Warner he wanted to adapt the Steinbeck novel, Warner gave him an unlimited budget, casting approval, and final edit. In early 1954 Paul Osborn, the writer working on the screenplay for *East of Eden*, talked Kazan into seeing Dean in *The Immoralist*, and Kazan, who knew Dean's work from the Actors Studio, was so impressed that he called him in for a meeting at Warner Bros.' New York offices. "He looked and spoke like the character in *East of Eden*," Kazan would recall. "When he walked into the office, I knew immediately that he was right for the role. He was guarded, sullen, suspicious, and he seemed to me to have a great deal of concealed emotion." After that meeting, which ended with Jimmy giving him a ride through the streets of New York on his motorcycle, Kazan sent Jimmy over to meet Steinbeck. "He *is* Cal," Steinbeck told Kazan on the telephone as soon as Jimmy left his apartment. So that was that. Warner Bros. announced Dean's casting on March 6, two days before Dean and Kazan boarded the airplane for Los Angeles. Now here Jimmy was, descending onto the city where his mother had died, where his father still lived, and where he hoped he would now finally become the star he had always wanted to be.

Kazan had a habit shared by few other directors. As part of his preparation for shooting a picture, he liked to learn as much as he could about the private lives of his stars. On the set, when he needed to elicit an emotion from an actor, he would often mention something from the actor's private life to make the actor respond in such a way that Kazan could get on film the emotion he wanted. He had used this technique effectively with Brando while they worked together both on Broadway and in films. The more he knew about the actor's thoughts and emotions, the better he could trigger the kinds of responses he had to have a character show in any given scene. In the short time he had known him, Kazan had gone out of his way to learn from Jimmy as much as he could about his life. So he was happy when they got into the limousine at the airport in Los Angeles and Jimmy wanted to know if they could stop by the hospital and see his father. At the hospital, Jimmy went inside and brought his father out to meet Kazan, who, as he watched the two of them interact, was astonished at the way Winton treated his son. Certainly Jimmy was showing off the famous director to let his father know that, yes, he had finally made it as an actor. But Winton wasn't impressed. Cold and distant, he appeared almost to resent the fact that Jimmy had stopped by to see him. "Obviously," Kazan would write, "there was a strong tension between the two, and it was not friendly. I sensed the father disliked the son." From his point of view as a director, Kazan could not have been more pleased. One of the main story lines in *East of Eden* involves the son, Cal, who is constantly trying to earn the love of his father, a stern and puritanical man unwavering in his moral commitments. While he stood outside the hospital, Kazan decided that he had rarely seen a father-son relationship as strained as Winton and Jimmy's. Suddenly Kazan knew that, if for no other reason than the past troubles he had had with his father, Jimmy was going to be able to play the part of Cal with arresting authenticity. Unfortunately Jimmy did not necessarily—consciously—see this, certainly not as clearly as Kazan did. Jimmy only knew that his father was still as reticent with him as ever, even though Jimmy had just come to California to star in a major motion picture to be distributed by Warner Bros. and directed by the most admired director working in the industry. Clearly Jimmy's (now) unqualified professional success was not going to win his father's affection. Jimmy was about to decide—and for good reason—that he was *never* going to win Winton's approval. "I thought [Jimmy] was an extreme grotesque of a boy, a twisted boy," was how Kazan put it. "As I got to know his father, as I got to know about his family, I learned that [Jimmy] had been, in fact, twisted by the denial of love."

As it turned out, Jimmy only spent one night in Los Angeles. Since Cal was supposed to be a healthy-looking farm boy and not a pale, washed-out New Yorker, Kazan ordered Jimmy to go to the desert and get a suntan. He also told him to gain some weight, about ten pounds. Because of this, on the morning after Jimmy had arrived in Los Angeles, he woke up early, ready to drive to the desert. Before leaving the city, he dropped in on someone who probably never expected to see him again—Bill Bast. Following the scene Bill and Jonathan had had in Jerry's Tavern in New York, Bill seemed to have resigned himself to the fact that his relationship with Jimmy was over. When Bill moved to Los Angeles, he must have thought that that would have ended whatever was left of his life with Jimmy. Yet here Jimmy was, the last person Bill expected to find when he answered a knock at his apartment door one morning. Bill invited Jimmy in so they could talk. At once, Jimmy told Bill that he had gotten a lead role in *East of Eden* and that he needed a good suntan for the part. Then he made Bill a proposition: Jimmy wanted him to go to the desert with him. Finally, after some soul-searching, Bill said he would go. If Jimmy worked his way into someone's life, it seemed, he was in it—until *he* wanted to get out. Bill, for one, was helpless in the matter. So the two of them packed Bill's suitcase, went over to a local rental agency to pick up a car, and started east, toward Palm Springs.

Jimmy and Bill stayed in the desert for a week, during which Jimmy worked on his tan every day. Finally they drove back from Palm Springs to Los Angeles so that Jimmy could see Dick Clayton, the agent at Famous Artists whom Jane Deacy had lined up to represent him on the West Coast. In their first meeting in Clayton's office, Clayton and Jimmy, who had brought Bill along, discussed a variety of subjects, from where Jimmy would live to the terms of his Warner Bros. contract. To start with, Jimmy would be earning one thousand dollars a week. Because Jimmy had so little money, the studio had agreed to advance him seven hundred dollars, which he would pay back at the rate of one hundred dollars a week. In effect Jimmy would receive the standard studio contract for someone in his position, the star of a picture who had no clout in the industry. Significantly better than the contracts supporting actors or bit players received, it was still substantially inferior to the contracts of established stars like Rock Hudson and Elizabeth Taylor. At the top of the Hollywood salary scale, they made one hundred thousand dollars a picture.

On April 7, Jimmy signed his Warner Bros. contract. By early May, he had used his newfound income to buy something he had always wanted—a sports car. Specifically he selected a red 1953 MG. It would be the first of four sports cars he would buy over the next eighteen months, each with a capacity to go faster than the one before.

On May 17, Paul Osborn finished the final draft of the screenplay for *East of Eden* and the picture was ready to shoot. The project had taken a long time to reach this stage of development. Warner Bros. had bought the film rights to the novel from Steinbeck in November 1952. For the rights to the book and for writing a screenplay, Steinbeck had been paid $125,000 plus a promise of 25 percent of the profits if the picture was made. However, the original script, which used the whole book as source material, was not successful dramatically. Because of this, the picture was put on hold. It was not until Kazan got involved and hired Osborn to write a screenplay based only on the last fourth of the novel that the project began to appear workable. Kazan's decision to use just the last fourth of the book was a risky move, but by focusing the story he was able to accentuate the novel's most compelling conflict, the struggle between two brothers—Aaron and Cal—as they vie for their father's love.

During the time Osborn worked on the final draft of the screenplay, Kazan had been making casting decisions. Dean would play Cal. That was set, although for a while Kazan had thought about using him for Aaron instead. For that role, Kazan finally cast an attractive young actor who, despite his dark features, resembled Dean enough for the two of them to look like brothers. Richard Davalos, a newcomer, had won the part over another unknown, Paul Newman. The decision was not easy. Kazan went so far as to have Newman and Dean do a screen test together, but in the end Newman lost to Davalos because Kazan believed the chemistry was better between Dean and Davalos. Two major parts remained—the father and the young woman, Abra, who becomes the object of affection for both brothers. Even though Dean and Joanne Woodward did a stunning screen test together, Kazan passed up Woodward to cast Julie Harris, a member of the Actors Studio whose talent he admired. In general, Kazan preferred intense, internal actresses over those he considered outward with their emotions. He and Tennessee Williams, for example, would fight over whether they should cast Barbara Bel Geddes (Kazan's choice) or Tallulah Bankhead (Williams's) in the stage production of *Cat on a Hot Tin Roof*, a fight Kazan won. Julie Harris was much more in Kazan's style than Woodward. Still, what a different picture it would have been if, besides James Dean, Kazan had cast in the picture's major roles for young actors Paul Newman and Joanne Woodward, who at the time were not yet married to one another.

In a way the most pivotal role in the script was the father. After he had seriously considered a number of older actors, among them Gary Cooper, Kazan selected Raymond Massey, an old-time Hollywood actor known for his social and political conservatism and his strong religious beliefs. In a community not overly populated with religious people, Massey was a bit of an oddball. By making this casting move, though, Kazan indicated that he knew exactly what he was doing. Dean, rebellious and bohemian, was sure to clash with Massey, uptight and paternalistic, just like the son and the father in the script were supposed to do.

With the final draft of the screenplay finished and the cast lined up, Kazan began to shoot *East of Eden* on May 27 in Mendocino, the town that served as Monterey in the picture. The cast and the crew lived at the Little River Inn, three miles north of Mendocino in a village called Little River. In the inn Jimmy stayed in room number 8. At one point

With Julie Harris, who received top billing in *East of Eden*

A still shot from *East of Eden*

during his stay, he was nursed by the owner, a Mrs. Reynolds, when he came down with a serious case of poison oak. In fact, Jimmy's bout with poison oak was so severe that he was confined to bed for several days. While he was sick, the shooting schedule had to be suspended.

Jimmy held up the shooting of the picture in a more subtle way as well, although what he did to cause the delay finally allowed him to give the performance Kazan knew the picture needed. Since he worked on almost pure instinct, Jimmy had to have time to prepare each scene before he did it, no matter how small the scene. What's more, because this was his first picture, he was not used to preparing for such demanding work. As a result Jimmy would often take an inordinately long time to get ready to do a scene. Kazan was patient. He had no choice; he was painfully aware of the fact that he had to get a career-making performance out of Dean if the picture was going to succeed. So he—and the cast and the crew—waited. They also had to get used to another one of Jimmy's idiosyncrasies, an inability, or unwillingness, to do a take the same way twice. Although Massey complained bitterly—"Make him say the lines the way they're written," he'd demand—Kazan gave Dean the freedom he needed to develop his character in the only way he knew how.

On June 4, the company moved from Mendocino to Salinas, a town in northern California not far from the Monterey peninsula. In Salinas, Kazan shot most of the outdoor scenes, especially those involving the bean fields. In the picture Cal invests in commodities—specifically beans—which end up increasing in value because of World War I. In an agonizingly tragic scene, Cal tries to use the money he makes from selling the beans to buy his father's love. His father rejects the money—and him. Perhaps some of the most memorable footage in the picture's final cut shows Cal lying in the dirt in the middle of the bean fields wondering if the beans will grow so he can sell them and make the money he believes he can buy his father's love with (he's wrong about the money, as it turns out). In some of these shots Jimmy stares longingly at the tiny bean plants. If Jimmy knew about anything, he knew what it was like to try to win a father's love.

On June 12, the production moved yet again, this time to the Warner Bros. lot in Burbank, where a complete amusement park had been built. In Burbank, most of the scenes were shot at night, but that didn't keep Jimmy from socializing with his friends when he could get away from the set long enough. As soon as Kazan found out about this, he put a stop to it; there was no way Kazan was going to let Jimmy become distracted, no matter how slightly, from his work on the picture. So Kazan forced Jimmy to leave the small apartment near the studio at 3908 Olive Avenue that he and Davalos had rented together and move into an apartment on the Warner Bros. lot. To ensure that nothing went wrong, Kazan even put Jimmy in the apartment directly across from his. That way, he could always keep an eye on him.

During the production of *East of Eden,* the Warner Bros. publicity department and Jimmy's handlers, specifically Dick Clayton, began to think about how they could generate the publicity they would need both to launch Jimmy's career and to give *East of Eden* a chance of becoming a financial success. In Hollywood the best way for an actor to get his name or picture in the newspaper was to go on a date. Warner Bros. wanted to present Jimmy to the public as a romantic leading man. He should have an edge, to be sure, but, above all else, he had to be the dream boyfriend girls across America could fantasize about. Clayton was determined that the public see Jimmy as virile, macho— and heterosexual. To accomplish these goals, it was decided that Jimmy should start dating attractive young actresses. When potential dates were considered, Pier Angeli's name kept coming up. A beautiful up-and-coming actress, she was shooting a picture called *The Silver Chalice*—Paul Newman had gotten a part in it after he was turned down for *East of Eden*—which would be released at about the same time as Jimmy's picture. The combination of Dean and Angeli seemed

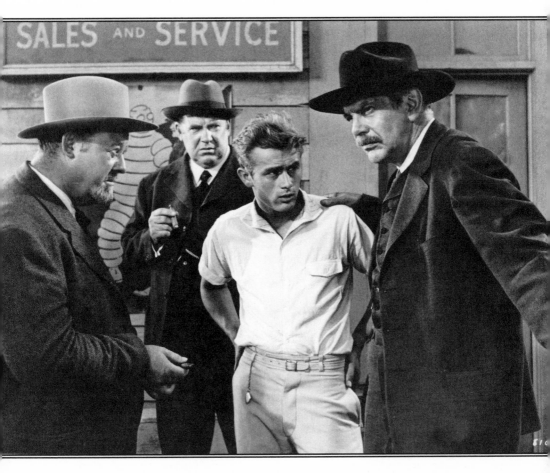

With Burl Ives (left) and Raymond Massey (right) in *East of Eden*

Cal tries to win the love of his father who rejects him.

just right, especially when they started to be photographed together. On film, they were the perfect couple.

Her real name was Anna Maria Pierangeli, and she was touted as one of *the* new actresses in Hollywood. She had a twin sister who was also an actress, but the person in her family who had the most influence on the way Pier conducted her life was her mother. Originally from Italy and devoutly Catholic, the Pierangelis kept a traditional household. The ultimate stage mother, Mrs. Pierangeli firmly controlled her daughters' private lives and their acting careers. In the beginning the relationship that had been arranged for Jimmy and Pier seemed to be accomplishing exactly what it was supposed to. "James Dean has the lead in *East of Eden* and you'll be hearing of him soon," said a gossip column item. "Pier Angeli, who isn't in the movie, has discovered him already." Other items also appeared. "Jimmy is different," Pier was quoted as saying in one curious item. "He loves music. He loves it from the heart the way I do. We have so much to talk about. It's wonderful to have such an understanding." Pier never went on to explain what exactly she meant by "different," although the reference to Jimmy listening to music "from the heart" implies a sensitivity that would not have been found in most Hollywood leading men at the time. Many show business insiders knew the main reason the Dean-Angeli romance was being played up the way it was. "Jimmy's much-publicized affair with Pier Angeli was purely platonic," an actor then on the scene would be quoted as saying, "a cover-up for his homosexuality." But that didn't stop the press from doing its part to help create a romance that may or may not have existed. "Do you think eventually you kids will get married?" Jimmy was asked once by a reporter. "Who knows?" was Jimmy's answer. On another occasion Jimmy said this to a reporter about his relationship with Pier: "Nothing complicated, just a nice girl for a change. I mean, you know, I can talk to her. She understands. Nothing messy, just an easy kind of friendly thing. I respect her. She's untouchable. We're members of totally different

Pier Angeli visits Dean on the set of *East of Eden*.

castes. You know, she's the kind of girl you put on a shelf and look at. Anyway, her old lady doesn't like me. Can't say I blame her."

The actual extent to which Jimmy and Pier became involved is unclear. Neither spoke frankly about their relationship before their deaths (Angeli died in 1971), so all that remains is circumstantial evidence. From the way they were photographed, they certainly seemed to be attracted to one another. Perhaps they were even in love. If they were, the affair developed so quickly it would be hard to imagine that the love was lasting or substantial. They did spend a lot of time together when they were not working. Jimmy even introduced Pier to several of his friends, including Gene Owen. "He brought Pier Angeli over to our house and spent the bulk of a Sunday," Owen says. "My husband and I were leaving for Europe soon and Pier was talking about how important it was to get to Italy. She wanted to get Jimmy there. She seemed to be deeply in love with him and he with her. I thought it was a solid romance."

Perhaps Jimmy *did* fall in love with Pier and, once they had become intimately involved, decided that he wanted to marry her. Through the years, Jimmy had had his random sexual encounters with women. With Barbara Glenn, the woman he introduced Jonathan Gilmore to that night at dinner in New York, he may have even had an all-out affair. "The sexual attraction was so powerful," Glenn later told a journalist. "There were a lot of people after Jimmy, men as well as women, but our physical relationship held." In fact, Glenn may have been the *only* woman with whom Jimmy had an ongoing sexual involvement since his relationships with women usually amounted to little more than one-night stands or brief flings. For a young man coming to terms with his sexuality, it is not at all uncommon for him to experiment with having sex with both men and women. In Jimmy's life, what he chose to do once his relationship with Pier had broken up— after all, this was the first time he was really supposed to have been in love—should have indicated to him the true nature of his sexuality.

If he *was* heterosexual, and his relationship with Pier should have proven this to him beyond a doubt, he would have become involved with another woman. Instead, when he did move on to his next affair some months later, Jimmy would be romantically linked to one of the most notorious homosexual men in Hollywood. To be fair to Jimmy, after seeing pictures of Jimmy in the press, the young man had become obsessed with him. "I want to spend the rest of my life with James Dean," the young man would tell one of his friends before he devoted all of his energy to becoming Jimmy's lover.

While Jimmy and Pier were dating, the shooting schedule for *East of Eden* continued. For Jimmy, a high point of the schedule occurred on the day Kazan invited his friend Marlon Brando, who was on a nearby lot shooting a picture, to drop by the *East of Eden* set. Naturally Jimmy was in awe of Brando. "Marlon . . . was very gracious to Jimmy," Kazan would write, "who was so adoring that he seemed shrunken and twisted in misery." In a photograph taken of the chance meeting, Kazan appears dour, Brando smiles demurely at the camera, and Julie Harris stares up admiringly at Brando. It is Dean, his body taut with tension, his mouth nervously clenched shut, who glances away from the three of them, his eyes fixed off in the distance.

Finally, on August 9, 1954, *East of Eden* wrapped after ten weeks of shooting. Dean had turned in a moving, inspired performance. The picture left him exhausted yet exhilarated. He knew he had achieved the level of acting that could establish him as an important young star. Not surprisingly, while creating that performance, he had left members of the cast and crew with decidedly mixed impressions. "Jimmy had only to act himself," Massey later wrote. "But that is a difficult role even for an experienced actor to play. A rebel at heart, he approached everything with a chip on his shoulder. The Method had encouraged this truculent spirit. Jimmy never knew his lines before he walked on the set, rarely had command of them when the camera

Marlon Brando stops by the set of *East of Eden* to see his friend and mentor, Elia Kazan. Dean and Harris join them for the photograph.

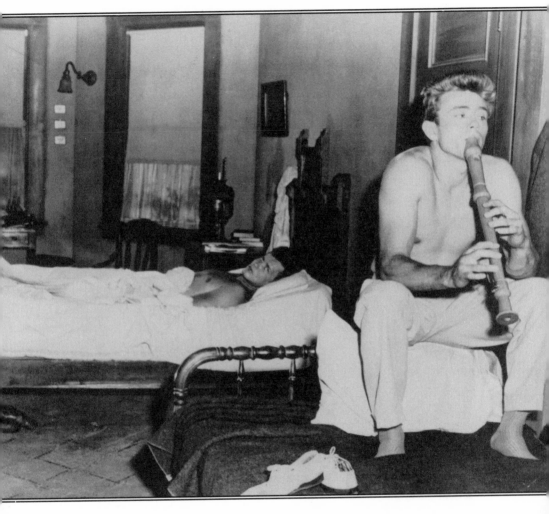

With Richard Davalos in *East of Eden*. The scene was
considered so homoerotic that studio censors would not
let Kazan include it in the final cut.

rolled and even if he had was often inaudible. Simple technicalities, such as moving on cue and finding his marks, were beneath his consideration." Kazan remembered similar breaches of professionalism on Dean's part. "A couple of weeks before the end of our shooting schedule," Kazan would write, "it was getting around that the kid on the *East of Eden* set was going to make it big. Jimmy heard the news too, and the first thing I noticed was that he was being rude to our little wardrobe man. I stopped that quickly." Yet Julie Harris remembers the more pleasant side of Dean. "I loved him," she says. "I looked forward to our scenes together. I admired him and I loved his talent. He surprised me in the day-to-day context because he was so brilliant, but it didn't surprise me because I *knew* he was brilliant. He was quite a charismatic human being and had a mixture of sexual attraction and great innocence, the same as Marilyn Monroe. I think that that was their appeal—that they were curiously untouched by their sexuality and remained innocent."

2. In August, once *East of Eden* had wrapped, Jimmy went back to New York to appear on an episode of the *Philco TV Playhouse*. Even though he stayed in the city only two weeks, his personal life had been altered drastically by the time he returned to Los Angeles. If he and Pier had had an affair, or if they were on the verge of having one, all that changed when Jimmy got back to Los Angeles and Pier broke the news to him that she was going to start dating other men. According to the gossip in Hollywood at the time, Pier's mother strongly disapproved of Jimmy because she thought he was rude and unkempt, an opinion not unlike the one Joan Davis had formed of him years ago when he was dating Beverly Wills. Mrs. Pierangeli objected to Jimmy for another reason too: He wasn't Catholic. But just as Joan Davis had, Mrs. Pierangeli had probably also heard at least some of

With Richard Davalos

the rumors about Jimmy's sexual history. There was no way Mrs. Pierangeli would have wanted her daughter to become involved with, or maybe even married to, a young man who had slept with as many men as Jimmy had. No matter what her specific reasons were, Mrs. Pierangeli demanded that Pier start distancing herself from Jimmy. Pier did this by dating other men. While Pier followed her mother's orders and saw a variety of men, Jimmy dated a handful of girls, mostly to keep his name in the newspapers. Usually Dick Clayton or someone at Warner Bros. arranged the dates. One in particular was with Terry Moore, an actress so determined to be a Hollywood starlet that she seemed consumed with the idea. In a photograph taken on the night of September 22, when he escorted her to the premiere of *Sabrina* at the Paramount Theatre, Dean, dressed in a tuxedo, obviously looks uncomfortable as he stands next to Moore, who clutches his arm tightly while she gives the camera her biggest—and phoniest— Hollywood starlet smile. In this photograph, one can see that on some level Dean was deeply contemptuous of the image-making process. But there he was with Moore, escorting her to a movie premiere for no other reason than to get his picture in the newspaper.

As the days passed, Jimmy and Pier saw less and less of each other. While they did go to the premiere of *A Star Is Born* at the Pantages Theatre on September 29, they were by no means as much of an item as they had been. Then, in early October, Pier had some more news for Jimmy: She had decided to marry Vic Damone, the popular singer. Jimmy was shocked. He could hardly believe what Pier had told him, not only because he had no idea she was serious about Damone (he was not even fully aware of the fact that they were dating) but also because Damone seemed to be such a strange choice. However, if Pier's mother had anything to do with the selection (and it's hard to imagine that she didn't), Damone was a sensible pick. He was pleasant and clean-cut. He was Catholic. But, beyond this, he was unequivocally heterosexual. It was reported by those who knew him at the time that

Dean escorts Terry Moore to the premiere of *Sabrina*.

Jimmy was crushed by the break-up of his relationship with Pier. In the mythology of James Dean that emerged following his death, Pier would be portrayed, whether she deserved to or not, as the "evil woman" who broke Jimmy's heart. In this scenario Jimmy became the spurned lover who was betrayed by the one true love of his life.

In October, even though Warner Bros. renewed his contract that month, Jimmy felt at loose ends about his career. *East of Eden* was well into post-production, but the picture was too far from its release for Dean to start doing any more serious publicity than he was at the moment, which usually involved showing up at movie premieres with dates like Terry Moore. Until the final cut of *East of Eden* was finished, Warner Bros. was not ready to cast Dean in another picture. Metro-Goldwyn-Mayer approached Warner Bros. about borrowing Dean for *The Cobweb,* a picture to be directed by Vincente Minnelli, but Warner Bros. turned MGM down. The picture would not be a good career move for Dean, Warner Bros. argued. (MGM cast John Kerr instead.) With no film project for Dean to do in the near future, Jane Deacy and Dick Clayton started to look for some television work for him. Unlike many actors, Dean had a studio contract that allowed him to appear on television. At the same time, Dean also began to take private acting classes with Jeff Corey, a local coach who taught out of his home in Los Angeles. Even in those classes, which were informal compared to classes at the Actors Studio, Dean stood out from his fellow students.

"I remember this one exercise he did," says Carol Easton, who was an aspiring actress at the time. "Everyone was into the Method, and this was a scene for two roommates. Jimmy Dean was told that his action was to tell his roommate, who had a serious drinking problem, to stop drinking. He was supposed to tell him this because he was so worried about him. So Jimmy prepared. And when he came onto the stage he was acting drunk. I thought, as most everyone else did, that he had misunderstood the instructions—that it was the other guy who

With Pier Angeli

was supposed to be drunk. Then what came out was this. The room-mate asked Jimmy why he was drunk and Jimmy told him that he was going to stay drunk until he promised to sober up. And that's how they played the scene. Which was an interesting twist."

By November, Jimmy began to get jobs on television. On the ninth he co-starred in "Padlocks," an episode of *Danger*. Immediately after that, in an old abandoned theatre in downtown Los Angeles, he began to rehearse for another television show, this one to star Eddie Albert and an actress who had been a child star (her most famous picture was *Miracle on Thirty-fourth Street*) but who was now trying to be taken seriously as an adult actress, Natalie Wood. (While he was filming *East of Eden* on the Warner Bros. lot, Jimmy had met Wood briefly when she came by to say hello from an adjoining soundstage where she was working.) An episode of *General Electric Theatre* (which was hosted by Ronald Reagan), the show was adapted from Sherwood Anderson's short story "I'm a Fool" and involved a poor farm boy, played by Dean, who pretends to be rich so that he can impress a wealthy girl, played by Wood. Sixteen and beautiful, Wood turned in an impressive "adult" debut when the half-hour show aired on November 14. Coincidentally, it was Dean who gave her her first on-screen kiss.

For Thanksgiving in 1954, Jimmy went to the home of Keenan Wynn to join other guests, among them Rod Steiger, Jim Backus, and Arthur Loew, Jr., for a holiday meal and an afternoon of friendly conversation. The twenty-fourth, however, was not so pleasant. On that day at St. Timothy's Catholic Church on West Pico Boulevard in a ceremony so elaborate that it could only have been Catholic, Pier Angeli married Vic Damone. The legend surrounding what Jimmy did or did not do on that day would grow as the years passed. It's said that he sat on his motorcycle in a driveway across the street from the church and gunned the motorcycle's engine when the couple appeared at the front door of the church following the ceremony. It's said that Jimmy fell into a serious depression in the days after the service when the reality

of what had happened sunk in. It isn't clear, though, how much of this
is legend and how much is fact, not unlike most of what went on between Pier and Jimmy.

Now that his association with Pier had ended, Jimmy decided to go to
New York for the holidays. Before he left, he did a *General Electric
Theatre* episode called "The Dark, Dark Hour" on the twelfth. Once
he had finished that job, Jimmy went first to Indiana, to spend Christmas on the farm with the Winslows, then on to New York. While he
was there, staying in the Sixty-eighth Street studio he still rented even
though he now lived most of the time in Los Angeles, he relaxed and
socialized with friends. Warner Bros. had finally set the release date
for *East of Eden*—it would come out sometime in March 1955—so
Jimmy was beginning to think about what kind of publicity he would
like to do for the picture. The studio had started placing smaller items
with magazines for their March issues, but Jimmy wanted something
really dramatic. What he wanted was to be featured in *Life*, the fore-
most mainstream American magazine at the time. To try to make this
happen, Jimmy asked Roy Schatt to send the magazine some photographs he had taken of him. When the magazine's editors looked at
the pictures, they contacted Schatt to tell him that while they liked the
shots they wanted something more masculine. Jimmy and Roy decided to do a new shoot in the hopes that they might come up with
some pictures that would be more appropriate to submit to the magazine.

On the day they got together to do the shoot—December 29,
1954—Jimmy neither shaved nor fixed his hair. He also wore a ragged
black wool sweater with a hole in the right shoulder. If *Life* wanted
him to be masculine, then he would be masculine. Indeed, the look
Jimmy affected was so dark and hard-edged that he appeared menac-
ing. As Ray started taking pictures, Jimmy felt himself responding
well. By now, with one major motion picture and countless television

shows behind him, he was comfortable in front of the camera. What's more, he trusted Roy as a friend and as a photographer to the point that he could let go of his toughness and reveal his sexual side. Jimmy must have known he was doing this too, for after they had finished one certain shot Jimmy asked Roy, "Don't I remind you of Michelangelo's *David?*" And Roy agreed that he did.

The photographs that came out of this session would be some of the most dark and sensual ever taken of Dean. In picture after picture he fixes his half-closed, seductive eyes on the camera as if he were staring at a lover. In more than one he pulls the neck of his sweater down with his hand, revealing a glimpse of his bare upper chest. In another shot he cocks his head and contorts his face—"Oh, this feels so good," he seems to be saying—as though he were nearing orgasm. If ever a subject made love to a camera, Dean did with this series of pictures. He and Roy were still talking about how well the shoot had gone two days later when they celebrated New Year's at Roy's apartment with a group of Jimmy's friends that included Marty Landau, Billy Gunn, and Bobby Heller. Soon after this, Roy submitted the photographs to *Life.* While waiting for the magazine's decision, Roy went with Jimmy to the rehearsals of "The Thief," an episode of *The U.S. Steel Hour* that Deacy had lined up for Jimmy to do. On the set Roy snapped some pictures, capturing Jimmy in a completely different mood than he had expressed in the series shot in Roy's studio. Unfortunately, several days later, the *Life* editors turned the photographs down. They were too brash and aggressive, the editors said, compared to the photographs they usually published in the magazine. Apparently, in their attempt to please the editors by making Jimmy look more masculine, Jimmy and Roy had gone too far.

After "The Thief" aired on January 4, 1955, Jimmy had to return to Los Angeles right away. Warner Bros. was about to decide what picture Jimmy would do next. It would probably be a youth-oriented vehicle called *Rebel Without a Cause.* Just as important, Kazan had finished editing *East of Eden,* so it was ready to be screened for test audiences. The advance publicity for the picture had also started to appear. Not surprisingly, the person who stood to benefit most from that publicity was Jimmy.

In January, *Look* ran "I Predict," a column featuring the new stars of 1955. One was Dean, who, the magazine said, "will be the most dynamic discovery since Marlon Brando." In February, *Vogue* mentioned Dean in a column, "The Next Successes." Calling him "thin, intense, with such strong projection that he is always noticed," the magazine contended that Dean—"a smash [in] *East of Eden*"—"was in." That same month, *Cosmopolitan* printed "James Dean—New Face With Future" by Louella Parsons. After she said that Dean "belongs to the Marlon Brando–Montgomery Clift 'school' of acting, the professionally unwashed, unmannered, unconventional actors' group that—East or West—flourishes under the brilliant direction of Elia Kazan," Parsons went on to speculate that "[y]ou won't be able to forget James Dean as Cal, the originality, force, and certainty of his interpretation of a highly complex role." For the article Dean had given Parsons an interview to which, she noted, he showed up two hours late and wore "a thick purple sweater, out at the elbows, and riding breeches, torn at the knee." When she asked Dean about acting, he had said: "I can play the Prince—if necessary. But I can't divert into being a social human being when I'm working on a hero like Cal, who is essentially demonic." In a fan magazine Parsons was even more boastful about Dean. "This twenty-year-old [sic] actor from Broadway, I guarantee you, will be the rave of the season after he is seen in *East of Eden.* It is what Dean projects on the screen that makes him my pick among the new actors for stardom in 1955. He is a great young actor. I predict a long and brilliant career for this screen newcomer." Still, after all this praise, Parsons could not help but add a dig. "Now, come on, young Mr. Dean," she wrote, "how about forgetting the Brando bit?"

As the early publicity pieces began to appear, Warner Bros. set up some sneak screenings of *East of Eden* around Los Angeles. Nicholas Ray, a Hollywood veteran, had been lined up to direct *Rebel Without a Cause*. At a party in Ray's suite at the Château Marmont one Sunday afternoon, Jimmy met an attractive dark-haired young photographer named Dennis Stock. Jimmy invited Dennis to one of the upcoming sneak previews of *East of Eden*. On the Wednesday night of the screening, Dennis sat in his seat in a theatre in Santa Monica, mesmerized by Jimmy's performance. When the picture was over, Dennis rushed outside and found Jimmy sitting on his motorcycle in an alley. Once he had told him how impressed he was by his acting, Dennis asked Jimmy if he could do a photo-essay on him. Jimmy said he would think about it.

The next morning over breakfast at Googie's, a popular hangout for young actors located next to Schwab's drugstore on the Strip, Jimmy and Dennis talked about a variety of subjects. After Jimmy had paid for breakfast, they walked out into the parking lot. "Get on," Jimmy said, meaning his motorcycle, "and let's go up into the hills. My agent's got a place up there with a beautiful view, and we can talk." Climbing on, Dennis held Jimmy tightly as Jimmy started off, speeding through traffic on their way to the Hollywood Hills. At Dick Clayton's house, Jimmy and Dennis sat outside on the ground in the yard so that they could look out over the hills while they talked. During the five hours they sat there, deep in conversation, they agreed on the concept for a photo-essay. Dennis would follow Jimmy around Los Angeles, then go on with him to Fairmount and New York, taking pictures of him in all three places. The essay would show where Dean, the new young star, had come from. Dennis felt fairly certain that *Life* would be interested in the concept—an idea, of course, that appealed to Jimmy. Knowing Roy had failed with *Life*, Jimmy hoped that Dennis, who worked with the highly regarded Magnum Agency, would have better luck. So he agreed.

Within a week, Dennis got a go-ahead from *Life* and started taking pictures of Jimmy. For two weeks he trailed Jimmy all over Los Angeles. In that time the only development that threatened to kill the assignment was Jimmy's decision to insist on being put on the cover. Because Dennis knew that Jimmy was not yet famous enough to appear on the cover of *Life*, he never even brought the issue up with the editors although he told Jimmy that he had and that they had refused. Jimmy sulked for a few days, but he wanted to be in *Life* so badly he resolved himself to being merely the subject of a feature story. Finally, during the first week in February 1955, Jimmy and Dennis left Los Angeles to go to Indiana.

In Fairmount, Dennis snapped roll after roll of pictures of Jimmy: on the farm, in town, in the local cemetery, in the motorcycle shop, in the Winslow farmhouse, in his old high school where he posed on the stage of the theatre in which he first acted. The highlight of the trip was Jimmy's appearance as the guest of honor at the Sweetheart's Ball held on St. Valentine's Day at Fairmount High School. That evening, Jimmy sat in on the congo drums with the George Columbus Combo, the band playing the dance, but the most exciting aspect of the occasion for Jimmy was the fact that the high school students treated him as if he were a celebrity. Even though *East of Eden* had not yet been released, word was already circulating through Fairmount that the movie was going to make Jimmy Dean a big star in Hollywood. So the local teenagers lined up to have Jimmy autograph their Sweetheart's Ball tickets. All the while, Dennis clicked away with the camera, something that did not go unnoticed by the teenagers. Jimmy Dean must be on his way to becoming important, they decided. He was being photographed for *Life* magazine.

Of all the pictures Dennis took of Jimmy in Fairmount, one sequence would become infamous. Jimmy got the idea one day that he wanted Dennis to take some shots of him in Hunt's Funeral Parlor. When they got there and Dennis began snapping pictures of Jimmy in

With Markie, back in Fairmount, February 1955

On the Winslow farm, February 1955

the back room where the new coffins were kept, Jimmy suddenly opened a coffin, climbed inside, and told Dennis to take some pictures of him sitting in the coffin. Since he didn't want to stifle Jimmy's spontaneity, Dennis clicked away. Most of the local residents of Fairmount expressed concern over the way Jimmy had changed on this trip. After all, no one in Fairmount went around wearing blue jeans and a suit jacket like Jimmy did now. But what people simply couldn't believe was that Jimmy Dean was crazy enough to have his picture taken in a coffin at Hunt's. The whole idea seemed so disrespectful, as if he were somehow making fun of the seriousness of death. There was no doubt about it. Jimmy Dean may have been a strange kid when he was growing up in Fairmount, but Hollywood had made him just plain weird.

Soon after Valentine's Day, Jimmy and Dennis left Fairmount for New York. There Dennis continued to photograph Jimmy: now in Times Square, on the street, in his apartment, in Jane Deacy's office with his accountant, at the Actors Studio, with Geraldine Page backstage at the theatre, with Eartha Kitt in her dance studio. When he was not doing work concerning his career, Jimmy did see a few people (he and Dick Davalos gave a party at the "21" Club for their friends), but at this point his social life came second. His career was most important. Of all the business-related activities, perhaps the most noteworthy occurred on the day Howard Thompson, a reporter for *The New York Times,* interviewed him at Jane Deacy's home. As Jimmy sat quietly in Deacy's apartment, Thompson asked him near the beginning of the interview if he had ever read the novel *East of Eden.*

"No, I didn't read the novel," Jimmy said. "The way I work, I'd much rather justify myself with the adaptation rather than the source. I felt I wouldn't have any trouble—too much, anyway—with this characterization once we started because I understood the part. I knew, too, that if I had any problems over the boy's background, I could straighten it out with Kazan."

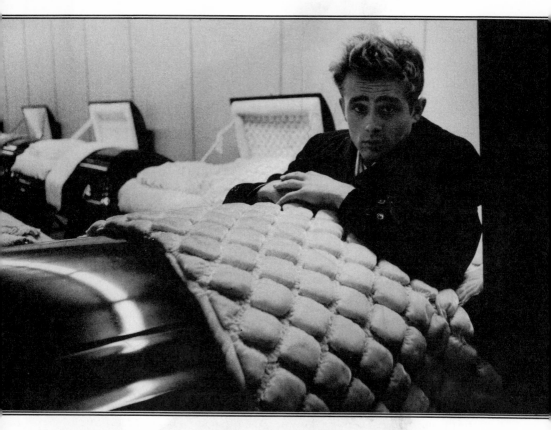

One shot from the sequence that would become infamous.
Hunt's Funeral Parlor, Fairmount, February 1955.

When Thompson questioned Jimmy about how he got involved in acting, Jimmy lit a cigarette, stood, and began pacing the room.

"To me," he said, "acting is the most logical way for people's neuroses to manifest themselves in this great need we have to express ourselves. To my way of thinking, an actor's course is set even before he's out of the cradle. Whatever abilities I may have, crystallized . . . in high school, when I was trying to prove something to myself—that I could do it, I suppose."

Thompson prodded him to talk more about his youth. "After graduation, I went to live with my father in Los Angeles—Mother had died when I was a kid—and just for the hell of it, signed up for a pre-law course at UCLA. That did call for a certain amount of histrionics. I even joined a fraternity on the campus, but I busted a couple of guys in the nose and got myself kicked out. I wasn't happy in law, either."

Next, Jimmy said, he "tried [his] luck in pictures." Then Whitmore sent him to New York to study with Strasberg, whom he described as "an incredible man, a walking encyclopedia, with fantastic insight."

What about the difference between New York and Los Angeles, the question every actor must answer?

"It just happens that I felt in cadence and pace better here as far as living goes. New York is vital, above all, fertile. They're a little harder to find, maybe, but out there in Hollywood, behind all that brick and mortar, there are human beings just as sensitive to fertility. The problem for this cat—myself—is not to get lost."

On March 7, a group of Dennis Stock's photographs appeared in *Life*. In the spread, entitled "Moody New Star," the first photograph shows Dean sitting in his uncle's barn. Dressed in a suit and tie, he stares at the camera. "In Sunday best Dean reads," said the picture's caption, "as he used to when a child after Sunday school, in uncle's barn." Then, in the other photographs, there is Jimmy with Julie Harris; with a pig on the farm; with his grandfather; with Geraldine Page in a dressing room; in a chair in the window of a furniture store near Rockefeller Center; among a herd of cattle on his uncle's farm; in his agent's office, his feet propped up on a desk, his head tilted to one side, his eyes, behind his glasses, shut. Finally, the last shot—Jimmy is walking down Times Square in the rain. Bundled in a heavy black overcoat, a cigarette dangling from his mouth, his face darkened by shadows, Dean looks off to his left. The large glassy puddle through which he is walking is broken here and there by tiny drops of rain.

On March 9, two days after *Life* published its piece, *East of Eden* had its official premiere in New York City at the Astor Theatre. The fifty-dollar-a-seat screening, the proceeds of which benefited the Actors Studio, featured a number of celebrity ushers, among them Marilyn Monroe, Eva Marie Saint, Marlene Dietrich, and Celeste Holm. Most of the major figures associated with the picture attended the premiere: Jack Warner, Elia Kazan, John Steinbeck, Raymond Massey, Richard Davalos, Jo Van Fleet. One, however, did not. Unable to stand the pressure caused by such a screening, or so he said, Dean had flown back to Los Angeles. "Why should I go?" he said to Christine White. "I know I was good, and having people tell me so would only embarrass me."

On March 10, immediately before the airing of "The Life of Emile Zola" on the show *Lux Video Theatre*, Jimmy was interviewed about *East of Eden* live on NBC. On April 5, *Look* ran a brief piece on *East of Eden*. "[I]ts big news is the debut of James Dean," the magazine said, "who overnight may become a star. . . . Because of a similarity in their acrobatic mannerisms, Dean inevitably will be compared to another Kazan actor, Marlon Brando." But of all the press generated by *East of Eden*'s release, the most fascinating piece was an interview Winton Dean gave to *Modern Screen*. Dean talked to the reporter around the time *East of Eden* came out—it is perhaps the only known print interview he would ever give—but the piece didn't appear for several months. In the interview Winton Dean spoke candidly.

Dennis Stock photographed Dean in New York City
in February 1955.

In his Upper West Side studio

My Jim is a tough boy to understand. At least he is for me. But maybe that's because I don't understand actors, and he's always wanted to become one. Another reason is that we were separated for a long period of time. From when he was nine until he was eighteen. Those are important, formative years when a boy and his father usually become close friends. Jim and I—well, we've never had that closeness. It's nobody's fault, really. Just circumstances. . . .

I didn't know what to do. How do you tell an eight-year-old boy his mother's going to die? I tried. In my own stumbling way I tried to prepare Jim for it.

Nowadays, he lives in a world we don't understand too well, the actor's world. We don't see too much of him. But he's a good boy, my Jim. A good boy, and I'm very proud of him. Not easy to understand, no sir. He's not easy to understand. But he's all man, and he'll make his mark. Mind you, my boy will make his mark.

3. Of the hundreds of people who saw the private screenings of *East of Eden* in Los Angeles, one of them, a young actor named Jack Simmons, was about to become a major part of Jimmy's life. While Jimmy did not know him personally, there was a good chance he had heard of him since Jack was a fixture of the Los Angeles homosexual scene. One of Jack's favorite bars was Tropical Village, a club just off the beach in Santa Monica. In the early fifties, TV Bar, as the Los Angeles homosexual set called it, was among the most popular bars in the city. It wasn't at all unusual to see Rock Hudson and George Nader, the objects of considerable gossip in Hollywood at the time, dancing with each other on the dance floor. Regulars had even seen Rock and George show up at the bar in drag. This was not at all out of character for the couple, who regularly gave drag parties

James Dean and his friend Jack Simmons

at Rock's house in the city. Jack Simmons had once tried to pick up Jonathan Gilmore at the TV Bar, long before Jonathan and Jimmy became friends in New York. "The first time I saw Jack Simmons," Gilmore says, "he was standing in front of the TV Bar in a bathing suit. And he had on an Indian belt. He also had a gigantic hook nose. He pursued me but nothing ever happened." One night some time later they were at a party, Gilmore also recalls, when Jonathan left and Jack came running out of the place. But Jonathan got in his car and drove off.

That was 1952. By the spring of 1955, Jack Simmons was living with James Dean, or rather James Dean was living with Jack Simmons. Jimmy had rented a place in the hills near West Hollywood— *the* homosexual neighborhood in Los Angeles—but he often stayed at Jack's apartment because it was closer to the studios. It would be hard to establish exactly when Jimmy and Jack became lovers. A part of the Googie's crowd, of which Jimmy was one of the more famous members, Jack had hung out with Maila Nurmi, a strange woman who made a living playing the character Vampira on a local television show. Though she was another figure on the Googie's scene, she got on Jimmy's nerves. He may have been weird himself, but Maila was *too* weird for his tastes. Regardless of Jack's friendship with Nurmi, Jimmy felt attracted to him, and after Jimmy came back to Los Angeles from New York to start shooting *Rebel*, he and Jack became romantically involved. More than likely, it was Jack who made himself available to Jimmy, for once he had seen pictures of Jimmy in the newspapers and watched a screening of *East of Eden* Jack would tell friends that he was going to pursue Jimmy, get him, and spend the rest of his life doing whatever Jimmy wanted him to do. Sadly, in the end, only the first two parts of Jack's plan came true.

Jimmy made another decision at this time. With his financial future now secure, he went out and bought two expensive items. The first was practical—a 1955 Ford station wagon, white with wood paneling on the sides—while the second was anything but—a white 356 1500cc Porsche Spyder Speedster convertible. He settled on this make and model because recently Jimmy had become interested in auto racing, and he could race this car. To pursue his new passion, he entered the Palm Springs Road Races on March 26. Driving the Porsche, he won the preliminary race but placed second in the finals. At this stage of his career, why would Jimmy have become involved in a sport in which he could be killed? "Death can't be considered," he told a friend, "because if you're afraid to die there's no room in your life to make discoveries."

For some time, Dean had campaigned for the part of Jett Rink in the adaptation of Edna Ferber's novel *Giant* that George Stevens was planning to do for Warner Bros. Finally Jimmy got the part. Like the rest of the cast, he was ready to begin shooting when a schedule complication with Elizabeth Taylor, another star of the picture, caused a delay in the start of production. Because it looked as though the delay would be a long one, Warner Bros. decided to let Dean go ahead and shoot *Rebel*, which was originally conceived by the studio to be a low-budget teen-oriented melodrama in the style of *Blackboard Jungle*. A picture about juvenile delinquency that had just been released in 1955, *Blackboard Jungle* was doing surprisingly well at the box office.

At Warner Bros. *Rebel* had had a long and complicated history. In 1946, the studio spent five thousand dollars to option a book called *Rebel Without a Cause* written by Robert M. Lindner, a prison psychiatrist, and published in 1944. The studio had optioned the book with the intention of getting Brando interested in the project, but he wasn't. Then in 1954 Nicholas Ray, a protégé of Kazan's known for directing such pictures as *They Live by Night, Knock on Any Door, In a Lonely Place,* and *Johnny Guitar,* got involved in the project in a peculiar way. He had written *The Blind Run,* a treatment about confused teenagers and juvenile delinquency in Los Angeles, that Warner Bros. had

Natalie Wood and James Dean. To many he would become the God of Teenagers.

With Sal Mineo, his costar in *Rebel Without a Cause*

thought enough of to buy. But the studio didn't like his title. So it was decided that Ray's treatment would be put with the title *Rebel Without a Cause*. (Lindner's book, a semi-fictionalized collection of case studies of disturbed adolescents, had nothing at all to do with the plot of the picture that was shot.) Once Ray had been signed on to direct, the studio hired Leon Uris in December 1954 to write the script. Uris worked on the project only long enough to be replaced by Irving Shulman. Then Ray saw an early screening of *East of Eden*, made up his mind that he wanted Dean to star in *Rebel*, and talked Warner Bros. into letting him have Dean. Even though Shulman had done a good job developing the script, Jimmy didn't like him, so he was replaced by Stewart Stern, a cousin of both Arthur Loew, Jr., and Leonard Rosenman. At the time, Stern had only one screen credit, but it was for *Teresa*, a picture that had made Pier Angeli a star and that had earned him an Academy Award nomination for best story. Working hard, Stern produced the final draft of *Rebel* rather quickly while Ray began to line up his cast.

With Dean as his lead—the studio finalized that decision in March 1955—Ray had to fill two other key parts. One was Plato, a young teenage boy who becomes interested in Dean's character Jim Stark; the other was Judy, Plato's female counterpart. For Judy, Ray chose Natalie Wood, Dean's co-star in "I'm a Fool." Under contract to Warner Bros., Wood had recently appeared in *The Silver Chalice* with Paul Newman and Pier Angeli. Even so, it was probably neither these credits nor the ones she had accumulated as a child star that got her a part in *Rebel*, but the fact that she was having an affair with Nicholas Ray. For Plato, Ray selected Sal Mineo, a pretty dark-featured fifteen-year-old boy who had already appeared in two Broadway plays (*The Rose Tattoo* and *The King and I*) and two pictures (*Six Bridges to Cross* and *The Private War of Major Benson*). When Ray had cast the minor parts—Jim Backus would play Stark's father, Ann Doran his mother, and Corey Allen his adversary—he was ready to start shooting.

On March 23, wardrobe fittings were finished. Filming began on the twenty-eighth. For four days, the picture's cinematographer, Ernest Haller, who had won an Academy Award for *Gone With the Wind*, as well as nominations for *Jezebel, All This and Heaven Too*, and *Mildred Pierce*, shot *Rebel* in black and white. Once *East of Eden* had opened nationwide on the sixteenth and performed unusually well at the box office, Warner Bros. decided to upgrade *Rebel* from a B to an A picture, which meant that it could be shot in color. Happy with this development, Ray and Haller prepared to start reshooting. Before they began, Jimmy made a wardrobe change. Originally he had planned on wearing a black leather jacket, but now that the picture was going to be shot in color he thought he should wear something colorful. As a result he picked out a red nylon jacket, the one item that, over the years, would be most associated with the picture.

While *Rebel* was being shot, romantic attractions developed between the cast, a not uncommon occurrence on a movie set. Supposedly, Natalie Wood fell in love with Jimmy. This may or may not have happened; it became apparent, though, that she did form a strong affection for him. (Sal Mineo would say she saw *East of Eden* thirty times—or more.) Regardless of what she felt for him, Jimmy didn't have an affair with Natalie Wood. Nor did he have an affair with Mineo, who told friends years later that he and Jimmy *had* slept together. Any physical involvement between the two of them would have had to occur during the filming of *Rebel* since Jimmy did not know Sal before the picture started shooting and never saw him again after it wrapped. There were even rumors circulating at the time *Rebel* was filming that Jimmy and Sal were having an affair; Roy Schatt heard the rumors in New York. To be honest, the chances of Jimmy's sleeping with Sal were small. More likely, Mineo became obsessed with Dean. While he was working on *Rebel*, Jimmy was almost exclusively involved with Jack Simmons. In fact, Jimmy went so far as to get Jack a small part in the picture. In an item in his gossip column, Sidney

Skolsky, whose daughter played a gang member in *Rebel,* hinted at Jack and Jimmy's relationship. "Jack is always around the house and set," Skolsky wrote. "He gets Jimmy coffee or a sandwich or whatever Jimmy wants. Jack also runs interference for Dean when there are people Jimmy doesn't want to see. There are many people trying to contact a nobody who becomes a star." For some people, the item came too close to revealing the truth about Jack and Jimmy; Skolsky almost identified Jack for who he really was—Jimmy's lover.

Of all the young homosexual actors in Hollywood—Tab Hunter and Anthony Perkins were just two—the press had decided to make an effort to call into question the sexuality of only one, Rock Hudson. Hunter and Perkins would even have an affair in the fifties, but the press seemed to focus its attention on Hudson, perhaps because he was such an easy target. After all, Hudson and George Nader were all but open about their relationship, going so far as to appear together regularly at bars in Los Angeles and San Francisco. Coincidentally, the first hint of trouble for Hudson came not long after *Rebel* went into production when *Movie/TV Secrets* ran an item taunting Hudson. "He is handsome, personable, intelligent, and a top-salaried actor—what's wrong," the magazine teased, "with Rock where the fair sex is concerned, we ask?" If this wasn't bad enough, *Confidential* also threatened to reveal Rock's homosexuality—and to name names. As long as these rumors were surfacing in publications like *Confidential* and *Movie/TV Secrets,* Hudson's handlers—specifically, his agent Henry Willson—did not panic. Then in October *Life* ran a cover story on Hudson, "The Simple Life of a Busy Bachelor: Rock Hudson Gets Rich Alone." In the story the writer suggested strongly that Rock Hudson should get married, now that he was becoming an established star. If he was not going to, he needed to tell his fans why. "[S]ince 1949 movie fan clubs and fan magazines have parlayed a $75-a-week ex–truck driver named Roy Fitzgerald into a $3,000-a-week movie hero named Rock Hudson," the *Life* story read. "But now they are beginning to grumble. Their complaints, expressed in fan magazine articles, range from a shrill 'Scared of Marriage?' to a more understanding 'Don't Rush Rock.' Fans are urging 29-year-old Hudson to get married—or explain why not." Young, handsome, rich, and still a bachelor, the fans seemed to be saying about Rock, what was he, homosexual?

What alarmed Willson, of course, was the fact that the story questioning Rock's sexuality had now made *Life*. One didn't have to read between the lines to figure out that *Life* knew more than what it had reported. How could the magazine not? Half of Hollywood had heard the rumors about the parties at Rock's house. Before a Rock Hudson party was over, there was always someone (and more often than not it was Rock) who ended up dressed in a ballerina outfit twirling about the living room. And who *didn't* know about Rock and George's escapades on the Los Angeles homosexual scene? As soon as the *Life* article hit the newsstands, Willson got worried. By November, he knew he had to do something to kill the rumors, so he arranged for Rock to marry Phyllis Gates, one of Willson's former secretaries. At the wedding ceremony, Willson made sure that a corps of photographers showed up. Then he had a photographer follow the couple on their honeymoon, going so far as to have pictures of them shot in their bedroom suite. But even *that* wasn't enough. After the honeymoon, Willson arranged for photographers to trail the couple during the first days and weeks of their marriage as they settled into their new home. It was as if Willson was now taunting the Hollywood press. *Okay, you wanted him married*, Willson was saying, *so he's married. Now snap away to your heart's content. Just make sure you publish these goddamn pictures in your newspapers and magazines.*

It goes without saying that the marriage of Rock and Phyllis Hudson didn't last. After a little over a year, the Hudsons filed for divorce. In the end the divorce didn't matter. Regardless of how brief the marriage was, the fact that Rock actually *got* married seemed to be all it took to assure the American public that Rock was, as Winton Dean had said about his son, "all man." In fact, Rock Hudson was homosexual before, during, and after the marriage. The marriage may have been a sham and the Hollywood press corps may have known it was a sham but Hudson had shown that he knew how to play the game an actor had to play to make it in Hollywood. No more news items about Rock Hudson's homosexuality would appear and Hudson would go on to have a long and successful career until his death from AIDS in October 1985.

Much of the Rock Hudson public drama would play itself out after *Rebel Without a Cause* had wrapped. Even so, rumors about Rock's sexuality were circulating throughout the summer and early fall of 1955 while Jimmy was filming *Rebel*. As a result Jimmy was careful about his private life. Though he was deeply involved with Jack Simmons, he occasionally saw Jonathan Gilmore, who had recently returned to Los Angeles from New York. "Jimmy and I did some stuff," Gilmore says. "Once or twice we went to my mother's house, but it was no big deal. We just embraced and moved toward each other. We'd lay on the bed together and jack off."

Oddly enough, it had been Jack who reintroduced Jimmy and Jonathan. One night at Googie's, Jonathan had run into Jack, whom he barely recognized as the person who had tried to pick him up once at the TV Bar because Jack had gone through so many changes, not the least of which was a nose job. As Gilmore would put it, Jack had turned into "this guy who kind of looked like Jimmy and had his nose done like Jimmy's and combed his hair like Jimmy's and wore clothes similar to what Jimmy would wear." Several nights later, in the parking lot of Googie's, Jack introduced Jonathan to Jimmy. When he did, he played up the fact that he knew James Dean, the movie star, completely unaware that Jimmy and Jonathan were already friends. As soon as Jack found out, he became jealous. Then, one afternoon, in a perverse move, he tried to seduce Jonathan when Jonathan stopped by to see Jack at his apartment. On this occasion, Jonathan was looking around Jack's living room and noticed something peculiar, a worn-out pair of Jimmy's boots that Jack had encased in a plastic box and placed on a set of bookshelves as though the boots were on display in a museum. That day, Jonathan was examining the boots when, without warning, Jack approached him and told him how attractive he thought he was. Before long, the boys were drinking whiskey from a bottle, a prelude to Jack's coming on to Jonathan. "Then," Gilmore remembers, "he stares at me and says, 'I'm going to kill myself if you tell Jimmy anything about this. I'm going to fucking kill myself.' So I told him that I was not going to tell Jimmy." After that, Jonathan left.

Maybe the strangest night of the late spring and early summer occurred a few weeks later. On that night, Jonathan and Jimmy picked up a one-legged girl at a bar and took her back to Jimmy's apartment on Sunset Plaza. There, as the three of them drank and smoked pot, Jimmy slipped into an unusually morbid mood. "Then Jimmy drew a face on the stump of her leg with lipstick," Gilmore remembers. "He draws the eyes, the nose, the mouth. And he starts kind of relating and talking to the face. Next he wants me to fuck her and he's going to sit in a chair and watch while I fuck her. So I fucked her while he watched. Then he had me take her to where she was living. And when I came back he was gone."

It was on a night similar to this one, though perhaps not quite so strange, that Jimmy opened up to Jonathan and started telling him about his early days in Hollywood. "You know, I've had my cock sucked by five of the big names in Hollywood," he said to Jonathan, "and I think it's pretty funny because I wanted more than anything to just get some little part, something to *do,* and they'd invite me to fancy dinners overlooking the blue Pacific, and we'd have a few drinks, and how long could I go on? That's what I wanted to know—and the answer was it could go on until there was nothing left, until they had what they wanted and there was nothing left."

Naturally, the Warner Bros. publicity department worked hard to create a public image for Dean that was much different from the person he actually was. At the time *Rebel* was being filmed, Lori Nelson, who said she was a girlfriend of Dean's, published a fan magazine article entitled "The Dean I've Dated." Obviously a part of the advance publicity campaign for *Rebel* that Warner Bros. was now carefully orchestrating, the article contained a paragraph in which Nelson offered her own brief examination of Jimmy's personality. "He was polite, shy and hesitant," she wrote, "and he stood off, scrutinizing and studying, and saying surprisingly little. For me, it was a pleasant surprise to find him so shy. Believe me—most of the men in Hollywood are anything but." Then she revealed to the reader how she felt after her first date with Jimmy, an occasion on which, she said, they went horseback riding, caught an early movie, and listened to records at a friend's house. "I went home with a real glow," she wrote. "Everything had been so real and honest, and so nice. There was none of that empty glitter you feel on so many Hollywood dates. . . . That first date was typical of all we've had since—relaxed, casual evenings spent doing something which we both enjoyed, and with no pretense. That's the Jimmy Dean I know—the person who's himself, no matter what the circumstances." If the person Nelson wrote about in this article was the Jimmy Dean she knew so well, then she had apparently never met that "other" Jimmy Dean, the one who at that very moment was seeing a boy who had had his nose fixed to look like his, who had a pair of Jimmy's worn-out boots enshrined in his living room, and who had stated that his one goal in life was to do whatever Jimmy wanted whenever Jimmy wanted him to do it. No doubt Lori Nelson would have had trouble recognizing this Jimmy Dean, the one who, as he said, had had his cock sucked by five of the big names in Hollywood. Her "real

With Ursula Andress

glow" might have dimmed slightly if she had found out that everything in Jimmy's life was not "so real and honest, and so nice."

That a story like Nelson's bore little relation to Jimmy's actual life and that the girlfriend in question (who was supposed to be in love with Jimmy) may have barely even known him caused the Warner Bros. publicity experts little concern. They only cared about shaping the proper image for Dean. To this end, the studio arranged for Jimmy to have other "girlfriends." One was Ursula Andress, a recent "discovery" Hollywood had made in Italy. Described in the press as "the female Brando" (even though her acting credits were nowhere near as impressive as Brando's), she and Jimmy did share an amazing resemblance. When the two appeared together in public, especially if they were wearing similar outfits, they almost looked like brother and sister, not lovers. Actually, they probably never *were* lovers. As he had with nearly all of his girlfriends, Jimmy most likely kept his friendship with Ursula on strictly platonic terms. But their relationship did serve a purpose. Because they made such an appealing couple, the Hollywood photographers loved to take their picture. Of course this was just what Warner Bros. wanted. With all the rumors about Rock Hudson, the studio certainly didn't want a scandal to erupt involving James Dean, their talented rising star who was just about to become bankable.

The shooting schedule for *Rebel Without a Cause* continued into May. Some scenes had to be shot over and over, especially the highly emotional ones, but that didn't delay the picture too much. Only once, when Jimmy came down with malaria—yes, malaria in Los Angeles in the mid-fifties—and had to stay in bed for several days, was the shooting schedule suspended. He did take off May 1 to race at Minter Field in Bakersfield, where he placed third. Otherwise Jimmy was on the set every day, ready to work. In fact, a number of people in the cast and crew would believe he had as much to do with the final cut of *Rebel*

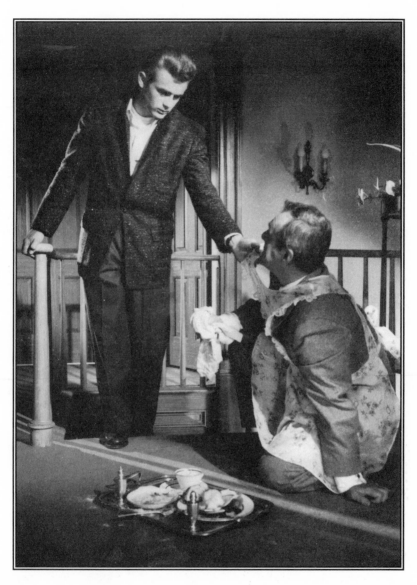

With Jim Backus, who played Jim Stark's father
in *Rebel Without a Cause*

On the set of *Rebel Without a Cause*

as Nicholas Ray did, so collaborative did Dean and Ray's relationship become during the filming process. Then again, unlike many actors, Jimmy seemed to understand the mechanics of filmmaking almost intuitively. Lately he had even started to say that in the near future he wanted to begin directing the pictures in which he appeared. Among the pictures he often mentioned directing was an adaptation of *The Little Prince.*

After *Rebel* had been in active production for close to two months, Ray finally wrapped the picture on May 26. Then, on May 28 and 29, Memorial Day weekend, Jimmy drove in the Santa Barbara Road Races. In the under–1500 cc. production event, he was running fourth in his Porsche when he blew a piston and was forced to drop out of the race.

On its most basic level, *Rebel Without a Cause* is a drama about a boy in conflict. Discontented and rebellious, he has had little luck fitting in with his family, his friends, his school. The main plot of the picture shows his attempt to resolve this conflict, even if he achieves only a partial resolution. Yet during the course of the picture a more intriguing story line emerges as a three-way romance forms between Jim, Judy, and Plato. The focus of both Plato and Judy's infatuation, Jim never really picks between the two; instead he seems to give both of them his love and allegiance. It's interesting to watch Jim's relationships with Judy and Plato grow independently of each other only to merge by the end of the picture. Many of the scenes with Jim and Plato were surprisingly homoerotic for 1955. Time and again, Plato stares lovingly into Jim's eyes as he tells him how much their friendship means to him. In the working draft of the screenplay, the implied love between the two boys was much more obvious. In one scene Jim and Plato were actually going to kiss. But when the industry censor spotted the kiss in the script, he balked. "It is of course vital," the censor wrote to Warner Bros., "that there be no inference of a questionable or homosexual relationship between Plato and Jim." Needless to say, the kiss was cut. So was the word "punk," which was at that time slang for homosexual. All that could be put on the screen, then, were Plato's romantic stares, subtle innuendos ("Where's your friend?" one gang member yells at Plato about Jim as three gang members rough Plato up; "Yeah, we got eyes for him, you know?" another says under his breath), and Jim Stark weeping at the end of the picture when Plato is killed.

In 1955, the picture every actor in Hollywood wanted to be in was *Giant*. When Edna Ferber's novel about the Texas rich was published by Doubleday in 1952, it became an immediate best-seller. Over the next five years, the book sold twenty-five million copies. Spanning forty years, *Giant* centers around the drama of the Benedict family, specifically the struggle between Bick Benedict and Jett Rink, an upstart Texas oilman whom Ferber based on Glenn McCarthy, the legendary wildcatter who, as a capstone to a career in which he became one of the wealthiest men in the state, built the Shamrock Hotel in Houston. The book was so popular that Ferber refused to sell its film rights to Hollywood unless she was made one of the picture's producers. Finally Warner Bros. worked out a deal with her in which she would share that job—and the profits—with George Stevens and Henry Ginsberg. Once Warner Bros. had finalized a contract with Ferber, *Giant* went into pre-production in 1953 with Stevens as director. At that time, having already made two pictures that were sure to be classics, *Shane* and *A Place in the Sun,* Stevens was one of the most respected directors in Hollywood. In due course Stevens hired Fred Guiol and Ivan Moffat to write the screenplay for *Giant.* Then over the next several months he lined up one of the most impressive casts ever assembled for a motion picture: Elizabeth Taylor, James Dean, Rock Hudson, Mercedes McCambridge, Chill Wills, Carroll Baker, Sal Mineo, Earl Holliman, Dennis Hopper, Jane Withers, and on and on.

On the beach in Los Angeles—a rare moment of relaxation

Dean washes his Porsche.

Eventually, after numerous delays, only one of which was caused by Elizabeth Taylor, *Giant* went into production in May 1955.

On the twenty-third, shooting started on the Warner Bros. lot in California. Before long, the production moved east to Virginia to film the early scenes of the picture with Bick and Leslie, the characters played by Rock Hudson and Elizabeth Taylor. Well behind schedule, *Rebel Without a Cause* wrapped on May 26, and, even though he was exhausted, Jimmy went directly into wardrobe and makeup tests for *Giant* in Los Angeles. During the three free days he had between *Rebel* and *Giant*, Dean took care of some personal business, specifically breaking off his relationship with Jack Simmons. Finally, on June 3, worn-out still and under doctor's orders to eat a high-protein diet, Jimmy joined the *Giant* production in Marfa, the tiny town in west Texas where most of the picture would be shot.

With the weather unbearably hot during the day and the town dead beyond imagination at night, the cast and the crew would endure six long weeks in Marfa. Most people affiliated with the picture stayed in town at the El Paisano hotel; everyone from both the cast and crew took their meals there. But the picture's major stars lived in homes rented from local residents. The actual shooting of the film took place in the countryside around Marfa, primarily on the Worth Evans ranch (which was used for Reata) and the Ben Avant ranch (which was Little Reata). In that part of the state, a Hollywood production company shooting a picture was such a novelty that it was not unusual for as many as a thousand people to show up on any given day just to watch what was happening.

From the start Dean found himself in serious conflict with Hudson and Stevens. Obviously, the friction with Stevens was potentially much more damaging to Dean than any disagreement he might have with Hudson. So far in his career, Dean had been able to experiment as an actor almost at will. Television directors gladly put up with his

quirks because he turned in such extraordinary performances, and
Dean's theatre experience to date had been brief but rewarding. In
Hollywood, Dean had worked with Kazan and Ray, two directors who
saw filmmaking as a collaborative art and allowed their actors to par-
ticipate actively in the process. George Stevens did not. A descendant
of a theatrical family from San Francisco who got his start in the business as a cameraman, Stevens believed, as he would say, that 25 percent of the creative process in filmmaking occurred in the editing
room, not on the production set. As a result he did not like his actors
to experiment with their acting, nor did he encourage them to change
their performance from one take to the next. Beyond this, in a Stevens
production an actor had to work through countless takes, since Stevens, famous for his obsession with trying to achieve perfection,
insisted on shooting every scene in a picture from numerous—
exhaustingly numerous—angles. The best of the countless thousands
of takes would then be woven together to make the final picture during
the months he and his crew of editors spent working in the editing
room. On the set, Stevens also demanded that his actors stay in
makeup at all times, even if he did not plan on using them on a particular day. Naturally Dean did not respond well to any of these demands. By the end of the first week, he and Stevens felt such
animosity toward one another that Stevens reprimanded him in front
of the cast and crew. Instead of bringing Dean in line, Stevens, by
scolding him, only made him sulk and seek solace from Elizabeth
Taylor and Mercedes McCambridge, the two actresses with whom he
became close friends during the filming. Like Geraldine Page, Jane
Deacy, and other women in his life, they were also surrogate mother
figures for him, not just friends.

Besides Stevens, Dean clashed with Rock Hudson, with whom he
and Chill Wills shared a house in Marfa. Through the years reports
would imply that the friction between Dean and Hudson centered
around their different acting styles. This is probably not the case

With Elizabeth Taylor in the "crucifixion" scene from *Giant*

Dean ties up Taylor on the set of *Giant*.

since Hudson did not *have* an acting style. What he achieved on film—and it *was* memorable, even remarkable—was affecting a sort of state of being. Rock Hudson did not so much act as *be there*. More probably, Dean and Hudson, who at present was having to deal with the rumors about his sexuality, were from opposite camps of the homosexual world. Jimmy would have hated Rock for his fey ways and his penchant for drag. A part of the "old" homosexual set, Rock would have been threatened by Jimmy's edgy and unconventional personality even as he was attracted by his sweet boyish looks.

Ultimately, because of his disagreement with Stevens and his dislike for Rock, Jimmy hated the time he spent in Texas on *Giant*. In a move that showed his contempt for the Hollywood power system that Stevens and Hudson were a part of, Jimmy spent a lot of his free time off the set socializing not with the picture's stars but with Bob Hinkle, the dialogue coach. During the day, when they weren't busy on the set with filming sessions that often went sixteen hours straight, Bob showed Jimmy rope tricks. "I taught him how to build a loop with the rope," Hinkle later wrote. "There's a lot more to it than just making a big loop. You have to work it so that you can throw it off your hand just right. Before we came back to Hollywood, Jimmy was an expert." At night, Bob and Jimmy would go rabbit hunting. In the five weeks *Giant* filmed in Texas, Bob and Jimmy shot a total of two hundred and sixty-one rabbits, plus two coyotes. "But more than shooting rabbits or coyotes," Hinkle wrote, "it was just being on that broad Texas plain under the bright stars and that strange bigness of Texas that was memorable. You feel it most at night, when it's quiet and lonely and there's no human being around to break the spell with talk."

On July 10, the majority of the cast and crew left Texas for Los Angeles. On the twelfth, once the second camera crew had finished filming Dean in the exterior shots in which he appeared alone, specifically the scenes in which Jett Rink strikes oil, Dean flew from Texas to join the company in Los Angeles. Back in California, the tension between

Dean and Stevens became even worse. On July 23, their conflict came to a head when Dean failed to show up on the set at all. Stevens's assistants tracked him down and discovered that he hadn't reported to the studio so that he could move into a house he had decided to rent in the San Fernando Valley. In Dean's defense, he had no scenes to shoot that day (and it *was* a Saturday). Stevens didn't care; he wanted him on the set anyway. Stevens got so angry with Dean that he told more than one associate he would never work with him again. He also instructed an assistant to draft a memorandum to Warner Bros. to complain about how difficult Dean had been to work with and to detail all of the occasions on which Dean had held up the production schedule, no matter how brief the delay. The memorandum, dated August 1, arrived on Jack Warner's desk at about the same time Dorothy Manners, who was substituting for Louella Parsons while she was on vacation, attacked Jimmy in her gossip column. On the fourth, Manners ran Dean's reply. " 'The trouble with me is I'm just dog tired,' said James Dean, the boy wonder I recently took over the coals for acting up on *Giant*. He went on sadly: 'Everybody hates me and thinks I'm a heel.' (Oh, come now—I wouldn't say that.) 'They say I've gone Hollywood—but, honest, I'm just the same as when I didn't have a dime. As I said, I'm just tired. I went into *Giant* immediately after a long hard schedule on *Rebel Without a Cause*. Maybe, I'd just better go away.' (Let's forget the whole thing, Jimmy. Stick around.)"

If Jane Deacy had anything to do with it, Dean *was* going to stick around. During the final weeks of shooting on *Giant*, as word spread through the industry that Dean was exceptional in *Rebel* and maybe even better in *Giant*, Deacy approached Warner Bros. about negotiating a new contract for Dean. She had several demands. First, Dean's present salary rate of fifteen hundred dollars a week had to be dramatically increased, perhaps to as much as one hundred thousand dollars a picture. Second, Dean would agree to do nine pictures for Warner Bros. over the next six years. Third, Dean wanted to establish his own

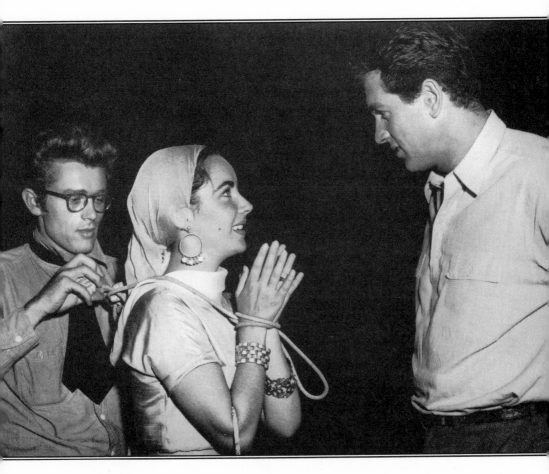

With Taylor and Rock Hudson. Dean and Hudson would dislike each other, but Taylor would be friends with both.

George Stevens directs Dean in his final sequence in the film.

production company at Warner Bros. through which he could develop film and television projects. Lastly, Dean would still be able to appear on television and do theatre. If Warner Bros. agreed to these basic terms, Dean would start the first of his nine pictures after he finished *Somebody Up There Likes Me*, a film biography of Rocky Graziano he was lined up to shoot for MGM. (The company had finally succeeded in forcing Warner Bros. to give up Dean for a picture when it loaned Elizabeth Taylor to Warner Bros. for *Giant.*) So, as he neared the end of production for *Giant*, which would eventually wrap on October 12 after 115 shooting days at a cost of $5.4 million, Dean was beginning to see himself for what he was—a demanding yet innovative actor who was turning into a major Hollywood star. Just six years ago, he had come out to Los Angeles from Indiana, Jimmy Dean from Fairmount. Now, at only twenty-four years of age, he had become what he most wanted to be, James Dean.

The
Little Bastard
and the
Little Prince

1. On the night of September 16, 1955, someone called the Hollywood Police Department to report a potential burglary in progress at Competition Motors. Officer Eddie Guzak happened to be near Competition so he got to the sports car dealership almost immediately. Years later, he recalled what he saw when he pulled up in his patrol car. "Who it was, see," Guzak said, "was Jimmy Dean. I asks him what he's doing there, and all polite-like he answers me that he wants to buy a car, and I says to him that he has to wait until they open. He wasn't drunk or nothing like that, and just as polite as he could be, but he just had to see his car. You work as a cop in Hollywood long enough, you see everything. But this was totally different. I give him a ride up to Hollywood and Vine and tell him to get on home."

Content with stealing a good look at the Spyder he had now decided to buy, Jimmy went home to bed and reported to work the next morning at the Warner Bros. lot. The main part of the production schedule on *Giant* had ended, but today Jimmy had to reshoot some scenes, common practice on a picture as long as this one looked to be—about three and a half hours. On this day, the seventeenth, because Stevens was redoing scenes from early in the script, Jimmy wore the costume of the young Jett Rink—jeans, denim shirt, boots, Stetson. His work going well, Jimmy at one point left the *Giant* set long enough to hurry over to another soundstage and fulfill a commitment he had made to film a television commercial for the National Safety Council. Because of his love of cars and racing, Dean had agreed to shoot the public-service announcement despite the fact that his Warner Bros. schedule had been hectic for the last eighteen months. Arriving on the set in costume, Jimmy brought with him one of his favorite props from *Giant,* the rope and the rock he needed to do the stunt Hinkle had taught him called the lasso trick. The commercial, shot in black and white, would be a short interview with Jimmy conducted in a nondescript office by the actor Gig Young. While Jimmy wore a cowboy outfit, Young was dressed in a plain dark suit. On screen, the contrast would be jolting, adding a surreal quality to the whole episode. That would be secondary, however, to the real focus of the commercial—Jimmy. What audiences saw as the two men spoke was vintage James Dean, for, even though he was supposed to be playing himself, Jimmy was acting every second the film rolled.

"Have you ever been in a drag race?" Young said after he and Jimmy had sat down next to each other in chairs.

"Are you kidding me?" Jimmy said. As part of the "business" of the scene, he smoked a cigarette.

"How fast will your car go?"

The camera held on Jimmy. He took the cigarette from his mouth. "Oh," he exhaled heavily, "in honest miles an hour, clocked, it'll run about"—a quick breath in—"hundred six, hundred seven."

Jimmy looked at Young. "You've won a few races, haven't you?" Young said dryly.

"Oh, one or two," Jimmy answered, cutting his eyes sheepishly.

On the set of *Giant*

"Where?"

"Well, I showed pretty good at Palm Springs." Jimmy rubbed his left eye before he rested his hand on the side of his face. "I ran at Bakersfield."

"We probably have a great many young people watching our show tonight," Young said, "and for their benefit I'd like your opinion about fast driving on the highway. Do you think it's a good idea?"

"That's a good point," Jimmy said. "I used to fly around quite a bit. I took a lot of unnecessary chances on the highway. And I studied racing and now I drive on the highway and I'm extra cautious 'cause no one knows what they're doing half the time." Jimmy shrugged his shoulders, then started playing with the rope. "You don't know what this guy is going to do—or the other one. On a track there are a lot of men who spend a lot of time developing rules and ways of safety. I find myself being very cautious on the highway. I don't have the urge to speed on the highway." The camera cut to Young as Jimmy continued to speak. "People say racing is dangerous, but I'll take my chances on the track any day than on a highway."

Jimmy briefly worked his lasso trick with the rope and the rock. Now it was time to go. "Well, Gig, I think I better take off."

Both men stood up, but before Jimmy could leave Young stopped him. "Wait a minute, Jimmy, one more question. Do you have any special advice for the young people driving?"

Then Jimmy looked straight into the camera.

"Take it easy driving," he said, waving both hands in front of him in little half shakes as if he were warning viewers to be careful. "The life you might save might be mine." In the line he stumbled over the two *mights* but not the *mine*. To punctuate the word he pointed to himself with one thumb.

His final gesture completed, Jimmy walked quickly out of the room and Young closed the door behind him.

*   *   *

A day or so later, Jimmy spoke with Lew Bracker, a friend who was an insurance agent, about a $100,000 life insurance policy he wanted to take out. He also brought up a subject clearly on his mind these days—the new Porsche Spyder. He couldn't wait to buy it, he said, and, once all his reshooting on *Giant* was done, get back on the track.

Jimmy kept his word about the car when on September 21 he went into Competition Motors and cut a deal with the company's owner, John von Neumann. For the tiny aluminum-bodied Spyder 550, whose serial number was 550-0055, Jimmy gave von Neumann his Porsche 356 Speedster as a trade-in and a check for three thousand dollars. The trade-in made the deal worth about seven thousand dollars—a lot of money, but worth it to Jimmy. Von Neumann had five 550s that he had imported from the Porsche factory in Germany where that year ninety had been built. A mere seventy-eight would be sold to the public. Made for the first time in 1954, the 550/1500 RS—the Spyder's official name—was a new model. Almost immediately, it had begun to dominate the racing events in which it was entered. With its ladder frame and a midship-mounted four-cam air-cooled four-cylinder engine, Jimmy's new 550 could easily hit its top speed of one hundred twenty miles an hour. Also, this particular car had widened brakes, just in case the driver had to stop quickly. It was said, in fact, that the car could stop on a dime. As Jimmy drove the Spyder away from Competition Motors, he was filled with pride. He had never spent his money on anything he wanted more.

These days Jimmy certainly didn't have to worry about money. At the moment Jane Deacy was finalizing a contract with MGM for Jimmy's appearance in *Somebody Up There Likes Me*. (He had already done wardrobe fittings for the picture although no starting date had been set.) In addition, Deacy had booked Jimmy for two major programs on NBC. He was to play the Welsh boy in "The Corn Is Green" on *Hallmark Hall of Fame*, a ninety-minute show that aired on Sun-

A publicity shot from *Giant*

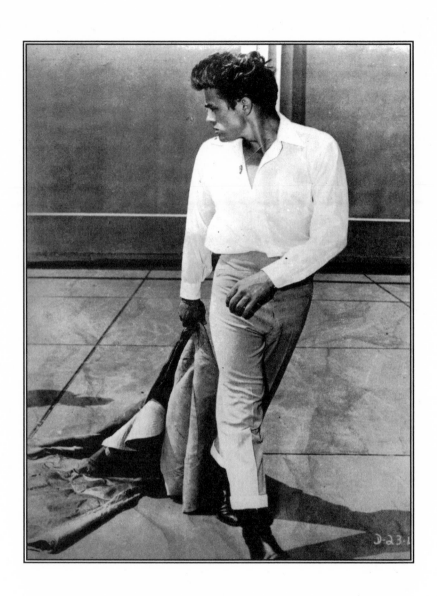

days, and the lead role in Ernest Hemingway's short story "The Battler," to be shown on a soon-to-debut TV anthology program, *Pontiac Presents Playwrights 56,* on October 18. Also, the producers of *The Perry Como Show* wanted Jimmy to come on the program and talk about his involvement in the filming of *Giant,* but no firm plans had been set for that appearance. While these jobs meant money and exposure for Jimmy right away, Deacy was about to shore up his long-term financial situation as well. She was scheduled to negotiate a new contract for him with Warner Bros. during the first week of October. Though he had earned the modest sums of ten thousand dollars for *East of Eden,* fifteen thousand dollars for *Rebel Without a Cause,* and twenty thousand dollars for *Giant,* it now looked as though Jimmy would be making, under the terms of his new contract, one hundred thousand dollars for every Warner Bros. picture he did. That was a staggering sum of money for 1955, but that's what Deacy thought she could get. In terms of salary, it would place him among the Hollywood elite. Jimmy could vividly remember his lean years in Los Angeles and New York. But those years were far behind him now. Today money was no object. He could afford the best Porsche had to offer.

On the night he bought his new Spyder, Jimmy took the car over to the Villa Capri, one of his favorite restaurants in Los Angeles. Years later, Patsy D'Amore, the restaurant's owner, would recall the evening. "That night—Jimmy just buy this car—seven thousand dollars he paid for it. Imagine! He pulled up like a bat out of hell and came running in, no necktie on. And he takes me out to show me the car. I didn't like it. I tell him he die in that car."

A day or so after he bought the Spyder, Jimmy took it to Compton so that George Barris, a highly regarded customizer, could add a few special touches to it. On the hood, the rear deck, and both doors, Barris painted 130, Dean's racing number. Then in script on the tail he painted "The Little Bastard," the name Jimmy had decided to give his car. A day or two later, Jimmy had a minor fender bender with a woman on Sunset Boulevard. To repair the slight damage to The Little Bastard, he took it back to Competition Motors.

It was around this time that Jimmy reached a decision about something that had been on his mind for a while. Now that he was on the verge of finishing up his reshooting on *Giant,* he would be free to drive again. There was a race up in Salinas on October 1, no more than a couple of weeks off. Though he had probably missed the deadline for entry, he would see if he could be worked into the field at the last minute. It had been some weeks since he had driven competitively and he couldn't wait to get behind the wheel in a race once again. Anyway, he had good feelings about Salinas, the small town in the northern part of the San Joaquin valley about three hundred miles north of Los Angeles, for it was there that he had shot part of *East of Eden.* The picture had established him as an actor. Maybe the race, if he won it, would establish him as a driver.

To make sure he was physically able to race, Jimmy went in to be examined by Dr. Irving Berman. On September 27, Berman wrote a letter to the Sports Car Club of America, Inc., in San Francisco to certify that he had given Jimmy a complete physical examination. Pronouncing Dean in "excellent" health, Berman reported that "his neuromuscular reflexes are all physiological," that "all organs and systems are normal," and that "he is therefore physically qualified to engage in competitive automotive racing."

In those final days of September, Jimmy drove the Porsche all over Los Angeles—to and from the studio, through the canyons, to the Villa Capri. He also visited with his family, since Marcus, Ortense, and his uncle, Charles Nolan, had come out from Indiana to spend some time with Winton. Mostly, though, he began to think about the upcoming race at Salinas.

Of all the people Jimmy knew who were involved with sports cars, perhaps the one he respected most was Rolf Weutherich. A twenty-

With Marcus, the kitten given to him by Elizabeth Taylor

In the final days

eight-year-old mechanic employed at Competition who had been trained at the Porsche factory in Zuffenhausen, he was nothing short of a world-class expert on cars, and because of this Jimmy had taken a special liking to him. As the day of the race in Salinas approached, Rolf told Jimmy that it was important for the Spyder to have at least five hundred miles on it before the race for the engine to be broken in properly. If Jimmy could put that many miles on it before the thirtieth, the day Jimmy had decided to drive up to Salinas for the race, he could tow the car. If the car hadn't gone that far, Jimmy would have to drive it to Salinas; the trip should finish breaking in the motor. The more Jimmy thought about it, the more he was about to conclude that driving the car to Salinas might be good for him too. Relatively unfamiliar with this Porsche model, Jimmy needed as much practice as he could get behind the wheel of the car, especially on the open road. Regardless of what happened, Rolf would be able to help Jimmy make up his mind at the last minute since, at Jimmy's request, he would be going to Salinas to work as his mechanic in the pit. Jimmy had also lined up two other friends—Bill Hickman, a stuntman, and Sandy Roth, a photographer who was taking pictures of Jimmy for *Collier's*—to go along as well, in case he needed someone to follow after him in the station wagon.

September 29 would be like most other days in his life recently although Jimmy did have plans to go to a party in Malibu that night. He put in some time at Warner Bros. where Lew Bracker, with whom he had been out palling around every night that week, showed up with papers for him to sign for his new life insurance policy. There was just one problem. If Jimmy died, Lew wanted to know, who should get the hundred thousand dollars? Jimmy had to name a beneficiary. "Make yourself the beneficiary," Jimmy told Lew. By law he couldn't, Lew explained, so they decided that Jimmy would think it over and tell him later.

That night, Jimmy took Marcus, the kitten Elizabeth Taylor had given him recently, over to Janette Miller, a friend who had agreed to keep it while he was gone. Along with vitamins and a Karo-syrup-and-evaporated-milk concoction he fed the kitten, Jimmy left instructions to take Marcus to the veterinarian the next week for his shots. Then Jimmy went to the Villa Capri for dinner. While he was there, he made a brief telephone call to a friend. After dinner he headed out to Malibu. Over the years, friends of Jimmy's would debate whether he actually went to the Malibu party. Some would say he did; others believed he didn't. There is evidence that he disappeared by himself on the night of the twenty-ninth. If he did go to the party, he probably also got into a disagreement with a friend who demanded that he be more open about his homosexuality. The friend must have been talking about all the dates on which Warner Bros. had been sending him lately. If nothing else, Jimmy could at least stop going on the dates. Wasn't he humiliated to be photographed with vapid Hollywood starlets? Did it not bother him that in the gossip columns the studio had him involved with one woman after another? No doubt Jimmy became angry with his friend because he knew his friend was right. He *did* feel cheapened by playing the Hollywood publicity game, but he did it anyway. He also had not stopped having homosexual sex even though he had broken up with Jack Simmons some time ago. As a friend of Dean's later revealed: "I knew a man—an intelligent, well-known composer—who told me one night over too many drinks that he went down on Dean in a speeding car on Mulholland Drive shortly before his death."

2. On the morning of September 30, 1955, Jimmy was awakened early, around 7:20, by Nikko Romanos, his landlord. Since July Jimmy had been living at 14611 Sutton Street in Sherman Oaks in the San Fernando Valley. For two hundred and fifty dollars a

month he rented a small log-cabin-style house that sat behind the larger house in which Romanos lived with his wife, Grace. This morning Nikko was just stopping by to check on the place. "Hello, Jimmy," Nikko shouted from the first floor in his thick Italian accent. Hungover from lack of sleep, Jimmy struggled up from the mattress on which he slept on the floor, walked to the balcony, and, swinging a leg over the rail, jumped to the main floor. Still wearing his pajama bottoms, he sat down and started banging on his bongo drums while he chatted with Nikko. After a few minutes, Nikko left and Jimmy, deciding not to go back to bed but to head on down to Competition, dressed for the day in blue slacks, a white T-shirt, a red windbreaker, shoes, and sunglasses. Ready for the trip to Salinas, he started packing the Ford station wagon. When he was done, he locked up the house and got in the Ford.

Leaving the house on Sutton Street behind, Jimmy drove the Hollywood Freeway as far as the Cahuenga exit. From there he cruised down North Vine, stopped briefly at Competition's Ventura Boulevard shop just to see what was going on, and finally arrived at a little after eight o'clock at the Competition location where he had bought his car. At Competition, Rolf was hard at work on Jimmy's Spyder, trying to get it ready for the race the next day. Jimmy wasted a couple of hours with Rolf until at a quarter to ten he was joined by Bill Hickman and Sandy Roth, who still planned on driving up to Salinas with him. Hickman would help out with the car (Jimmy often counted himself lucky to have as a friend a stunt-car driver for a major studio) and Roth would do what he had been doing now for weeks—shoot more photographs of Jimmy. In fact, there had been talk that after Salinas Jimmy and Roth would go on up to San Francisco where Roth would finally wrap up his *Collier's* photo-essay.

At ten, Jimmy's father and his uncle, Charles Nolan, arrived at Competition. Jimmy wanted to take his father for a ride in his new car but Winton wouldn't go. Finally Charles Nolan agreed to, after much cajoling, and Jimmy took him around the block two or three times. Shortly before noon, Jimmy drove his father and uncle in the station wagon through Hollywood to West Hollywood to Patsy's Pizza, located in the Farmer's Market on the corner of Fairfax Avenue and Third Street, so that the three of them could have lunch. No doubt Jimmy had picked Patsy's because the pizza parlor was owned by Patsy D'Amore, who also owned the Villa Capri. Over lunch, which went quickly since he had to get on the road, Jimmy tried to talk his uncle into going with him to Salinas, but the family had already decided what they were all going to do. Marcus and Ortense were heading back to Indiana that day and Charles Nolan planned to drive down to Mexico. Busy with his own life as always, Winton would stay in Los Angeles. Unable to convince anyone from his family to go with him to Salinas and watch him race, Jimmy drove them all back to Competition.

There, he sat in the station wagon for a bit while he told his father and uncle good-bye. As soon as his family left, Jimmy and Rolf turned their attention to the question of how the four of them would get to Salinas. They could all ride in the station wagon and tow the Spyder on a flatbed trailer Jimmy had borrowed. Or two could ride in the Ford and two in the Porsche. Since Jimmy had put only about two hundred and fifty miles on the car—nowhere near the five hundred Rolf had strongly suggested—it was decided that Jimmy would drive the Porsche and Rolf would ride with him. Sandy and Bill would follow after in the station wagon and pull the empty trailer. With this arrangement, Jimmy could also get some practice driving the Porsche on the open road under the supervision of his mechanic. Their plans made, the four men got in the cars and started off. When they stopped briefly for gas, Roth photographed them all. Once both cars were filled up, the four men headed out.

It was about 1:30.

*   *   *

The two cars sped down the Ventura Freeway to Sepulveda Boulevard, then to Route 99, on which they headed north, away from Los Angeles. Jimmy led the way, but the station wagon trailed fairly close behind, never falling back by more than four or five minutes. At around three, the four men stopped at Castaic Junction to have a snack at Tip's Diner. They didn't stay long. Soon they were back heading north on Route 99, Jimmy still ahead of the station wagon.

At about 3:30, somewhere south of Bakersfield, Jimmy hit a downgrade and got the Porsche up to sixty-five. When he did, he caught the eye of California Highway Patrol Officer Otie V. Hunter, sitting on the side of the road, who turned on his siren and pulled the Porsche over. Tall and husky, Hunter strolled up to Jimmy, who looked at him in the kneecaps from his seat in the Spyder. Hickman had stopped the station wagon behind the Porsche and watched as Jimmy tried to talk Hunter out of giving him a ticket. Jimmy explained that he was not going that fast. Other cars, even buses, had passed him on the highway doing eighty-five. Jimmy could just imagine what the press would make out of his getting a speeding ticket not two weeks after he had shot a commercial for the National Safety Council warning teenagers against driving fast on the highway. It did no good. As migrant workers harvesting onions in a field nearby stopped to watch, Hunter wrote Jimmy out a ticket for going sixty-five in a fifty-five-mile-an-hour zone. The ticket ordered Jimmy to appear in court on October 17, 1955, in Lamont. It also recorded the facts that the weather was "clear" and that the road conditions were "good." Hunter never recognized Jimmy even though Jimmy identified his employer as Warner Bros., told Hunter he was on his way to race in Salinas, and signed his name to the ticket. Jimmy was sure he had been given a ticket because he was driving a sports car, but then Hunter, once he had told Jimmy to take the rest of his trip more slowly, turned and walked back to the station wagon only to give Hickman a ticket too.

Back on Route 99, Jimmy continued north into Bakersfield. In the town, just large enough to be packed with traffic late on a Friday afternoon, Jimmy had to slow down to creep through red light after red light. As they had in Los Angeles and at other spots along the way, people stopped to stare at Jimmy. Which was not surprising. It wasn't often that a person saw a sports car like Jimmy's—no top, no bumpers, sleek, expensive-looking—come cruising through town, much less a Porsche Spyder 550. Outside of Bakersfield, Jimmy, happy to be out of traffic, drove much faster than he had up until now. More than once he pressed the accelerator all the way to the floor just to see how the car would respond. At Wasco, he turned left off Route 99 onto 466. It was getting late, some time before five o'clock. Jimmy had wanted to be in Salinas early that evening so he could get plenty of rest for the race the next day, particularly since he had been out the night before at the party in Malibu. He picked up the speed, driving west.

At Blackwell's Corners, located at the intersection of Route 466 and Highway 33, Jimmy glanced over at the parking lot of a gas station–restaurant and spotted a gray Mercedes 300SL that looked familiar, so he pulled off the road and stopped. As he had expected, the car belonged to Lance Reventlow, Barbara Hutton's nineteen-year-old son, who was also scheduled to race at Salinas. In the parking lot Jimmy and Lance chatted briefly while Rolf flagged down the station wagon, now following farther and farther behind as Jimmy drove faster. While he showed off his speeding ticket, Jimmy bragged to Lance that on one particular stretch he had gotten his new Porsche up to one hundred thirty. He also brought up the National Safety Council commercial he had made about speeding. Pretty ironic that he should do a commercial like that, wasn't it? Finally the two young men agreed to have dinner later that night in Paso Robles, a town about thirty-five miles east of where they were now. They could drive it in half an hour, or less if they went fast enough.

Sandy had gone inside and bought a bag of apples. When he offered Jimmy one from the bag, Jimmy took an apple and ate it as he finished up his conversation with Lance. Then Jimmy went in the station to use the men's room and buy a Coke. Back in the parking lot, he challenged a young man driving a Corvette to a race, but the young man wouldn't even think about it. The Porsche looked too fast for him. Jimmy didn't try to argue. Instead he and Rolf got back into the Spyder and started west on 466.

The sun was setting.

Jimmy sped on into the coming twilight. Despite the descending darkness, he had not yet turned on his headlights. He bore down on the road, entering into San Luis Obispo County and continuing on the narrow winding two-lane highway toward Polonia Pass. Then just west of Cholame, the next town coming up according to a sign they passed, Jimmy got behind a car that was moving considerably more slowly than he was. His instinct was to gun it and try to pass the car. But when he veered into the left lane and pulled up even with the car, he saw a Pontiac heading straight for him. Instantly Jimmy realized he was trapped. He could not move to his right because of the car he was passing, yet he was not going to be able to get around that car before he hit the Pontiac. All three cars kept moving. No one seemed to know what to do. Finally the Pontiac cut suddenly to its right and ran off the side of the road. This allowed Jimmy to speed ahead and pass the car. Jimmy was going so fast—somebody would say he had to have been doing a hundred and twenty although that was probably an exaggeration—that he could barely see the stunned looks on the faces of the family of four riding in the Pontiac.

In a way Jimmy and Rolf were lucky to be alive. They could have easily had a head-on collision with the Pontiac. They were no doubt feeling light-headed as they sped out of Polonia Pass toward the intersection of 466 and 41 where eastbound 466 could turn left into 41, which made the roads form a Y. Jimmy didn't know how fast he was going. He just drove on into the light gray of the approaching sunset.

Then in the left-hand lane coming at him he saw it—a huge tank of a car, a black-and-white Ford sedan that, as far as Jimmy could tell, was going to make a left off 466 onto 41. This meant, of course, that he would have to cross Jimmy's lane. If the driver of the Ford saw Jimmy, naturally he would wait until Jimmy passed before he made his turn onto 41. "That guy's gotta see us," Jimmy said to Rolf as they sped down the road. "He's got to stop." No sooner had Jimmy said those words than the sedan went through a series of moves that happened so quickly Jimmy had little chance to respond. The Ford began its left turn, straightened somewhat to end up facing Jimmy head-on in *his* lane, and started to stop. It was as if the driver of the Ford was positioning his car as a roadblock in Jimmy's lane. In the split second before he was going to hit the Ford, Jimmy chose not to use his brakes but floored the Porsche so that he could speed up quickly and swerve around the other car. This would have been the approach any well-trained sports car driver would have taken to avoid a wreck. Yet the geometry of the two moving objects was simply not right. Jimmy couldn't swerve away enough from the Ford to miss it. So the driver's side of the Spyder slammed into the driver's side of the Ford. To people driving nearby, the violent crash sounded like a small explosion. The Porsche careened off onto the shoulder of the road and came to a halt close to a telephone pole. The Ford, one huge mass of weight, slid on down the asphalt of 466, stopping eventually.

The force of the impact threw Rolf from the car into a field some distance away. Jimmy would have probably been thrown from the car too, but in the wreck his feet got stuck between the clutch and the brake pedals, so instead his body was slung over onto the passenger seat. When the Porsche had come to a halt, Jimmy's arms and legs lay awkward and limp. Slumped over the top of the door, his head hung loose; the collision had thrown Jimmy's head back violently, breaking his neck. Though Jimmy's chest had been impaled on the steering wheel, the broken neck would prove to be the injury that killed him. As Rolf lay on the ground, Jimmy struggled to breathe. His breaths were as faint as his fading pulse. Down where the Ford had slid to a stop, the driver of the car sat slumped over the steering wheel in a state of shock.

Two cars arrived at the wreck site at almost the same time. One was the car Jimmy had passed only seconds ago, nearly causing an accident. The driver of that car, John Robert White, an accountant from Pasadena, got out to look at the wreck. So did the driver of the other car. When White saw how badly Jimmy was hurt, he returned to his car and drove off to find a telephone. As the other motorist, Tom Frederick, began to look after Rolf and Jimmy, the driver of the Ford, who had somehow gotten out of his car, wandered about aimlessly. Within seconds, more cars stopped and people began to gather around Rolf and Jimmy. Before long, White returned. Then almost immediately a siren sounded off in the distance. In no time the ambulance arrived and Paul Moreno, its driver, and Collier Davison, his assistant, hopped out. They removed their two gurneys from the back of the ambulance, leaving one on the ground next to the car and rushing toward the two injured men with the other. About this time, Patrolman Ernie Tripke pulled up. Moments later, he was joined by Patrolman Ron Nelson. It was now twenty past six, twenty-one minutes after Tripke had first heard the accident reported on his car radio. The two police officers set up flares before they joined Moreno to see how they could help attend to the two injured men.

Soon Sandy Roth and Bill Hickman arrived. Years later Roth still remembered what he had seen on that late September afternoon. "As I drew near I saw what I thought, at first, was a roadblock," Roth would say. "I saw a strange car. Neither that car nor the passenger seemed damaged. Then I saw the Porsche. It was smashed, completely. Rolf was lying on the ground, crying: 'Jimmy, Jimmy!' through bleeding jaws and shattered teeth. Rolf's legs and arms were broken.

I saw Jimmy. He was thrown back behind the wheel and I knew he was dead. His neck was broken. There was very little blood on him, only a small cut where his eyeglasses had been."

Roth may have been sure Jimmy was already dead, but Moreno believed he was still just barely alive. Rushing to the Porsche, Hickman helped Moreno pull Jimmy from the mangled mass of aluminum. Then Bill held Jimmy's warm body while Moreno and his assistant got ready to carry him to the ambulance on a gurney. "When I first got to him, I thought he was alive," Hickman would recall, "because there seemed to be air coming from his nostrils. His forehead was caved in and so was his chest." While Bill cradled Jimmy close to him, Roth stood back from the wreck and started to snap photographs. Even as Jimmy approached death in Hickman's arms, if he was not already dead, he was being captured on film. One person or another had been taking pictures of Jimmy for most of his adult life. Somehow it seemed appropriate, though certainly morbid, that a photographer was on hand to record the moment for history.

Eventually Moreno and his assistant placed Jimmy on a gurney and carried him to the ambulance. Next they put Rolf on a separate gurney and slid him into the ambulance beside Jimmy. Finally, with its siren wailing, the ambulance set out for War Memorial Hospital in Paso Robles. Hickman followed right behind in the Ford. On the way to the hospital, the ambulance was sideswiped by another car. Moreno pulled the ambulance over long enough to see that the minor accident had caused little more than a dent in the fender. Then he got back behind the wheel and headed on to Paso Robles.

At the hospital, Dr. Robert Bossert, the physician on duty, had been alerted by radio to be ready. As soon as the ambulance lurched to a stop at the emergency room entrance, Moreno and Davison, met by Bossert, slid Rolf out of the car and carried him into the hospital. "You better check the fellow in the ambulance first," Moreno told Bossert. Climbing inside, Bossert examined Jimmy. He could tell sim-

The crash site

Dean is carried to the awaiting ambulance. Turnupseed's Ford
sits in the near distance.

ply by looking that Jimmy had a broken neck. He confirmed this by moving Jimmy's head back and forth; when he did, the bones in Jimmy's neck made a faint grating noise. Without even having Moreno remove Jimmy from the ambulance, Bossert pronounced Jimmy dead on arrival. If he had not died instantly at the time of the crash, Bossert said, he had died very soon after that. An attending physician at the hospital would later tell the press that Jimmy had died at about 5:30 as a result of a broken neck, that he had several broken bones and lacerations over his whole body, and that he had been left "terribly battered" by the force of the collision. Bossert would put his findings in a written report. "[Dean] was dead," Bossert wrote, "and gross examination revealed fractured neck, multiple fractures of forearms, fractured leg and numerous cuts and bruises about the face and chest. I believe that he died of these injuries and that death came at the time, or shortly after the accident."

Once Bossert had gotten out of the back of the ambulance, Moreno shut the door and drove over to Kuehl Funeral Home. Paul Merrick, the coroner and sheriff for Paso Robles, would eventually examine Jimmy's body. On the death certificate, Merrick described the disease or condition directly leading to death as "Broken neck." Antecedent causes included "multiple fractures of upper and lower jaw, multiple fractures of left and right arm, internal injuries." The time of death was set at "5:45 P.M." In addition, Merrick stated that the accident took place in the town of Cholame and in the county of San Luis Obispo. The accident's exact location was "One mile east Cholame at Highway 466 and 41 junction." Kuehl Funeral Home would handle the funeral services. Burial would take place in Grant Memorial Park in Marion, Indiana.

Back at the hospital, doctors were working frantically on Rolf, who had numerous cuts and broken bones and a leg fractured so severely that as the doctors took him into surgery they were not sure if they could save it. Meanwhile, at the accident site, Ron Nelson and other members of the California Highway Patrol were trying to sort out what exactly had happened. Quickly they determined that the driver of the Ford was Donald Turnupseed. A four-year veteran of the navy who had served on a hospital ship during the Korean War, he was now, at twenty-three, a freshman electrical engineering major at California Polytechnic Institute. Turnupseed had been on his way from school, he said, to spend the weekend with his parents at their home in Tulare. Dean had died and Rolf had sustained life-threatening injuries—in the end Rolf survived and the doctors were able to save his leg—but Turnupseed had suffered no more than a few cuts and bruises. He didn't even need to go to the hospital, although eventually a doctor would examine him to make sure he was all right. He was, however, in a state of shock. As he wandered about the scene of the accident and as he talked to highway patrol officers, he kept mumbling to himself over and over, "I never saw him. I never saw him."

According to Turnupseed, sometime between 5:30 and 6:00, he had been traveling east on Highway 466 when he reached the Y-turn onto 41 that he needed to take to go to Tulare. He had made the left-hand turn from his lane, that is to say he cut in front of Jimmy, because he never saw the gray sports car coming, or so he contended. On the surface, this made sense. After all, it was twilight, the time of day when the sky goes gray, almost the same color of Dean's Porsche. Low-slung and moving fast, the Spyder had blended into the approaching twilight. It didn't help matters that Dean had not yet turned on his headlights, which Turnupseed would have surely been able to see. In Turnupseed's version of the event, Jimmy's Porsche simply slammed into his Ford. The first detail Turnupseed remembered seeing was the passengers in the Porsche throwing up their arms in front of their faces to shield themselves from the crash.

There is no doubt Dean was speeding, though no one knows exactly how fast. The family of four he had run off the road just before the accident would swear he was doing at least a hundred. Others who clocked his time from Blackwell's Corners to the wreck site would guess he was going about eighty at the time he came down the hill heading toward Turnupseed's Ford. Most probably, he was traveling faster than fifty-five, the legal speed limit. Even so, what Turnupseed would never address fully was why after he started his left-hand turn he had angled back to the right and slammed on his brakes in the middle of Jimmy's lane. His actions imply strongly that he *did* see the car coming. Otherwise, why would he veer the Ford back slightly to the right? Why would he slam on his brakes? Why did he not simply carry out his turn unaltered? The fact that he did not go through with the turn he had started indicated that something made him change his mind. That something, more than likely, was a glimpse of Jimmy's Porsche heading right at him.

So this is what seems to have happened. Traveling east on 466, Turnupseed slowed down to make his left-hand turn onto 41. After he cut his steering wheel, he may have seen at the last instant a gray flash of a car speeding toward him. His initial instinct seems to have been to cut his wheel back to the right and try to get out of the way. But it was too late. The car was too close. Instinctively he slammed on his brakes, as almost any motorist would if he was about to be in an accident. It was probably this final action, his slamming on his brakes, that set up the Ford as a sort of metal wall for the Porsche to slam into. If Turnupseed had cut his wheel to the right and hit his gas pedal, *not his brake,* quite possibly the Ford and the Porsche could have barely missed each other.

Turnupseed would always say that he never saw the Porsche coming before it actually hit his car. He was probably smart in sticking to his story. If he had seen the Porsche and had not done everything in his power to get out of Dean's way, he could have been charged with manslaughter. After all, even though there was no question that he was speeding, Dean *was* in the lane he was supposed to be in. What's

Dean's Porsche after it had been towed to a junkyard

more, since the junction did not have a stop sign, he was required to do nothing more than what he had done: continue driving down the road. It was Turnupseed who had made the improper turn into incoming traffic. It was Turnupseed who was in the wrong lane. It was Turnupseed who did not succeed in maneuvering his way out of the path of the Porsche. No doubt Turnupseed was guilty of committing a simple human error. If he had seen the car coming at the last split second, he probably just panicked as anyone in that situation would have, and chose the worst series of moves to make to prevent an accident from happening. Then again, he was young. He was not a professional driver. He was just a college student on his way home for the weekend when he found himself involved in a wreck that would eventually become one of the most notorious of the twentieth century.

In the end Turnupseed was lucky. Because Dean died, an inquest had to be held. But no one connected with the investigation of the accident for that inquest faulted Turnupseed. The wreck was blamed solely on Dean because he was driving too fast. Highway Patrol Officer Nelson would submit the following accident report: "I received a call at 5:59 P.M. It occurred on US 466 at the intersection of 41, September 30, 1955. It was a side-swipe, head-on collision. There were two persons injured and one killed. Number One injured was Donald Gene Turnupseed, driver of Vehicle Number One. Number Two injured was Rolf Wütherich [sic], a passenger in the Dean car. The dead was James Byron Dean, dead-on-arrival at the hospital." *A sideswipe head-on collision. Injured was Donald Gene Turnupseed. Injured was Rolf Weutherich. Dead was James Byron Dean.*

That night, Sal Mineo, Natalie Wood, Nick Adams, and Dick Davalos were having dinner in a restaurant in New York City not long after James Dean had been pronounced dead in California. At one point during their meal, the conversation turned to Jimmy, the friend they all had in common. Someone mentioned that Jimmy couldn't wait to start racing the Porsche he had just bought. If Jimmy doesn't slow down, someone else said, he's going to be in a serious accident within a year. Obviously the dinner party did not know that even as they spoke their portent had already come true. They wouldn't find out until the next morning when the radio and the newspapers picked up the story. Dean's death permanently affected the lives of his four friends who were having dinner that night in New York City, yet no friend of Dean's would remember September 30, 1955, more than Roth and Hickman. "The last time I saw him," Roth would recall, "Jimmy was feeling wonderful. He'd just gotten the car and he was thrilled. It was the first time he had a break, a period free from moviemaking for a long time." Hickman's recollections would be much more poignant. "In those final days, racing was what he cared about most," he said two decades after the accident. "I had been teaching him things like how to put a car in four-wheel drive, but he had plenty of skill of his own. If he had lived, he might have become a champion driver. I'm sure I was his closest friend [in Los Angeles], but I never really knew him that well. Sometimes I think I didn't know him at all. We had a running joke: he'd call me 'Big Bastard' and I'd call him 'Little Bastard' "—the reason Jimmy named his Spyder what he did. "I never stop thinking about those memories."

In the days and weeks following his death, friends remembered Jimmy's own thoughts about dying. "In a certain sense I am [fatalistic]," Jimmy once said in a radio interview with Jack Shafer. "I don't exactly know how to explain it, but I have a hunch there are some things in life that we just can't avoid. They'll happen to us probably because we're built that way—we simply attract our own fate . . . make our own destiny. . . . I think I'm like the Aztecs in that respect too. With their sense of doom, they tried to get the most out of life while life was good. And I go along with them on that philosophy. I don't mean that 'eat, drink and be merry for tomorrow we die' idea, but something a lot deeper and more valuable. I want to live as intensely as I can. Be as useful and helpful to others as possible, for one thing. But live for myself as well. I want to feel things and experiences right down to their roots . . . enjoy the good in life while it is good."

3. On Saturday, October 1, 1955, the banner headline of the *Marion Leader-Tribune* read "James Dean Is Killed in Automobile Wreck," with a subheadline that said "Fairmount Man Died in Traffic Accident in West." That's how most people in Marion and Fairmount learned that Jimmy Dean had died, if they had not already heard through normal gossip channels. On the night of the accident, the news had filtered through Hollywood, but it had also reached Fairmount.

Soon after Dean was pronounced dead, an operator at War Memorial Hospital telephoned Warner Bros. where a night watchman took the news—James Dean had been killed in a car wreck—and called Henry Ginsberg. Immediately Ginsberg put in a call to Dick Clayton. He passed the news on to Jane Deacy, who had just checked into the Château Marmount in Los Angeles so that she could begin renegotiating Dean's Warner Bros. contract the following week. Clayton decided to drive over to Winton Dean's house to break the news to Winton before he heard it from someone else, or, even worse, on the radio. While Clayton spoke to Winton, Ginsberg contacted other people, among them George Stevens. Stevens and several actors were sitting in a screening room at Warner Bros. watching part of a rough cut of *Giant* when Ginsberg's call came in. Stevens spoke on the telephone. As soon as he hung up, he had the screening-room lights turned on and announced to the actors, "I've just been given the news that Jimmy Dean has been killed." One of the actors in the room was Elizabeth Taylor. "There was an intake of breath," Taylor would one day write. "No one said anything. I couldn't believe it; none of us could. So several of us started calling newspapers, hospitals, police, and morgue. The news was not general at that time. After maybe two hours the word was confirmed." Taylor took Dean's death hard. The next day she threw up in her dressing room; then she broke down weeping and almost passed out. Finally she had to be hospitalized.

Two people who did not know about the death on Friday night, or, for that matter, even on Saturday after the story hit the newspapers, were Marcus and Ortense Winslow. Following their month-long visit to Los Angeles, the Winslows set out for Indiana that Friday as planned at around the same time Jimmy headed for Salinas. So when the accident took place, the Winslows were on the road themselves. At some point along the way, something odd happened to Marcus. As he was driving down the road, either Friday night or Saturday morning, an announcer came on the radio and started to report a story about a young actor who had been killed in a car accident. Suddenly, before the announcer could give the details of the story, before he could describe the accident or name the actor, Marcus reached down and switched off the radio. In the back of his mind, he had a feeling that the dead young actor could have been Jimmy. If it was, Marcus did not want to know anything about it until he got home. As it happened, Marcus and Ortense reached Fairmount early Monday evening. By then, almost everyone in town knew about the death. Their daughter Joan met them at the farm and told them the news. Inside, Marcus reached Winton on the telephone in Los Angeles. Winton had wanted to bury Jimmy next to Mildred in the cemetery in Marion— that's why Dean's death certificate read the way it did—but Marcus felt strongly about burying Jimmy in Park Cemetery in Fairmount. With little prodding, about as much as it took for him to give up Jimmy when he was nine, Winton agreed to let Marcus bury him where he wanted. Winton would accompany Jimmy's body back on the flight to Indianapolis. Marcus would start making plans for the funeral, which, they decided, was to be held on Saturday.

*　*　*

At 10:17 on Tuesday night, an ambulance from Hunt's Funeral Home met the airplane carrying James Dean's body in Indianapolis. The body was taken to Hunt's, located on Main Street in Fairmount, where by Thursday night it was laid in state. Many people came to view the body, which proved not to be possible since the casket remained closed. Almost all of the visitors were from Indiana, although the family did expect, the local newspapers reported, people from New York and Hollywood to come in on the weekend for the funeral. A rumor began to circulate around Fairmount that several stars were flying in, maybe even Elizabeth Taylor.

On that same day, the *Fairmount News* ran as its lead story "James Dean Killed As Result of California Car Accident." After a subheadline, "Fairmount Is Stunned To Learn of Tragedy Which Claimed Native Son; Head-on Collision Near Intersection Causes Fatality Friday," the article detailed the basic facts of the story. It concluded with what amounted to an apology for the way many townspeople had thought about Dean through the years. "Jimmy Dean contributed a lot in the 24 short years he lived," the article stated. "A great many people, who didn't understand him, called Jimmy eccentric. Perhaps he was. But then again, when a person becomes so wrapped up in something he forgets everything else but that one thing. When he lets off steam it is apt to be outside the regular bounds of activity, according to the measure of society. His homefolks understood him, though. And they'll miss him."

True or not, on Saturday, October 8, Dean's homefolks turned out en masse for his funeral. Fairmount had never before been the site of a gathering so large. Because the Fairmount Friends Church held only six hundred, people lined up early for the service, scheduled to start at two o'clock in the afternoon. In no time, every seat was taken. The remaining crowd, another twenty-five hundred, flowed out into the street in front of the church. The Winslows had decided to have

The grave site

the funeral at the Fairmount Friends Church, instead of Back Creek, because it was much larger. Still, since a mob was expected, speakers had been wired up to broadcast the service to the people who would have to stand outside. To conduct the services, the Winslows had chosen Xen Harvey, the local minister who had spoken at Jimmy's graduation, and James DeWeerd, now the minister at the Cadle Tabernacle in Indianapolis. The *Fairmount News* had found newsworthy the method by which DeWeerd would actually get to the funeral. "Dr. DeWeerd, who has a telecast at Cincinnati shortly before services begin at 2 o'clock," the newspaper reported, "will be flown in the private plane of Buford Cadle to Marion Airport and is scheduled to arrive there at 1:45. He will be met by a state police patrol car and be driven to the Friends Church." In the end DeWeerd's arrival would cause more of a stir than anyone else's. While Elizabeth Taylor, Edna Ferber, and the cast of *Giant* sent flowers, they did not attend the service. Only Henry Ginsberg and Steven Brooks, a Warner Bros. publicist, traveled to Fairmount. Nearly all of the estimated three thousand people who came to Dean's funeral were from Indiana. Even so, it was a crowd so huge—the largest in Grant County's history, not just Fairmount's—that thirty policemen were needed to direct traffic.

Shortly before two o'clock on the afternoon of October 8, the hearse pulled up in front of the Fairmount Friends Church and the casket containing the body of James Dean was carried in by the young men the Winslows had picked to be pallbearers. They were Paul Smith, Robert Pulley, Whitey Rust, Robert Middleton, James Fulkerson, and Rex Bright, all friends of Dean's from high school. Inside the church, the Deans sat behind the Winslows in the front pews. Like everyone else, they watched as the casket, still closed, was put into place. Then the service began. In his eulogy DeWeerd dwelt on the past. According to DeWeerd, as the *Fairmount News* would quote him, Jimmy "was not a problem boy but simply a boy with problems who knew how to seek council [sic] from men older and wiser than himself." DeWeerd continued: "Dean's life should be a lesson that what we put into our memory no one can take away. He was wealthy with memories in his short life." In closing, DeWeerd became philosophical. "The only worthwhile things are the things that outlast life here," he said. "Fame, wealth, and pleasure are false goals. [Jimmy's] in the hand of a just and merciful God and we are content to leave him there." Next, Harvey spoke. Calling his eulogy "The Life of James Dean—a Drama in Three Acts," Harvey described Dean's death as "only the end of Act Two and the beginning of Act Three." "The career of James Dean has not ended," Harvey concluded. "It has just begun. And remember, God Himself is directing the production."

Following the ceremony, most of the three thousand people went to Park Cemetery to watch the burial. There, at the open grave, they found another five hundred people who, sure they couldn't get into the church, had bypassed the funeral and come directly to the cemetery. When the burial was over, the crowd finally broke up. Throughout the rest of the afternoon, a steady stream of people, about two hundred in all, dropped by the Winslow farm to pay their respects to the family. At one point Marcus was standing in the barnyard chatting with friends when Henry Ginsberg and Steven Brooks came up to tell him they were leaving to catch their plane. Marcus stared at them. "I don't want another damn Valentino," he said flatly. Brooks agreed with Ginsberg that Dean wouldn't be made into another Valentino. "When will all this die down?" Marcus wanted to know. "Maybe in a couple of months," one of the men from Warner Bros. had said.

In the coming days, it became apparent that, no matter what anyone from Warner Bros. thought, "all this" would not die down "in a couple of months." Within days of the funeral, the *Fairmount News* printed a special edition. On the front page, an editorial read: "Because of the overwhelming demand for this week's issue of the *Fairmount News*, which contains exclusive material concerning the brief, brilliant career of James Dean, we have sold all of our regular copies, even though we printed several hundred extra. Consequently, we decided to publish this special edition to try and meet the public's demand. We, as members of the staff, would like to take this opportunity of expressing our sympathy to the bereaved family of Jim Dean. Words can not begin to express emotions during periods of time such as this but Jim Dean and his influence on Fairmount will never be forgotten." On that same page, an essay by James DeWeerd appeared. It read in part:

A native son who startled the nation with a brilliant flash of genius was brought back home this week for last rites. His brief career was as bright as a meteor which flows like a golden tear down the dark cheeks of night. . . .

It is in the grass roots of Grant County from which he made his start that the body of this restless youth has been returned to rest.

James Dean's path, to those of us who knew him best, was steep and rugged and was covered with sandpaper instead of velvet. As he said in a letter to a friend, "We are impaled on a crook of conditioning. A fish that is in the water has no choice that he is. Genius would have it that he swim in sand. We are fish and we drown. We remain in one world and wonder. The fortunate are taught to ask why. No one can answer."

Several days later the Associated Press reported that James Dean's estate, valued at $105,000, mostly because of the life insurance policy he had taken out shortly before his death, had named as administrators Carl Coulter and William Gray. They were selected by Winton Dean, who had been established by the Superior Court of California to be his son's, to quote the Associated Press, "only direct heir." Through the years, critics would observe how ironic it was that the man who did more than anyone to keep James Dean from becoming an actor would finally end up being the one person who benefited most financially from Dean's decision to ignore his advice.

On October 11, 1955, a jury headed by foreman D. H. Orcutt met in the courthouse of the county of San Luis Obispo as part of a coroner's inquest. They listened to evidence presented by Assistant District Attorney Harry Murphy. They also heard a lengthy examination of Donald Turnupseed, who continued to insist that he never saw Dean's car coming. Then the jury deliberated and concluded that Turnupseed bore none of the blame for the wreck that killed James Dean. In short, even though Turnupseed's Ford was in the process of skidding to a stop in the middle of Dean's lane when the two cars collided, the jury ruled that the event that had caused Dean's death was an accident. Specifically the coroner's inquest report read:

We find the deceased was named James Dean and that he came to his death on the 30th day of September, 1955, at Cholame in the County of San Luis Obispo, State of California by injuries received in an accident at the intersection of highways 41 and 466, according to the evidence presented, in a two car collision. We find no indication that James Dean met death through any criminal act of another, and that he died of a fractured neck and other injuries received.

Valentino
Redux

1. As of October 1955, James Dean was considered little more than a promising young actor with exceptional potential. He was not, by any means, famous. At Warner Bros., a steady trickle of fan mail came in for him, but that was it—a trickle. This made sense. So far in his career, he had appeared on Broadway twice; acted in some two dozen television shows, a handful of which had brought him minor recognition in the press; and co-starred in one picture, *East of Eden,* in which he was given second billing under Julie Harris. Only with the release of *East of Eden* did he get his first real burst of publicity—fan magazine articles, mentions in national gossip columns, short but enthusiastic write-ups in magazines like *Look, Life, Vogue,* and *Cosmopolitan,* and a brief profile in *The New York Times.* And he *had* attracted attention. Witness this from François Truffaut, writing in *Cahiers du Cinéma:* "James Dean . . . *is* the cinema in the same sense as Lillian Gish, Chaplin, Ingrid Bergman. James Dean has succeeded in giving commercial viability to a film"—*East of Eden*—"which would otherwise scarcely have qualified, in breathing life into an abstraction, in interesting a vast audience in moral problems treated in an unusual way." Still, Dean had not generated the volume of publicity he needed to become well known. It certainly didn't compare to the press coverage that followed his death, a portion of which was almost hysterical in tone. If Dean was a rising young actor with a potentially spectacular career ahead of him when he died, he had become eighteen months later, after the media blitz that resulted from the accident and the release of *Rebel Without a Cause* and *Giant,* one of the most idolized actors in America. Not since the death of Rudolph Valentino a quarter century before had the American public become so obsessed with a dead actor.

Even more strange, the myth that formed around Dean in 1955 and 1956 did not fade away as the years passed, nor did it confine itself to the United States. During the fifties and sixties, Dean's fame grew around the world, especially in England, France, Germany, Holland, Italy, Spain, Sweden, Finland, and Japan. By the 1980s, he had become, along with Elvis Presley and Marilyn Monroe, one of the three most famous American popular cultural figures, an astonishing feat for an actor who had made only three pictures in a career much shorter than either Presley's or Monroe's. "If a man can bridge the gap between life and death," Dean had said to Bill Bast, "if he can live on after he's died. . . . To me the only success, the only greatness . . . is in immortality." In the eighteen months before his death, James Dean created a body of work, no matter how slight it might have been, that gave him the chance to achieve immortality. In his three film performances, he was so original in his creative aspirations and so near perfect in the execution of his craft that he created pieces of art that would last long after his death.

The extraordinary reaction to Dean's death started with his obituaries. Picked up by both the Associated Press and the United Press International, the story about the promising young actor killed in a car wreck was wired to newspapers all over America. Many papers devoted ma-

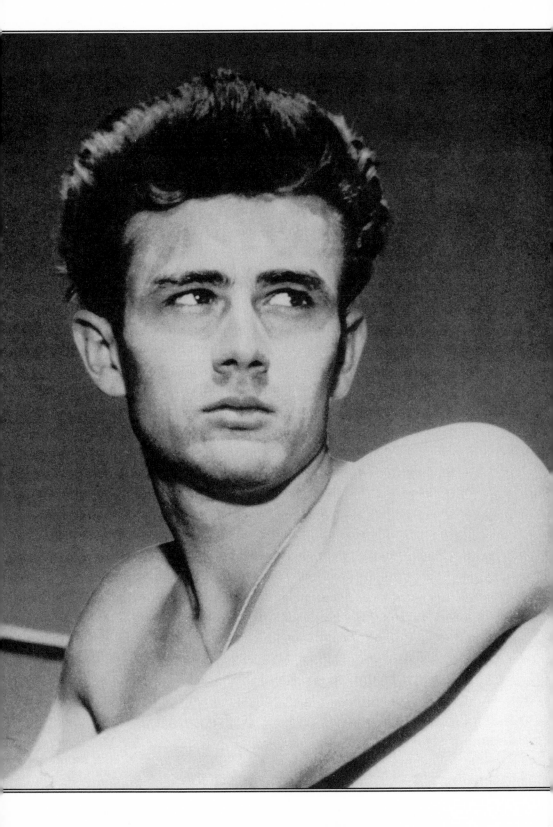

jor space to the story; some put it on the front page. In "James Dean Killed in Crash of Sports Car in California," the *Providence Journal* described Dean as an actor "who shot to film prominence with the leading role in John Steinbeck's *East of Eden*." In "Film Star James Dean Dies in Head-on Crash," the *New York Journal American* stated that "Hollywood is stunned today over the tragic auto crash death of brilliant young actor James Dean." In "Death of Star James Dean In Crash Stuns Hollywood," the *New York Post* said that "James Dean, the spectacular young movie star who'd been forbidden to indulge his sports car craze while working on a film was dead today after a head-on crash." Even *The New York Times*, which rarely reports the death of unestablished actors, ran an obituary. "James Dean, Film Actor, Killed in Crash of Auto," a write-up illustrated by a still shot from *East of Eden* in which Dean never looked more youthful, noted the mere facts, but, even so, the piece was significant. By running it, the *Times* seemed to be endorsing Dean's importance as an actor.

The next week, following the *Times'* lead, *Time* and *Newsweek* reported Dean's death, an almost unheard-of development for an actor with his modest credentials. While *Time* called Dean the "most promising young cinemactor of 1955," *Newsweek* said his "portrayal of a brooding, inarticulate adolescent in the movie *East of Eden* [had] rocketed him to stardom." Almost every article of any length compared Dean to Marlon Brando. One paper printed Dean's standard reply. "When a new actor comes along, he's always compared to someone else," Dean was quoted as saying. "Brando was compared to Montgomery Clift, Clift to someone else, Barrymore to Booth and so forth. I can only do the best kind of job I can—realistic acting. They can compare me to W. C. Fields if they want to." Even in his death notices, the line of descent was being established: Montgomery Clift, Marlon Brando, James Dean. By dying, Dean had been elevated, on the basis of just one picture no less, to the best of his generation.

Considering the tone and sheer number of the obituaries, Warner

Bros. executives knew they were going to have to deal with a unique situation. For months, the company had been planning for the November 1 release of *Rebel Without a Cause*. Naturally the entire publicity campaign had been based on the fact that when the picture came out Dean would be alive to promote it. After a series of meetings, the studio's executives decided to make only two small changes in the advertising campaign. Obviously Dean would no longer be referred to in the present tense in all press material. Second, the studio would drop from its newspaper ads the line "The overnight sensation of *East of Eden* becomes the star of the year!" Otherwise, Warner Bros. would go ahead with its advertising campaign as planned and hope that its staff would be able to handle the predicament of releasing a picture in which the star with whom the audiences were supposed to identify was dead.

In late October, the advertising campaign began when Warner Bros. ran a two-page spread in *Variety*. Illustrated by six still shots from the picture, all of which featured Dean prominently, the ad called *Rebel* "Warner Bros.' challenging drama of today's teenage violence." Referring to Dean's character, it said: "He was new on the block, the pretty girl belonged to the leader of the gang, and the leader of the gang called him 'chicken' to his face. THIS IS THE WAY A TEEN-WAR STARTS!" But the ad's most important detail appeared to be tagged on as an afterthought. "Sneak L.A. showing had audience completely spellbound!" a tiny inset box revealed. "Deafening applause at finish and all comments 100% raves! Showmen, you've got a sensation." Studios routinely hype their pictures, but this ad was unusually accurate. Preview audiences *had* been extremely responsive to the picture. Only days before, on October 11, at the Paramount Theatre in Los Angeles, an audience applauded on and off throughout the screening. "[The preview] was very impressive," Henry Ginsberg wrote to Marcus Winslow after seeing it, "and of course Jimmy's performance was outstanding. . . . I phoned a few people in the Press Department to get the reaction of the reviewers and the public who were present. All were unanimous in their praise of Jimmy's fine work." It was only a matter of time to see if critics and audiences across the country would respond the same way.

Warner Bros. didn't have to wait long. Almost all reviews were favorable; many of them praised Dean lavishly. In *Saturday Review,* Arthur Knight contended that Dean "reveals completely the talent latent in his *East of Eden* performance." The *New York Daily News* claimed Dean was in "complete control of his character." *Variety* went so far as to call Dean "a talent which might have touched the heights." Of the few negative reviews, one was Bosley Crowther's in *The New York Times.* In it Crowther accused Dean of "imitating Marlon Brando," a tendency that may "be a subtle commentary but it grows monotonous." But audiences ignored reviews like Crowther's. Instead they responded so enthusiastically to the picture, but mostly to Dean, that it became clear to Warner Bros. that the picture was going to be nothing short of a phenomenon.

What about Dean's Jim Stark caused audiences to react the way they did? From the opening scene that runs behind the credits, when Dean curls up in the fetal position on a sidewalk and plays with his toy monkey, he is vulnerable, rebellious. Previously, Hollywood leading men, actors like Gary Cooper in *High Noon* or Humphrey Bogart in *Casablanca* or John Wayne in any of his pictures, projected the image of being strong, independent men who got whatever they wanted in life, *when* they wanted it. Not Jim Stark. In the first part of the picture, Jim is a confused young man who hates his parents, despises authority of any kind, but wants desperately to fit into the world around him. If Wayne and Cooper personified action, Dean, in *Rebel,* personified *re*action. He doesn't shape his world; it molds him. Finally, when Judy and Plato become central figures in Jim's life, which happens as the main story line of the picture unfolds, he softens and becomes more sympathetic. By the end of the picture, as he tries to save Plato from his seemingly inevitable death, the audience pulls for Jim so strongly that it empathizes with him when the catastrophe finally happens: The police shoot Plato on the observatory steps and he dies. Jim Stark looks at Plato lying on the concrete—his socks, one red and one black, do not match—and he begins to cry. Since the boys have known each other for less than twenty-four hours, Jim is weeping not so much for Plato as for the very loss of innocence.

While they sat in darkened movie theatres all across America, audiences identified with this emotion. Watching Dean's beautiful alluring face flicker on the screen, they too mourned a loss—his. A person couldn't see this picture without being aware that each scene in it contained a dead man, that he was killed just weeks earlier in a tragic (and probably avoidable) car accident, and that he was only twenty-four years old when he died. It created an eerie, otherworldly feeling. It was as if James Dean was speaking from the afterworld, and his audience listened to every word he said. "We were watching," Joy Williams would write, "the intense, doomed performance of a dead youth, a myth, the myth of those who would wish to see themselves dead without dying. Dean was dead, predead, dead upon our discovery of him. His vivid presence projected a fathomless absence. It was thrilling."

At the time of the picture's release, a teenage girl pointed out another key aspect of Dean's appeal: What he was saying reflected the feeling of many young people. "To us, Dean was a symbol of the fight to make a niche for ourselves in the world of adults," she wrote. "Something in us that is being sat on by convention and held down was, in Dean, free for all the world to see." Another teenage girl put it more poetically. "Oh Jimmy, we love your meteor spirit, lighting a dark sky too briefly. That spirit, courageous, rebellious, proud and yet lost and gentle and lovable; the essence of tormented youth—of a generation to which we too belong, and which we can understand."

*   *   *

On November 25, *Collier's* ran Sanford Roth's photographic essay on Dean. In an accompanying article entitled "The Late James Dean," Roth wrote: "His death was front-page news. But the stories were something more than a tribute to a newcomer whose career stopped at the edge of greatness. They were also testimony to the pressures that today keep youngsters like Jimmy in constant warfare with the status quo." Then there were the photographs: Dean twirling a pistol on the set of *Giant;* Dean lassoing Elizabeth Taylor; and "the last picture taken of Jimmy alive"—Dean driving down the highway in The Little Bastard. Although it was interesting in itself, the *Collier's* spread only served to focus attention on what was becoming obvious: Dean had captured the imagination of a growing audience of adoring fans.

In the weeks after his death, fans in New York and Los Angeles ransacked locations where he was known to have lived, searching for any memento of him. They mailed him letters in care of Warner Bros.; during the fall as many as several hundred letters a week poured into the studio, dramatically more than the handful a week he had received before his death. They sent flowers to his grave in Fairmount, especially on the thirtieth of the month. At times, local flower shops could barely keep up with the orders. But mostly they went to see his picture. In the fall of 1955, all across the country, teenagers lined up to see *Rebel Without a Cause.* Some fans saw it twenty or thirty times—or more. Before Dean, Hollywood had not witnessed a dead star worshiped to this extent since Valentino.

In due course the entertainment business establishment recognized Dean for this achievement. The Hollywood Foreign Press Association voted him a special posthumous Golden Globe Award. The French magazine *Cinémonde* named him best foreign actor for 1955. On the national television show *The Colgate Variety Hour, Modern Screen* gave him its Special Achievement Silver Cup Award for 1955. (Not long after that, in a letter to the magazine, Ethel Dean wrote: "Mr. Dean and I would like to thank you and the people who made it possible, from the bottom of our hearts for our Jimmy's award. . . . I do not know how these things are handled, but nothing could make us happier than to be able to have his award to treasure forever. Do you think this would be possible? Do you know who has it now?" The letter was signed "Mr. and Mrs. Winton A. Dean.") On February 9, 1956, *Lux Video Theatre* televised the *Photoplay* Gold Medal Awards on which Dean was presented a posthumous special achievement award. Charles and Emma Dean, along with Winton—he had apparently been informed of this ceremony—sat in the audience as the show was broadcast from the Beverly Hilton hotel. Also in February the Academy of Motion Picture Arts and Sciences nominated Dean for a best actor Oscar for *East of Eden,* a nomination both fans and critics felt he deserved. Many members of the press, notably Hedda Hopper, speculated that Dean might actually *win* the Academy Award, the first time the Oscar would have been given posthumously. The possibility of this historic development overshadowed all other honors Dean received in and around the spring of 1956, even his nomination for best actor for *East of Eden* by the New York Film Critics Circle and his being named best foreign actor by the French Film Academy.

As Dean received these professional accolades, his fans continued to show their devotion. In January 1956 alone, Warner Bros. got over three thousand letters for Dean; by July, seven thousand letters a month were coming into the studio. Fans did more than just write to Dean in care of Warner Bros. They called television stations to demand that they rerun old programs in which Dean had appeared. They searched out specialty stores to buy pictures of Dean, which sold faster than pictures of any other Hollywood star. Some fans went to the Laurence Hutton Collection at Princeton University to see the life mask of Dean that had been placed alongside the masks of Garrick, Booth, Thackeray, Keats, and Beethoven. Other fans purchased sculpted busts of Dean in stores and through the mail. Its price: thirty dollars for the cast-stone version, one hundred and fifty for the bronze.

At this time Dean also became the subject of numerous one-shot magazines, publications that devoted an entire issue to one actor. With names like "The Real James Dean Story," "Jimmy's Own Scrapbook" (readers could find out "How He Lived/How He Loved/How His Genius Flowered/Why He Died/Why He Lives On"), and "Jimmy Dean Returns!" ("Read His Own Words from the Beyond"), these magazines sold out as soon as they hit the newsstands. One that promised Dean's message from the afterlife sold 500,000 copies within weeks. Many of these one-shot magazines contained articles with purposely suggestive titles, such as "James Dean's Black Madonna," "The Girl James Dean Left Behind," "Is Dean a Dandy?" and "Jimmy Dean Is Not Dead." ("Genius never dies," according to this article. "It lives on in the hearts and minds and memories of the people who have been touched by it.") In *Photoplay,* which serialized William Bast's article "There Was a Boy" in its September, October, and November issues, readers could join the James Dean Fan Club by following the instructions included in an advertisement. "To perpetuate the memory of a great actor," the ad said, mail in one dollar. That dollar bought an eight-by-ten glossy portrait of Dean ("suitable for framing"), four scenes from *East of Eden,* four scenes from *Rebel Without a Cause,* eight poses of Dean ("wallet size"), and a membership card. This was just one of some fifty fan clubs that formed around Dean in the years after his death. The James Dean Memorial Club, the Lest We Forget Club, the World Wide James Dean Club (headquartered in London, it had branches in America and Australia)—so many sprang up that it was hard for fans to decide which to join.

That on March 21, 1956, Dean lost the Oscar to Ernest Borgnine for his performance in *Marty* only galvanized the devotion of Dean's fans. Even Hedda Hopper, who was not known for having a sympathetic side, became so angry over the Academy's vote that she wrote a column in which she demanded that the Academy give Dean an honorary Oscar the next year. As it happened, Hopper was merely speaking for the legions of Dean's fans who still mailed letters to Warner Bros. (the studio received 5,863 in May 1956), still made pilgrimages to his grave in Fairmount (as many as five hundred a day now showed up to put flowers on the grave or just to look), and still sent off for pictures and memorabilia. The latest item to catch on was a knockoff of the red nylon zip-up jacket Dean wore in *Rebel Without a Cause,* which fans could buy through a mail-order offer for $22.95.

By June, the story of Dean's obsessed fans had become so newsworthy that the national media picked it up. On June 18, *Newsweek* ran "Star That Won't Die," an article that detailed how Warner Bros. was being flooded with fan mail, how in London *Picturegoer* had announced that Dean had won its poll as the leading actor of 1955 for *East of Eden,* and, in one of the most ghoulish developments to occur after Dean's death, how Dr. William S. Eshrich of Burbank, California, had bought the wreckage of Dean's Porsche for one thousand dollars, reassembled it, and was charging fifty cents a head for people to see it as he toured the car around the country in shopping malls. Some fans, it was reported elsewhere, pulled pieces of aluminum off the wrecked car for keepsakes. It was a practice as odd as buying paper wrappers said to have been peeled from gum Dean chewed, a hobby fans also pursued. "Many Dean fans even refused to believe he is dead," *Newsweek* reported, "and this part of the legend promises to be as durable as the same talk about Hitler. Dean, according to this gospel, was only mutilated in the smashup, but so badly that he is being kept out of sight in a hospital, against his will."

As strange as it may seem, even though published pictures of the accident site showed Dean's Porsche as little more than a twisted mass of metal, some fans actually believed that Dean had not been killed in the wreck. In Fairmount, the police posted guards at Dean's grave periodically because the family feared someone might dig it up just to prove he wasn't dead. To these doubting fans, Dean was not dead but living in a sanitarium, either of his own volition or against his will. Once he had restored his good looks with plastic surgery, this rumor went, he would resume his career, much to the pleasure of his fans. "The fantastic climax of the Dean legend," Herbert Mitgang wrote in *Coronet,* "is the oft-repeated rumor, perpetuated by movie columnists, which calls for the resurrection of James Dean himself, in person, alive. According to this weird story, first given currency in a gossip column, when Dean crashed, his face was badly mutilated. Since then, he has been in hiding, undergoing facial repairs. Someone else supposedly was buried in his place; and when *Giant* is released, Dean, almost as good as new, will reappear."

In a different scenario of Dean's death circulating at this time, not only did he die he, in effect, committed suicide. The line of reasoning went like this: He should not have been driving a race car on the highway because of its construction (made of lightweight aluminum, Dean's car had no top and an inferior grade windshield), nor should he have been driving as fast as he was. Since he had been, he was obviously flirting with suicide. "It is difficult if not impossible for the people who knew and loved Jimmy Dean to believe that he felt his search for personal happiness to be so futile that he might have entertained thoughts of suicide," *Photoplay* speculated in "The Truth Behind the Rumors That James Dean Committed Suicide!" "And yet, anyone who observed him closely could not help but be aware of the black moods that closed down on him so suddenly, shuttering him away from everyone." The evidence in the *Photoplay* article, like the rumors themselves, was decidedly speculative, but that didn't stop Dean's fans—and magazine editors—from making the accusation. In the end, the rumors only added to the Dean legend.

By September, the month that *Photoplay* readers voted Dean their "most favorite" actor, *Time* took note of what it called "a weird new phenomenon . . . loose in the land," "a teenage craze for a boyish Hollywood actor named James Dean." Then again, *Time* could hardly miss the Dean phenomenon. The James Dean Foundation, which had been incorporated in Fairmount in the summer of 1956, was now in full operation; its goals were to raise one million dollars to support young actors trying to get into show business and, by doing this, to provide "a living memorial to James Dean." *Life* ran "Delirium Over Dead Star," an article that recounted the actions of some of the more bizarre Dean fans. Nick Adams was so harassed by fans (one woman who wanted some of Dean's possessions that Adams owned left burned wax effigies on his doorstep) that he started sleeping with a loaded revolver under his pillow. George Stevens received letters from fans threatening him if he cut one single frame of Dean from *Giant*. And still the letters poured into Warner Bros. Some of them were almost pathetic. In one, a young woman wrote: "Jimmy darling, I know you are not dead. I know you are just hiding because your face has been disfigured in the crash. Don't hide, Jimmy. Come back. It won't matter to us."

On Sunday, October 7, 1956, a remembrance service was held at Park Cemetery in Fairmount to mark the first anniversary of Dean's death. At four o'clock in the afternoon, two thousand people watched as James DeWeerd laid a wreath, sent by Dean's fans from West Germany, on his grave. "We are grateful," DeWeerd told the crowd, "as the citizens of Fairmount, that from our town in our state of Indiana and in our times, James Dean, one of our young men, has earned world acclaim in his chosen field of dramatic arts. On behalf of the James Dean fans of West Germany, we place this wreath in his honor, on this, the first anniversary of his untimely death, and dedicate this gesture of international goodwill in appreciation of his talent forever and to his memory." Afterward, Marcus Winslow unveiled a portrait of Dean by Robert Ormsby. When the service ended, the audience stood in silence for more than a minute before it surged toward the grave briefly, broke up, and moved on.

Not surprisingly, with all of these developments, the Dean myth would not stop. On October 16, 1956, *Look* put Dean on its cover.

Dressed in a cowboy hat, a denim shirt, and a vest, Dean cuts his eyes away from the camera just enough to make it impossible for the reader not to look at him. Next to his face, the magazine ran the headline "James Dean: The story of the strangest legend since Valentino." Inside fans found a large spread of pictures of Dean—on the *Giant* set, at home in Fairmount, in the middle of a sculpting lesson. The article recapitulated why Dean had become so popular in the year since his death. Then it concluded: "This [adulation] was not a requiem to a dead star. It was a tribute to a living legend."

Naturally, before long, the television networks cashed in on the Dean phenomenon. In November, two networks ran repeats of three programs in which Dean appeared. NBC showed "Harvest" on *Robert Montgomery Presents* while CBS replayed "I'm a Fool" on *General Electric Theatre* and "The Unlighted Road" on the *Schlitz Playhouse of Stars*. When *Time* noted the repeats on November 26, it observed that "TV last week hysterically joined the weird posthumous cult of James Dean, by featuring the late young actor on three shows on two networks." To prove that "all three shows exploited the Dean legend for frankly commercial purposes," *Time* quoted an unnamed network executive. " '[Dean is] hotter than any body alive,' cried one NBC executive." Apparently. "Harvest," *Time* reported, "bludgeoned the opposition with a sizable 24.3 Trendex rating."

There was one additional reason the repeats had done so well: *Giant* had opened, and Dean was more popular than ever.

2. Following an almost unprecedented advance publicity campaign, *Giant* premiered in New York City on October 10 and in Los Angeles on October 17. The picture, which Warner Bros. marketed as a controversial portrait of the Texas rich, received wide review coverage. Yet even with this cast—"a cavalcade" of stars, the

A publicity shot from *Giant*

picture's trailer promised—almost every notice centered on the most newsworthy fact surrounding the release of the picture: that it was James Dean's last.... "It's Dean, Dean, Dean," raved *Saturday Review.* "It is the late James Dean as Jett Rink that the audience will be watching—and there are many who will be watching with fascination and love. For as everyone knows, this young man who died in an auto smashup has caused a mass hysteria at least equal to that caused by Valentino." The *New York Herald Tribune* brought up Dean and his cult as well. "His earlier depiction of the amoral, reckless, animal-like young ranch hand will not only excite his admirers into frenzy, it will make the most sedate onlooker understand why a James Dean cult ever came into existence." *Time* was not to be outdone. "James Dean ... in this film clearly shows for the first (and fatefully the last) time what his admirers always said he had: a streak of genius." Even *The New York Times*'s Bosley Crowther, who a year ago had dismissed Dean's performance in *Rebel* as a bad Brando impersonation, could not control himself. Pointing out that *Giant*'s running time of three hours and seventeen minutes was "a heap of time to go on about Texas, but Mr. Stevens has made a heap of film," Crowther concluded that "Mr. Dean plays this curious villain with a stylized spookiness—a sly sort of off-beat languor and slur of language that concentrates spite. This is a haunting capstone to the brief career of Mr. Dean." One of the few bad reviews of the picture appeared in *The New Yorker.* "Texas," John McCarten wrote, "which is apparently a state that resembles an American Legion convention in permanent session, is described at great length and to no particular purpose in the WarnerColor film called *Giant.*" As for Dean, McCarten snipped: "Muttering to himself, and wearing a large Stetson low on the bridge of his nose, he proves that Stanislavsky is just as much at home among the cattle as he ever was off Broadway."

All across America, audiences ignored reviews like McCarten's and lined up to buy tickets. At the same time, magazine and television shows clamored to cover the picture's release. One of the most unusual controversies to emerge involved *The Steve Allen Show* and *The Ed Sullivan Show*. An admirer of Dean, Allen had scheduled a tribute to Dean for his October 21 program; on it, he planned to show a film clip while Marcus and Ortense Winslow watched from the studio audience. But in early October word leaked out that Ed Sullivan was going to air his own segment on *Giant*—on October 14, one week before Allen's. When he found out, Steve Allen fumed. In *The New York Times* on October 14, he charged Sullivan "or someone in his organization," with stealing his idea for the segment. Sullivan defended himself by saying that "everything Allen has charged is a complete lie." Then he added: "I won't take his word for anything anymore." Allen was angry because Warner Bros. had agreed to let Sullivan use a clip from *Giant* and because the Winslows had committed to be on Sullivan's show even though Allen was under the impression that they were going to appear on his show exclusively. The controversy, as it was reported in the press, was resolved when Allen moved up his tribute to October 14 and when he decided to shift the focus of his segment from *Giant* to the release of the record album *The James Dean Story,* a project on which Allen had worked as narrator.

Of course, there was more to the story than the press reported. Actually, the dispute between the television shows grew out of a misunderstanding between the two offices of the James Dean Memorial Foundation. Logically, the foundation's home office had been set up in Fairmount, where the Winslows were unusually public with their appeals for money for its support. In "You Can Make Jimmy Live Forever," an as-told-to article that appeared in a popular fan magazine, Marcus Winslow openly asked for money to finance the James Dean Foundation. The organization, Winslow said, intended to underwrite three scholarships, establish a James Dean museum, and sponsor a summer drama festival. To do all of this, the foundation needed to raise one million dollars, a huge sum in 1956. In the article Marcus addressed his inability to allow Jimmy to become a memory. "We could never forget for long, because there'd always be somebody at the door who'd been to the cemetery to visit Jim and wanted to spend a bit of time with us. [Ortense and I] thought it would end after a while. We thought that Jim would be left to rest quietly, but we should have known better. All his life, Jim always did the opposite of whatever we expected of him." Finally Marcus made his pitch. "Jim's death is tragic and meaningless to me now. It will always be tragic, but it does not need to be meaningless. With your contributions, you can make Jim live forever."

Letters containing donations poured into the foundation's Main Street office in Fairmount. Two hundred thousand dollars in contributions arrived during the first eight months it was open. The foundation's board and advisory committee included people who had been important to Dean, among them Xen Harvey, James DeWeerd, Adeline Brookshire, Xen Edwards, Marcus Winslow, and Winton Dean. They all agreed that an appropriate creed for the foundation should be "Encourage talent, recognize achievement, reward genius." While the Fairmount office flourished, the board decided to open an office in New York. To do so, the board hired Vivian Coleman, a writer, and Kent Williams, a friend of Dean's, to run the office. At the New York staff's first meeting, which was held at the Bird 'n' Glass restaurant, Coleman announced that the goal of the foundation was "to aid in every way possible talented persons in all fields of artistic endeavor." In order to raise money to support this goal, Coleman approached several celebrities—Sammy Davis, Jr., Frank Sinatra, Natalie Wood, Robert Wagner, Cliff Robertson, Sal Mineo, and Nick Adams—and asked them to perform in benefit shows in New York and Hollywood. Coleman arranged for Sammy Davis to appear on Steve Allen's tribute; in return, Allen had agreed to contribute forty thousand dollars to the foundation. For his money, Allen expected an exclusive—and the Winslows. Then, without the knowledge of the

New York office, Lester Johnson, who ran the Fairmount office, cut a deal with the Sullivan show. In exchange for an appropriate contribution, the Winslows would appear on *The Ed Sullivan Show,* not *The Steve Allen Show.* In the end the Winslows appeared with Sullivan and Allen aired his tribute starring Sammy Davis on the same night as Sullivan's, but the conflict between the two offices of the Dean Foundation proved to be severely damaging.

The squabbling over fame and money detracted only somewhat from the real appeal of the release of *Giant*—the chance to see James Dean in not just his final part but the first performance that allowed him to show the full range of his talent. The early scenes with Dean are hypnotic. While Rock Hudson, as Bick Benedict, rants and raves on the screen, Dean, as Jett Rink, quietly steals the picture from him. The audience becomes captivated by his singular version of the drifter cowboy. When Dean serves Elizabeth Taylor tea in his shack—this legitimizes him in the viewer's eyes—he is now ready to enter the picture's real world, the world of commerce. Which he does, in the oil business, only to end up beating Hudson at the game of making money. The final scenes with Dean are stunning, alarming. As Rink gains more power than Benedict, he is corrupted by the system, although he seems to be more than willing to be corrupted. By the end of the picture, Rink is reduced to a stammering, mumbling drunk who's obsessed with money and a desire to get back at Benedict in any way he can, going so far as to date his daughter if he has to.

Dean is unnerving in his portrayal of an aging Howard Hughes-esque eccentric. Both fans and critics pronounced *Giant* Dean's masterpiece. Even George Stevens found words of praise. "[Dean] was a good boy and he filled the bill perfectly," Stevens told *Time.* "He wasn't always a joy to work with, but find me any actors who aren't difficult. You gamble along with young people and hope their performance comes off. We gambled with Dean and we won."

On February 18, 1957, James Dean was nominated for his second

Academy Award. Since he had lost for *East of Eden,* he seemed to have a good chance to win for *Giant.* But Warner Bros. made a disastrous strategic error. Instead of placing him in the best supporting actor category, for which he would have easily qualified and probably won, the studio touted him as best actor. Apparently, Academy members did not feel his part in the picture deserved a best actor award. (Dean was on-screen only forty of the picture's one hundred and ninety-seven minutes.) When the ceremony took place on March 27, Yul Brynner won for *The King and I.* Anthony Quinn won best supporting actor for *Lust for Life.* Now Dean would never be able to win an Academy Award outright. It was a loss almost too painful for Dean's fans to accept. Many continued to lobby—Hedda Hopper among them—for the Academy to give him an honorary award.

3.   It was inevitable that someone would shoot a documentary on Dean. That person was Robert Altman, then a young unknown filmmaker. The documentary, *The James Dean Story,* was released by Warner Bros. in the fall of 1957. Following the enormous commercial success of Dean's three pictures, Warner Bros. obviously hoped the documentary would cash in on Dean's popularity. Some reviews discussed this. "In view of [Dean's legend], it is difficult to determine whether *The James Dean Story* is simply a shrewd exploitation piece or a sincere tribute from the company for which he worked," Arthur Knight wrote in *Saturday Review.* "Perhaps it is a bit of both." Other reviews did not question the motivation behind making the documentary but focused on the Dean myth. In *The New York Times,* Bosley Crowther, now a virtual champion of Dean, said that because "intimations of immortality run all through [the picture] . . . it should be irresistible to the Dean fans." In London, the *Observer* expanded on this idea. "So sedulously has the legend been built up, that in James Dean a generation mourns its own demise. He has become the symbol of frustrated youth, of mixed-up kiddery, revolt and loneliness. *The James Dean Story* was certain to be made some time, somehow. Perhaps . . . we should be thankful it has not been made more mawkishly."

In the eighty-two-minute documentary, Altman traces the major events in Dean's life by intercutting clips from Dean's pictures and television performances with on-camera interviews with people who knew him. A narrator, Martin Gabel, provides essential plot points missed by interviewees. Tommy Sand's "Let Me Be Loved" is the theme song. Of all the people Altman talked to—Marcus and Ortense Winslow, Charles and Emma Dean, Adeline Brookshire Nall, Lew Bracker, and others—none even approaches the subject of Dean's sexuality. This was still 1957; the same pressures that kept Dean from publicly dealing with his sexuality while he was alive prevented his family, friends, and colleagues from discussing the topic now that he was dead. In all of the articles that appeared on Dean in the years immediately following his death, not one mentioned his homosexuality. The grieving lovers, the one-night stands, the would-be romances—they were all women.

Not long after the release of *The James Dean Story*, the James Dean Memorial Foundation had more problems. Still angry about the Sullivan-Allen fiasco, Coleman shut down the New York office. In leaving, she said angrily that she believed Fairmount was more interested in "promoting Fairmount [than in] doing something constructive in Jimmy's memory." The foundation produced one play, *Our Town*, directed by Coy Bronson and starring Markie Winslow, at a small theatre in Indiana; it also funded two scholarships to the Neighborhood Playhouse School for the Theatre in New York. But by the summer of 1957 the foundation was in trouble. With Coleman gone, the organization lost the support of all the stars who had agreed to help with benefit performances. Eventually the Fairmount office fell into financial trouble, and the "fitting living memorial to the budding genius who spent his youth among us," as one Fairmount board member described the foundation, shut down for good. It had been in existence just eighteen months. Some townspeople didn't believe that internal conflict had brought down the foundation. They suspected the worst. "It was a big scam," a Fairmount resident would recall. "I heard one man"—someone not directly affiliated with the foundation board— "absconded with one hundred thousand dollars. No one said anything because they were so embarrassed. A lot of people around here had red faces."

While the drama over the foundation unfolded, the Dean cult remained as vital as ever. In *Esquire* magazine's 25th anniversary issue (October 1958), John Dos Passos, best known for his epic novel trilogy *U.S.A.*, published "The Death of James Dean." "James Dean is three years dead but the sinister adolescent still holds the headlines," Dos Passos wrote at the beginning of the prose poem. Dean did, too, for a while longer at least. But since no studio had any new Dean material, the Dean mania began to diminish some time after that. Many skeptics believed Dean would eventually lose his appeal altogether. In fact, in the early sixties, some Dean-related projects met with mixed success. For example, in 1961, James Fuller's stage version of *Rebel Without a Cause* received bad reviews—and closed quickly. So, by 1965, on the tenth anniversary of Dean's death, reporters were starting to announce the end of the Dean hysteria. On September 29, the *New York Post* printed "Decade Has Dimmed James Dean Luster," an Associated Press article that contended "the Dean craze has all but vanished, apparently the victim of malnutrition."

Maybe, but that same year *Variety* ran a story about the recent deaths of two teenage girls who killed themselves in a suicide pact because, according to the note they left behind for their parents, "this was the anniversary of the day Jimmy died" and they could not go on living without him. So, even though no new Dean material was forthcoming, a hard-core Dean cult continued to exist, whether or not the popular press wanted to acknowledge it. In 1965, there were still seventeen James Dean fan clubs in Germany alone, and many more operated in the United States. The club members' devotion to Dean had not faded over the years. Indeed, many fans remained almost religious in their worship of Dean. Therese J. Brandes, the president of the James Dean Memory Club, which was based in New York City, wrote a poem that summarized the feelings of most fans. The poem was included in a huge ad the James Dean Memory Club ran on *Variety*'s obituary page shortly after Dean's deathday in 1966. Published under the phrase "In Memory of the Late James Dean," the poem read: "The years are now eleven,/Since you've been in heaven,/There are some who say,/Your memory has faded away,/Many more than some are saying today,/Your memory is surely here to stay."

By the early 1970s, it became clear that fans like Therese Brandes were right. On the fifteenth anniversary of Dean's death, Warner Bros. rereleased *Giant*, and the crowds lined up to see it again. Dean's legacy was enduring even if his popularity had temporarily faded. Social critics took notice. When they tried to explain Dean's lasting appeal, they pointed to the political and social conflicts America had gone through in the sixties. Because Dean symbolized rebelliousness and discontent, radicals from the sixties could embrace him. They did too, especially toward the end of the decade. Some observers felt Dean probably even inspired *Easy Rider,* one of the most influential cultural documents of the sixties. If so, it wouldn't be surprising since Dennis Hopper, the picture's director, made no qualms about his admiration for Dean. "This scene of The Establishment versus The Youth"—the climax of *Rebel Without a Cause,* when the Los Angeles police shoot Plato as Jim Stark cries out that he has the bullets to the gun Plato is holding—"somehow seems to be an early version of the deaths in *Easy Rider,*" Elroy Hamilton wrote in the *Chicago Sun-Times* in January 1971, "and, perhaps, of those at Kent State, though the intervening years seem to have added the extra ingredient of hatred."

As the years passed, Dean's legend became more established. In 1974, the Eagles recorded "James Dean" for *On the Border,* their first album. In 1975, on the twentieth anniversary of Dean's death, fans organized memorial services in several American cities, among them New York and Los Angeles. In Fairmount, in two rooms over the Western Auto Store, the town had recently opened the Fairmount Historical Museum, which featured a display of Dean memorabilia; on the anniversary of Dean's death, fans streamed into the museum to see the Dean exhibit. In December 1977, Universal Pictures released *September 30, 1955,* an autobiographical picture, written and directed by James Bridges, that examines the way Dean's death affects the life of one young man. That same year, Seita Ohnishi, a wealthy Japanese businessman, paid for the construction of a memorial to Dean in Cholame, California. Built in front of the town's post office, the memorial consisted of a metal structure wrapped around a Tree of Heaven. Ohnishi decided to build the monument to Dean, which cost fifteen thousand dollars, after he made three trips from Tokyo to the site of Dean's fatal car wreck. On the shiny silver monument Ohnishi had workmen engrave the following words: JAMES DEAN, 1931 FEB 8– 1955 SEPT 30 PM 5.59.

One of the most gruesome developments in the Dean legend occurred on the night of February 12, 1976, four days after what would have been Dean's forty-fifth birthday. Around ten o'clock that evening, Sal Mineo was stabbed to death in the garage of the apartment complex in which he lived in West Hollywood. He had just returned home from a rehearsal of an upcoming production of *P.S. Your Cat Is Dead* by James Kirkwood. Residents of the apartment complex heard Mineo shouting "My God! My God! Help me!" He had died by the time the police arrived. He was thirty-seven years old. In the press reports of the murder, one unidentified source suggested that the crime might

those are feelings I can understand, but I just knew that I was feeling something that I didn't feel with anything or anybody else.

Mineo's revelations were not as startling as they would have been years earlier. By the mid-seventies, as the gay rights movement became a dominant social force in America (in fact, the movement had given society the word "gay"), homosexuality was more accepted, at least in certain segments of the population. To underscore the fact that as much as 10 percent of the country was gay—a number suggested by more than one survey—magazines began to reveal famous men who had lived their lives in the closet, an early form of outing. Dean was depicted in the gay press as just such a person—a gay man who pretended not to be to the public. *The Advocate* even published the infamous pornographic picture of a young man, said to be Dean, perched in the branches of a tree. Nude, he stares suggestively as he plays with his erection. Some friends of Dean's would insist that it was not Dean in the picture but someone who looked like him. Even so, if one studies the picture carefully, the boy in the tree seems to be Dean, and posing nude with an erection would not have been unthinkable for Dean, who was nothing if not an exhibitionist and an iconoclast. "A couple of years ago," *The Advocate* said of the picture, "[the] alleged photo of Dean was selling in New York like hotcakes, purported to be a scene from a gay porno movie that Dean made before he became a star. It is difficult to say who is attached to that mammoth, erect cock, but to millions of men and women, it sure looks like Dean, a giant in more ways than one." Most probably, it was the nude picture Dean wrote to William Fox about back in September 1952.

In the seventies and eighties, at least two books about Dean documented his homosexual activities, but only as evidence that he was bisexual. Fans could not accept the idea that Dean was gay—and, apparently, neither could authors. Naturally the residents of Fairmount rejected the notion, for despite all the social changes that had taken place in the country, Fairmount remained as conservative as ever. On October 9, 1980, in the same issue in which a story about a memorial service for James Dean appeared on its front page, the *Fairmount News* published a short but damning editorial on gay rights. Called "Homo Power," it read:

> The Justice Department is seeking from Congress legislation which would permit the immigration into the United States of admitted homosexuals. Worse, the department is winking at the present law which provides that any prospective entrant who admits being a homosexual must be barred from entering.
>
> Acting Immigrant Commissioner David Crosland recently admitted a new policy that went into effect in August, 1979. Under the policy, no one is excluded unless a voluntary admission is made!
>
> Thus the Carter Administration is playing politics on this front. In this connection, the recent Democratic Party platform included, for the first time, a plank on homo rights, signifying the growing political influence of homos in the U.S.

4. If there were any doubts about whether the Dean myth would last, those concerns ended in September 1980 when thousands of fans showed up in Fairmount to commemorate the twenty-fifth anniversary of Dean's death. Martin Sheen spoke at a memorial service held in the Wesleyan Campground Tabernacle. James Dean "created," Sheen told the huge audience, "one of this century's most unique inventions—himself." On the thirtieth Sheen led a procession of a thousand fans on a march to Dean's grave in Park Cem-

etery. "When I was in acting school in New York years ago," Sheen later told a reporter, "there was a saying that if Marlon Brando changed the way people acted, then James Dean changed the way people lived. He was the greatest actor who ever lived—he was simply a genius."

Throughout the eighties, Dean's fans continued to worship him. In the early eighties, Will O'Neil, a retired air force purchasing agent from Hawthorne, California, organized the James Dean Memorial Run. To mark the anniversary of Dean's death, O'Neil led a caravan of about one hundred vintage cars along the same route Dean took from Los Angeles to Cholame on the day he died. "We felt [Dean's rebelliousness] was something we could honor with our cars," the *Los Angeles Times* quoted O'Neil as saying, "a way to take that last trip with him in our mind."

On February 18, 1982, *Come Back to the Five and Dime, Jimmy Dean, Jimmy Dean,* a play written by Ed Graczyk and directed by Robert Altman, opened on Broadway at the Martin Beck Theatre. It starred Sandy Dennis, Karen Black, Kathy Bates, and Cher. With the same cast, Altman shot a film version of the play, also released in 1982. In March 1983, Warner Bros. rereleased *Giant* yet again. This time it played at the Beacon Theatre in New York City, and, as they had since 1956, fans lined up to see it. Soon afterward, in France, the sculptor Yasuo Mizui began work on *Wall of Hope,* the second memorial commissioned by Seita Ohnishi, the Japanese businessman obsessed with Dean. At a cost of two hundred thousand dollars, the monument was to be built in France and reassembled in Cholame. "James Dean was the brief, living manifestation of a new era," Ohnishi wrote in 1981 to explain his devotion to Dean. "There are some things, like the hatred that accompanies war, that are best forgotten. There are others, like the love inspired by this young actor, that should be preserved for all time."

On September 30, 1985, the thirtieth anniversary of Dean's death,

Warner Bros. rereleased *Rebel Without a Cause* and *East of Eden* in thirteen cities. As *Giant* had earlier, the double bill played to packed houses. This year, because it was a special anniversary, West Hollywood and Los Angeles declared September 30 James Dean Day, but, naturally, the largest celebration in the country occurred in Fairmount. Recently the town had started calling the annual event that acknowledged the day of Dean's death Museum Days/Remembering James Dean. Each year the crowds in Fairmount had grown larger. By the mid-eighties, town officials planned for fifteen thousand people to show up for Museum Days. At the celebration fans could enjoy a variety of activities, among them the James Dean Run, the James Dean Rock Lasso Contest, the Grand Parade, the James Dean Lookalike Contest, the James Dean Bicycle Tour, the James Dean Memorial 10K Run, a screening of Dean's three pictures, and a memorial service at Park Cemetery. Over time, some fans began to attend Museum Days year after year. One, a motorcycle fanatic, became famous because he chose not to reveal his real name but to go by the pseudonym Nicky Bazooka. "The leather-clad motorcyclist," a local newspaper reported in 1985, "who is believed to be from Bloomington, has come to the Fairmount cemetery each year for about ten years and places a wreath on Dean's grave, and in recent years has led the procession from the memorial service at Back Creek Friends Church to Park Cemetery."

Over the years Dean's grave at Park Cemetery has been the site of some strange episodes. In 1980, the Fairmount police caught a teenage boy from Europe trying to sleep on the grave. When the police ran him off, the boy wept as he left the cemetery. One night in 1991, Officer Carl Adams discovered a couple who were, Adams told a journalist, "getting ready to have sex on the grave." He made them gather up their clothes and leave. A few years earlier the police had had to break up a different sort of meeting—seven Ball State University teachers holding a séance over the tombstone. Then, not long after what would have been Dean's fifty-fifth birthday, a local journalist discovered Mary Johnson, a fifteen-year-old fan, sitting on a rock in front of the grave. She was reading "A Country Pathway" by James Whitcomb Riley, one of Dean's favorite writers, until the pathos of the moment took over and she broke down crying. "I'm a diehard James Dean fan," Johnson told the journalist, "but I don't consider myself obsessed."

Most fans are not so consumed with Dean. They show up at the grave, take some pictures, meditate a few minutes, and leave. Some women kiss the gravestone, smearing it with lipstick. Many fans bring gifts for Dean—a note or flowers or a pack of cigarettes. Occasionally a famous fan arrives. Morrissey, the former lead singer of The Smiths, who wrote the book *James Dean Is Not Dead,* came to Fairmount to shoot a video for his single "Suedehead," a cut from his solo album *Viva Hate.* Then, one night in the summer of 1988, Bob Dylan, who had just played a concert in Indianapolis, arrived in Fairmount unannounced. Besides the grave, Dylan stopped by the museum, which had relocated to a two-story house on Washington Street.

Many residents are not happy about the fans' coming to Fairmount. "The people who come to Museum Days are not the kind of people we know around here," Clyde William Smitson says. "One year I saw this guy who had his hair shaved on both sides and sticking straight up in the air. Looked like he had a spike in his head. Had on a great big old wool overcoat. Why do you need that sort of stuff in Fairmount? There are a lot of weird people who come here. I would guess that they come from the East some place. Him and the three that were with him. Half of them you couldn't tell whether they were male or female. Simple-looking people, but not us country folks." A large group of residents is equally disturbed that it's Dean who has gotten all this attention through the years. "They think he slept his way to fame—especially homosexually," Jack Raup says. "Homosexuality is really off the roll, and sleeping with other people is off the roll, even though they may have been out there doing it. In Fairmount, what someone did in 1860 is still an issue—with some people."

A lot of locals believe that Dean's homosexuality was the reason a bust of Dean by Kenneth Kendall, mounted on a brick pedestal in Park Cemetery not far from Dean's grave, disappeared after it was dedicated back in 1956. "It didn't hardly stay but seven weeks," remembers Ann Warr, past president of the Fairmount Historical Museum and Fairmount's historian. "Why, that baby didn't last long enough for me to get out there and get a picture of it." According to Fairmount gossip, a veterans' group stole the bust to show their anger over a monument being built to Dean—who had avoided the draft by saying he was a homosexual—and not to them. It's hard to know if the story is true since the bust never turned up and no group ever claimed responsibility for taking it.

The Kendall bust wasn't the only Dean monument to disappear. On the morning of April 12, 1983, the Park Cemetery groundskeeper showed up for work as usual only to notice something odd: James Dean's tombstone was gone. Confused about what to do, he called the Winslows, who reported the stolen tombstone to the police. But even they were puzzled. Why would someone steal James Dean's tombstone? What could the thief possibly do with it? Before the police began their investigation, the tombstone turned up. As he drove home from work on the evening of May 6, Guy Ellis spotted it near the corner of Grant County roads 400 East and 1100 South. The tombstone was sitting on top of a tree stump.

The Winslows had the stone returned to Dean's grave. In three weeks, though, it was stolen again. This time the police weren't so lucky. Months passed and the stone was not found. Many fans, some of whom had come from as far away as Europe and Japan, were horrified to find Dean's grave marked by a makeshift wooden cross. "It was a disgrace to think there was no tombstone," says Ann Warr, who worked at the museum at the time. "People would come in and complain that it was a disgrace. I'd say, 'We're not the immediate family.' We felt like if the father wanted a tombstone out there he'd see to it. Well, we began to get embarrassed and I talked to the manager at Wearly Monuments. So they didn't charge for the replica." Put into place in late May 1985, the replacement stone looked exactly like the original, only this stone was fastened to its base with super-hold glue and steel-rod bolts.

Finally, on the morning of Sunday, May 24, 1987, in Fort Wayne, Indiana, firefighter Gary Wymer was taking out the trash from Station Number Ten when he discovered the original tombstone sitting near a Dumpster. That afternoon, Marcus Winslow, Jr., picked up the stone and took it back to Fairmount. "It was good to know it's not in the bottom of a river somewhere," a local newspaper quoted Winslow as saying. "And it's just kind of the last piece of a puzzle. But I have no idea what we're going to do with it. We really never expected to get this back. Maybe somebody's conscience started bothering them." That was exactly what had happened. Not long after the stone reappeared, the man who stole it with the help of two friends wrote a letter to a Fort Wayne newspaper explaining why he had. "You have heroes," said the man, demanding anonymity. "How would you like to see their grave messed up? What would you think if you went to their grave and saw people had spray painted their lovers' names all over and were snorting cocaine off the stone, like they do at Jim Morrison's grave? . . . [At first] people had chipped [Dean's] stone away and we thought that was an insult to do something like that. We'd rather take it away entirely than have it die a terrible death. . . . I just want the family to know I didn't mean to hurt anyone, and I did it out of admiration and the fact that the tombstone was going to hell. A lot of us consider Dean to be one of the finest actors who ever lived."

*   *   *

By the late eighties, Dean was as popular as ever. So many companies had capitalized on his image—Maxell tapes, Converse sneakers, the Adolph Coors Company, Levi Strauss, to name just a few—that the Winslows hired Curtis Management in Indianapolis to license the name James Dean. "Someone wanted to market vials of what was supposed to be authentic James Dean sweat," Mark Roesler of Curtis once said. "I don't know where these people found his sweat but, like other objectionable projects, our company was forced to take them off the market." Dean sweat is one of the handful of projects Curtis has kept off the market. In the past few years, Curtis allowed Dean's image to be used on posters, T-shirts, jogging outfits, ashtrays, postcards, pillowcases, sunglasses, trinkets—the list goes on and on. Since it has taken over, Curtis generates between two and three million dollars a year. That money is split between the Winslows and Winton Dean.

In 1990, for the thirty-fifth anniversary of Dean's death, thirty thousand people attended Museum Days. "Fairmount is the only town this size, except for maybe old town Jerusalem, that people from all over the world come to," says Jerry Payne, a Fairmount resident. "But they come from around the world and then they come back." After she had observed this phenomenon for years, Ortense Winslow couldn't help but express her bafflement. "We've had kids come from France, from Japan, from all over America," she once said. "They've seen his movies on television and say they had to come. I've burned thousands of letters and I've got thousands left. I just wish somebody would tell me what it's all about."

5. On the makeshift stage in the parking lot of the Citizen's Bank, Jeff Nelson, a nineteen-year-old actor from West Covina, California, strutted in front of the screaming crowd and did,

as the John Mellencamp song goes, his best James Dean. He was followed by Travis Feldman, a nineteen-year-old McDonald's manager from South Bend, Indiana; Jim Sorg, a twenty-three-year-old bank teller from Fort Wayne; Larry Ledgerwood, a twenty-four-year-old pottery-maker from Clay City; and Scott Brim, a thirty-three-year-old model from White Plains, New York. Like Nelson, they all wore blue jeans, a white T-shirt, and a red windbreaker, Dean's outfit in *Rebel Without a Cause*. Like Nelson, they all "did" Dean—tilting the head down slightly, squinting the eyes just so, hunching the shoulders. As each of the five preened across the stage, the audience of fifteen hundred—so large it filled the parking lot and spilled out onto Main Street—cheered wildly, as if it were James Dean himself on the stage and not some impersonator young enough to be his son. Of the twenty-three original contestants, these were the five finalists in 1992's James Dean Look-alike Contest, one of the most popular events at Museum Days.

"What do you think of our contestants, folks?" the down-home announcer drawled into the microphone. "You wanna see them again?"

With the crowd roaring, each contestant did Dean one more time. Finally the audience voted for a winner by applauding for the contestant it liked best as the announcer went down the line and held his hand above each one's head. The judges—one was Marcus Winslow, Jr.—decided Jeff Nelson was the runner-up, Jim Sorg the winner.

Offstage, Nelson wasn't disappointed, just happy he had showed so well his first year. Sorg was shocked by his win since he had entered the contest only on a dare from friends at work. Was he a Dean fan? "I am now," he said. But the night's big winner was Travis Feldman although he didn't know it yet. Within days, Megan Foley, a casting agent who had flown in from Los Angeles for the contest because a national search had not turned up a Dean look-alike, would cast Feldman in a McDonald's commercial to be shot and aired in Australia. In the commercial a McDonald's employee daydreams about be-

coming James Dean—and in his dream he does. It seemed
appropriate that Foley found her Dean look-alike in Dean's hometown. "I've spent many nights in the mirror," Feldman said, explaining how he got the Dean moves down. "I've almost memorized
Rebel."

Of the thirty thousand fans who came to Museum Days, most would
admit that Dean is at least an idle interest of theirs. "You have to love
him," says Heather Thatcher, a Fairmount high school student who
was crowned Museum Days Queen for 1992. "I've grown up around
James Dean. Anyway, I love the way he acts. He's so mysterious.
Those eyes!"

But for a group of fans known as the Deaners, James Dean is more
than an idle interest, he maintains a central place in their lives. Why
do these fans feel so deeply about Dean? "For some, there's an element of religion to all of this," says Del Rey Loven, an artist from Chicago in his thirties. Take Bobby Dean, a thirty-year-old car restorer
from Colorado Springs, Colorado. "When I was young I used to think
James Dean was the God of Teenagers," he says. In fact, his worship
of Dean was so strong that in 1986 he had "the crucifixion scene from
Giant"—the notorious sequence in which Dean uses a shotgun for the
horizontal plank in the cross and poses like Christ at the crucifixion,
with Elizabeth Taylor kneeling at his feet—tattooed over his entire
back at a cost of twelve hundred dollars and enormous pain. "It was
my way of giving something back to Jimmy," says Dean, whose last
name is not Dean, although he uses it. "To show how much he has
given to people."

Bryan DeLuca sees a spiritual quality to Dean as well. "Jimmy was
so eternal," says DeLuca, twenty-one. "He's never going to die. His
spirit is in all of us." When DeLuca talks about Dean, it becomes
clear that, for him at least, he means this literally. "I had a dream that
I was walking around and Jimmy was there. I could hear him saying

that my body was perfect for his soul and that he wanted to enter my body. I felt him in my dream coming in me, almost merging with me. Now sometimes I actually feel Jimmy right here." He points to his heart. "It's like a very warm, strong feeling. Sometimes I don't even feel like myself. I feel like another person. To be honest, I've never told this to anyone before besides my wife."

If there's a common trait among the Deaners, it's an ability to identify with their hero. Arnold Siminoff, a housekeeping worker at Caesar's casino in Atlantic City, thinks he and Dean had much in common. "We were born the same year," he says. "Also, he was an only child whose mother died. I was an only child whose mother died." Among Deaners, Siminoff is well known for his penchant for taking long walks (he often walks the ten miles from his hotel in Marion to Fairmount) and his simple, uncompromising love for Dean. "My first dream was to come to Fairmount, and that came true in 1980," he says. "Now my second dream is to live here for good. Maybe my second dream will come true like my first. God willing."

At one o'clock in the afternoon on Wednesday, September 30, 1992, three days after Museum Days ended, Tom Berghuis, a longtime Dean fan from Flint, Michigan, stood behind the podium at the front of the Back Creek Friends Church. In the late fifties, commemorative services were held in this church each year on Dean's deathday, but during the sixties and the first half of the seventies the services stopped. Then in 1976 Adeline Brookshire Nall organized a service. She continued them each year after that. Nall was master of ceremonies until 1992. Upon being confined to a wheelchair, she turned over those duties to Berghuis. Even so, down near the podium, she sat in her wheelchair, taking everything in.

As he looked out over the congregation crammed into the tiny church, Berghuis addressed the first issue. "Absent among us today," he said, "is a friend from New Jersey, Arnold Siminoff. Everybody knows Arnold, the fellow in the red jacket and cowboy hat. More than once I've driven down here from Marion and I'd seen Arnold walking. I'd stop and ask him, 'Arnold, why are you walking?' and he'd say, ' 'Cause I want to go to Fairmount.' " With this, Berghuis introduced Becky Byington, Arnold's friend, to explain his absence. "Arnold was operated on this morning for bone cancer," she said, holding back her tears, "and that's why he can't be with us today. So he asked me to read his poem for Jimmy." The poem was called "From the Heart."

The program continued. David Loehr, a collector of Dean memorabilia, read a long published quote written by Dean and polished (and probably rewritten) by the Warner Bros. publicity department. Describing Dean as "a normal kid," Adeline Brookshire Nall shared "two highlights" from the years she taught him. Jeff Nelson read a passage from *The Little Prince*. Berghuis did too, commenting before he started that the book "needs very little introduction among Dean fans." Bob Pully, a high-school classmate of Dean's, recalled the time he, Dean, and some friends accidentally set a field of dry grass on fire. "Jimmy was just another Indiana boy like the rest of us," Pully said. Then Berghuis called for "a moment of silence" for Dean, which he ended by looking up to the back of the church to see "an awesome view . . . Mr. Nicky Bazooka."

For years Bazooka had been appearing at the September 30 service, though no one knows exactly who he is or where he comes from. The name is made up. The outfit—a Harley Davidson jacket, motorcycle pants, boots, a cap, all black—is hardly one he wears every day to work. He rides the motorcycle—a Triumph with the license plate "9-30-55"—one day a year, September 30. The rest of the time it's said to be kept in storage in Fairmount. But for decades now, like clockwork, he has shown up at the James Dean Memorial Service at Back Creek Friends Church, usually around 1:30. He'll ride the motorcycle past the church out front, gunning the engine as he does. Next he'll park the bike, come inside, and stand near the doors at the back of the church. Once he's introduced, he'll walk down to the podium and say a few words about James Dean. The Deaners have come to depend on Bazooka suddenly materializing each year. "In life, you can count on two things coming every year," as Loehr puts it, "Santa Claus and Nicky Bazooka."

That day, after being introduced, Bazooka decided to talk about himself. "When I first came to town and inquired about James Dean, people were not really wanting to know much about him," he said, his inflection much more polished than that of the biker he's dressed up to be. "They had heard enough and all that. I had a year to think about it and I thought, If I can do something to kind of stir up the hornet's nest a little bit, maybe people'll be a little more interested. I've had this stuff"—the jacket, the pants—"since it was in vogue. So I gathered it all up and got my motorcycle and thought, What if I stick a big bunch of flowers on the front of it and did a thing like Rudolph Valentino's black lady?" The audience laughed. Then Bazooka changed the tone of his remarks. "And I'll continue to come back as long as folks want me to to celebrate the life and art of James Dean. Some of us knew Jimmy and some of us loved him and all of us are inspired by him. For most of us, two out of three ain't bad."

As the audience applauded, Bazooka slipped a blue scarf from his neck, placed it around Adeline Brookshire Nall's, and kissed her on the cheek. "It's time to go," Berghuis said. Slowly the crowd of fans filed out of the church into the parking lot. Now sitting on his motorcycle, Bazooka kick-started the engine and headed off in a slow creep. Led by Bazooka, the fans, four or five abreast, fell in and set out on their quarter-mile march to Park Cemetery. Local motorists, aware of this yearly tradition, pulled off to the side of the road out of respect as the procession passed. At the entrance to the cemetery, Bazooka waited, his motorcycle's engine idling quietly, until the fans had made their way through the cemetery to Dean's grave. Then he drove over to the grave. Unfastening the spray of flowers tied to the bike's handlebars, he placed the flowers on the tombstone. After pausing to kneel at the stone, Bazooka got back on his bike and cranked it up. "See you next year, Nicky," a fan shouted out over the roar of the engine. Finally Bazooka sped down the cemetery's narrow dirt path, pulled onto the main road, and, without ever looking back, quickly disappeared from sight.

6. By the spring of 1992, several people who had been close to James Dean had died. In 1963, Beverly Wills, who was comedienne Joan Davis's daughter and one of Jimmy's first Hollywood friends, died in mysterious circumstances at the age of twenty-nine of a drug overdose; suicide was not ruled out. In 1968, Nick Adams, who had a small part in *Rebel Without a Cause,* died of a drug overdose at his home in Beverly Hills. In September 1971, Pier Angeli, divorced from Vic Damone since 1958 and desperate for a comeback picture to help revitalize her stalled career, died from an overdose of barbiturates. An apparent suicide, she was thirty-nine. On July 24, 1972, Lance Reventlow, with whom Dean was supposed to have dinner on the day he died, was killed in a plane crash. On February 12, 1976, Sal Mineo was murdered in Los Angeles. On April 6, 1976, Marcus Winslow died in Fairmount from old age. In June 1979, Nicholas Ray died, a slow agonizing death from cancer. On the evening of July 20, 1981, Rolf Weutherich, the mechanic who had survived the accident with Dean, lost control of his car on a wet road outside of Heilbronn, Germany, and smashed into a tree. Like Dean, he was dead on arrival at the hospital. On the night of November 29, 1981, Natalie Wood, dressed in a nightgown and down jacket, was wandering about the deck of her yacht docked off Catalina Island when she fell overboard into the lagoon's cold water and drowned. Robert Wagner, her hus-

band, and Christopher Walken, their friend, both of whom were onboard below deck, never heard her screaming for help. On October 2, 1985, Rock Hudson died from AIDS. In October 1991, Ortense Winslow died in Fairmount from old age.

As of the spring of 1992, Adeline Brookshire Nall, now living in a nursing home in Marion, was holding up well although she had developed a trick hip. On the March evening I spoke with her in her nursing home room as I did research for this book, she seemed lively and alert. Before we finished talking that night, she got tired and asked to meet a second time. On my way out, she mentioned that Winton Dean, who years ago had moved from California to Florida, where Ethel died, now lived in Marion in a nursing home too. "Would you ever want to go by and visit him?" I asked her. "Sure," she said. "I haven't seen Winton in years."

So Mrs. Nall set up a time for me to pick her up—a Sunday afternoon—and on that day I drove her across town to the Colonial Oaks Retirement Home, the retirement community whose most famous resident is Winton Dean. Modern, brick, well kept, it's probably the nicest nursing home in Marion. I had been told by numerous people that, under strict orders from his family, the nursing home staff would not allow anyone to see Winton Dean. In the past he had become so exasperated by the Dean phenomenon that he refused to speak with journalists—or fans for that matter—who wanted to know more about his son. Legend has it that Winton Dean once moved when a journalist found out where he lived. True or not, the story underscores the extent to which he has gone over the last four decades to distance himself from his son or his son's legend. I could not imagine what would happen at the nursing home when Mrs. Nall and I arrived. For all I knew, a nurse would summarily show us the door.

That day Mrs. Nall and I got lucky. The nurse on duty, a business-like woman dressed in starched whites who seemed instantly to regress twenty years when we approached her, had had Mrs. Nall for speech at Fairmount High. "Oh, Mrs. Nall," the nurse gushed. "You were my favorite teacher at Fairmount."

"Mrs. Nall would like to see Winton Dean," I said, seizing the chance to take advantage of the nurse's momentary lapse into sentimentality. I held on to Mrs. Nall's arm tightly, not just because her trick hip makes her prone to falling down, but because I wanted the nurse to know that I was with her.

"Go right on back," the nurse said, smiling happily at her favorite former teacher.

Slowly, Mrs. Nall and I made our way down the long corridor to Winton Dean's room. When I looked inside, I spotted him sitting, his back ramrod straight, in a reclining chair watching television. Although I could not see the set, I could certainly hear it, all the way out in the hallway.

As impatient as ever, Mrs. Nall started inside the room, pulling me along with her. At first Winton Dean didn't respond when he glanced up to see two people, one of them a stranger, suddenly walk in on him. He just looked at us. Then he motioned for us to come on into the room, so we did. "Winton," Mrs. Nall said. "Do you know me?" Dressed neatly in brown corduroy pants, a brown-and-white plaid shirt, tan zip-up jacket, and a cap, Winton Dean said nothing. I couldn't help but think how peculiar it was for Winton Dean, sitting in his nursing-home room on a Sunday afternoon, to be wearing a cap. As if to answer Mrs. Nall's question, he cracked a smile, letting her know that he *did* remember her even if they had not seen each other in years. I pulled up a chair so Mrs. Nall could sit down beside his recliner. No sooner had she sat on the chair than Winton Dean—he still had not spoken a word—reached over and took one of Mrs. Nall's hands in both of his. His actions were slow and deliberate. It was as if he had to consider doing something fully before he actually did it. I perched on the edge of his bed, which was neatly made up. Behind me, the television roared. Judging from how high the volume was, I had to assume Winton Dean, now eighty-four, had lost much of his hearing. The voices of the announcers were shouting. It was when I listened briefly to what they were saying that I realized Winton Dean was watching figure skating.

"You're looking good, Winton," Mrs. Nall said, leaning in to him so he could hear her over the television.

"You too," he said. Because of his age and his hearing, he spoke slowly, painfully slowly. He would also wait discernibly before he answered a question, again as if he had to consider saying something fully before he could say it. When he did speak, his voice was scratchy and rough. His words crackled. The two of them talked about Fairmount. They compared nursing homes. They discussed friends they had in common.

We were there thirty minutes, then forty-five. I got the sense they both knew that by talking about almost any other subject they could think of, they could avoid the one—James Dean, Winton's boy, Mrs. Nall's pupil—that had most changed the direction of their lives. Finally Mrs. Nall explained to Winton Dean who I was, a journalist "writing a book about Jimmy." Once she determined he was not bothered by my presence, Mrs. Nall continued on, now turning to Jimmy.

"You know, Winton," Mrs. Nall said in her soft clipped voice, "you don't have anything to be ashamed of with Jimmy. Marcus and Ortense did a fine job with him."

Winton Dean just sat there. Through the years no one had been more reluctant to talk about James Dean than his father. Today was no different. A look of genuine pain took over Winton Dean's face as he started to think about his son. In fact, he sat there for so long I decided that, once again, he was not going to talk about Jimmy. I was planning a tactful way for Mrs. Nall and me to leave when he finally spoke. "I feel pretty sentimental about Jimmy," Winton Dean said.

He still clasped Mrs. Nall's hand in both of his.

"I know you do," Mrs. Nall said, "but Jimmy had a good life here on the farm. And he was a joy to have in class."

There was another long pause. "I don't remember Jimmy being good at academics," his father said. "He wasn't a very studious person."

"No," Mrs. Nall said. "But he was good at other things."

Winton Dean picked up the cue Mrs. Nall had given him. "I do remember Jimmy being pretty good at athletics," he said.

"And dramatics!" Mrs. Nall added, her voice rising with enthusiasm. "I never had a better student. There was genius about that boy."

Again, Winton Dean waited before he spoke. "It took people a while to realize that Jimmy could do the plays he was good at."

Now Mrs. Nall paused. "But really, Winton," she said, "you have nothing to be ashamed of."

Finally the weight of the moment got to him. What Mrs. Nall was saying had brought back a rush of memories. Winton Dean's eyes filled with tears. It was all he could do to keep from breaking down. "I guess," he said, his voice quivering as he tried not to cry, "I am guilty of making some wrong turns along the way." If he was ever going to make an admission about how he felt over the way he treated his son, if he was ever going to admit to anything at all, this was it. The manner in which he spoke the sentence indicated that Winton Dean had said everything he was going to say, no matter how brief it was. *I guess I am guilty of making some wrong turns along the way.* During their entire conversation, not just the last exchange but the whole time they had talked, Winton Dean had never let go of Mrs. Nall's hand.

"You did the best you could do," Mrs. Nall said, summing up. "The best you could do." The look on his face was pained, and painful to see.

Soon Mrs. Nall and I left the nursing home, and Winton Dean went back to watching figure skating on television. Later, after I had said good-bye to Mrs. Nall in her room, I headed for my hotel in the rental car. When I turned on the radio, David Bowie was singing. *Rebel, rebel. Do you know what I mean? Rebel, rebel.* And as I drove I could not help but remember a comment Andy Warhol had once made about James Dean. "He's not our hero because he was perfect," Warhol said, "but because he perfectly represented the damaged but beautiful soul of our time." Which is why Dean remains relevant. He was the quintessential angry young man who did not fit into the society around him. He was the unloved hoping to find love. He was the fragmented personality trying to make himself complete. In the era of postmodernism, what Joan Didion calls a time "of atomization . . . [when] things fall apart," James Dean is the one actor who most represents the societal and cultural forces that produced him—a beautiful if damaged presence who lived just long enough to become legend.

7. Since his death in 1955, one of the main areas of discussion about James Dean has been his sexuality. During the last eighteen months of his life and in the years following his death, numerous young women, such as Pier Angeli, Lori Nelson, and Betsy Palmer, came forward to suggest that they had been romantically involved with Dean. If they didn't state this directly, they carefully avoided making any denial on the subject. But at the same time another line of thinking was put forth, though in a much less public way. At a party in New York, I once asked an established Hollywood producer familiar with Dean and his legacy to describe Dean's sexuality. "Well, he lived his life basically as a homosexual," the producer had said, obviously uncomfortable talking about the subject. When I pushed him to elaborate on his comment, he balked, then quickly left to talk to someone on the other side of the room. Why did he respond this way? Because he did not in any manner want to help debunk the myth that Hollywood, his industry, had spent years—decades—

creating. And is *still* creating. In 1990, Dennis Hopper wrote the following in an introduction to a picture book on Dean consisting of still
shots taken from Dean's three Warner Bros. pictures: "I find it unfor-
tunate that the two biographies that have been written about James
Dean say that he was gay. James Dean was not gay. The two great
loves of his life in Hollywood were Pier Angeli and Ursula Andress.
Pier Angeli married Vic Damone. Jimmy sat in the rain on his motorcycle outside the church. She'd asked Jimmy to marry her. He'd asked
her to wait until he saw how his career was going. Ursula Andress met
John Derek and proceeded to parade him on the set of *Giant* after
Jimmy refused to marry her for the same reason."

Naturally others have speculated that Dean was bisexual. Dean
himself seemed to have suggested this possibility when he said,
"Well, I'm certainly not going through life with one hand tied behind
my back." But what was he really? It is not unusual for a young gay
man still coming to terms with his sexuality to have affairs with
women. Some even marry only to accept their true sexual preference
afterward. Was James Dean a classic example of a young man who
would have lived an openly gay life-style but couldn't because of the
pressures put on him by society? Did he suppress his true sexual feelings, become involved with a woman—Angeli—since he was "supposed" to, and fall in love with her in the process? If he did do this,
we can only imagine the psychic torture through which he must have
lived. That torture would help explain the sort of behavior he regularly
displayed off the screen: intense anger, a contempt for authority, and
frustration over not fitting in.

Finally, would this have affected his acting, which is, after all, the
reason we still care about him? In each of his pictures Dean plays a
character in deep conflict. In *East of Eden*, Cal Trask struggles with
the way he feels toward his parents. In *Rebel*, Jim Stark fights similar
emotions, though in a different time and place. In *Giant*, through
much of the picture Jett Rink tries to carve out a niche for himself in

a society that shuns him first because he's poor, and then, once he gets rich, because he's not from the proper class. In short, each Dean character is a misfit attempting to learn why he's so out of step with the world around him. Maybe Dean's own inner struggle caused him to delve more deeply into his subconscious and explore his creative talents. There is no question that Dean revolutionized contemporary acting. Was he able to engage his artistic impulses to the extent he did because he was in conflict over how to deal with his own sexuality? No true artist fits into the world in which he lives. If he did, he would cease to be the observer and become the observed. One could argue that James Dean used this sense of angst, caused by his inability to live the life he wanted to lead, to spur him on as he relentlessly pushed the boundaries of his art.

Acknowledgments

I would like to thank James Stein, Marcy Posner, Tom Kazar, and Krystl Hall at the William Morris Agency; Maura Wogan and Martin Garbus at Frankfurt, Garbus, Klein, and Selz; Margaret Tufts, whose help with library research was invaluable; Steven Diamond, who expertly researched the enormous body of James Dean photographs; Julie Grau, who was supportive with her friendship; Paul Scott, who gave me insights into the craft of acting; and Dr. Richard Shepard, who has now seen me through three difficult books. I am grateful to the Biography Seminar at New York University, of which I am a member, where a portion of one meeting in the spring of 1993 was devoted to my work on James Dean. Also, I would like to acknowledge Cyndi Stivers at *Premiere* and Roger Alton at *The Guardian* for whom I wrote an article on Museum Days/Remembering James Dean, a part of which is included in "Valentino Redux." Finally I would like to thank Stephen Friedman at the PEN American Center for the generous advice he gave me when I needed it.

I received research materials from the Fairmount Historical Museum, the Fairmount Public Library, the Houston Public Library, the

James Dean Gallery, the Marion Public Library, the Museum of Television and Radio, and the Performing Arts Library of the New York Public Library. For interviews and other help, I would like to thank Sylvia Bongiovanni, Hugh Caughell, Tony Cichiello, Dick Clayton, Linda Cummins, Winton Dean, Carol Easton, Megan Foley, William Fox, David Garfield, Zina Glad, Jon Harned, Julie Harris, Lianne Hart, Venable Herndon, Val Holley, Steve Josephson, Frances Kiernan, Ralph Levy, David Loehr, Ronald Martinetti, Elizabeth McBride, Sylvia Miles, Dona Munker, Adeline Brookshire Nall, Vivian Nathan, Jeff Nelson, Gene Neilsen Owen, Jerry Payne, Bob Pully, Jack Raup, Roy Schatt, Bertha Seward, Jane Sheldon, Jayne Skinner, Clyde William Smitson, Saundra Webb Smitson, Ruth Wilson Stegmoller, John Stix, Lois Underhill, Richard Vincent, Ann Warr, Harry Warr, Christine White, Marcus Winslow, Jr., Larry Wood, and Nancy Wood. Of the Dean fans whom I interviewed I would like to thank Tom Berghuis, Scott Brim, Bobby Dean, Ana DeLuca, Bryan DeLuca, Travis Feldman, Larry Ledgerwood, Del Rey Loven, Arnold Siminoff, Jim Sorg, and Heather Thatcher. Naturally I would have liked to speak with Donald Turnupseed to ask him about the circumstances of the accident that killed James Dean, but when I called his home in Tulare, California, on the afternoon of July 31, 1993, identified myself, and told him I was writing a book on Dean, he said brusquely, "Oh, we wouldn't be interested in talking." Then he hung the telephone up.

I was also helped by reading *James Dean* by William Bast, *The Unabridged James Dean* by Randall Riese, *The James Dean Story* by Ronald Martinetti, *The Death of James Dean* by Warren Newton Beath, *James Dean: A Portrait* by Roy Schatt, *A Life* by Elia Kazan, *Montgomery Clift* by Patricia Bosworth, *The Drama of the Gifted Child* by Alice Miller, *A Player's Place* by David Garfield, *Haywire* by Brooke Hayward, and *Marilyn* by Norman Mailer. Jonathan (now John) Gilmore provided me with ample source material about his friendship with Dean, including diary entries and hours of conversation; I could not have written some parts of "Ten Thousand Horses Singing," "Broadway and the Motorola," and "James Dean" with as much detail as I have if I had not had Gilmore's cooperation.

The title for this book was taken from a Helnwein painting based on a Dennis Stock photograph; the photograph appears on page 152.

Finally, at Viking, I am indebted to Amanda Vaill, who acquired the American rights to this book in the summer of 1991, and to Al Silverman, who took an interest in the book, and Dawn Seferian, who edited it with sensitivity, understanding, and skill.

Photo
Credits

Copyright 1987 Seita Ohnishi/Photos by Sanford Roth: pp. ii, 212, 216, 220, 225, 226, 233, 234, 245, 246, 250, 307

Jonathan Gilmore: p. 124 (top and bottom)